Pussycats

By Martin van Creveld

DLVC Enterprises

Pussycats

Why the Rest Keeps Beating the West— and What Can Be Done About It

By Martin van Creveld

DLVC Enterprises

Library of Congress Cataloguing-in-Publication Data

Van Creveld, Martin, 1946
Pussycats,
Why the Rest Keeps Beating the West—
and What Can Be Done About It

First Edition: 2016
ISBN: 978-1533232007

DLVC Enterprises
POB 2766
Mevasseret Zion
90805 Israel

Bring forth the mighty men, let them press forward, let them rise up. Beat your plowshares into swords and your pruning hooks into spears. Let even the weak man say, I am a mighty warrior.

Joel 3.9-10

List of Contents

Preface i

Introduction: The Record of Failure 1

Chapter I. Subduing the Young 13
  1. A Tale of Two Childhoods 13
  2. "They Can't Handle It" 15
  3. Prohibit and Censor 24
  4. Becoming Infantilized 30
  5. "From Austria Came a Man" 35

Chapter II. Defanging the Troops 42
  1. "To Horse, to Horse!" 42
  2. The War on Men 46
  3. A Government of Lawyers 60
  4. The de-Militarized Military 65
  5. Soldiers into Mercenaries 73

Chapter III. Feminizing the Forces 79
  1. In Pursuit of Equality 79
  2. *Amazones Antianeirai* 87
  3. Retaining Privilege 93
  4. In the Land of Doublethink 103
  5. The End of Masculinity 113

Chapter IV. Constructing PTSD 118
  1. "Seek, and You Shall Find" 118
  2. Achilles in Vietnam 124
  3. From Soldiers' Heart to Combat Fatigue 131

4. The Great Epidemic 139

5. Damaged Goods? 145

Chapter V. Delegitimizing War 152

1. Of Might and Right 152

2. The Rise of Rights 157

3. The Demise of Duty 163

4. Learning to Say No 168

5. The Absolute Evil 176

Conclusion: Hannibal *intra Portas* 184

Thanks 200

Endnotes 201

Index 230

PUSSYCATS

Preface

I am one thing; my books are another. A few of my relatives, friends, and students have died in war, so I know a little of the sorrow and the grief it invariably brings. I have been under fire a couple of times, so I know a little of what it feels like. And I have heard, from no great distance, the sweetest, most melodious sound there is—that produced by the guns of one's own side when they finally start firing back. But I have never worn my country's uniform, nor served in its army, nor fought in any of its numerous wars, big or small, let alone exercised command over soldiers. The reason why, unlike most of my fellow-citizens, I did not do even the first of these things is because I was born with a cleft palate. Back in 1964, when it was my turn to be drafted, that was considered a sufficiently serious problem for the IDF (Israel Defense Forces) to disqualify me on medical grounds.

At the time few Israelis, least of all young ones, doubted that the IDF was the greatest organization God had created since the beginning of the world. This made being rejected a serious blow to my ego. It also brought in its wake some more or less unpleasant, and more or less humiliating, social and administrative problems. Later, though, once I had chosen my profession as a military historian, it made me think seriously about some of the things I had and had not missed. Here I want to put some of my thoughts on paper.

War is a practical activity above all. The objective is not to engage in reflection, nor to join "the chattering classes," nor to produce learned papers. It is all about "this little dumb business of victory," as the early twentieth-century German chief of staff, Field-Marshal Alfred von Schlieffen, once put it.[1] Undoubtedly it contains many things that can only be learned by experience. The best teacher of war is war. Yet experience is not everything. To quote another and much greater Prussian soldier, Frederick the Great: Had that been the case, then the best commander ought to have been the mule that carried Prince Eugene of Savoy (1663-1736), the Austrian commander who defeated both the French and the Ottomans, on campaign. Nor is experience of war necessarily the same thing as the ability to understand it, analyze it, and describe it to others. Has there ever been anybody who did so better than Homer, the blind bard, did?

Besides, rarely is one person's experience broad enough to cover all the relevant fields. That is why whoever fails to study the experience of others is a fool. It is study, and study alone, that can put experience into the proper perspective, so as to take the mind out of the familiar groove and provide it with the wings without which it cannot deal with the new and unexpected. The later the date, and the more complicated war grew, the clearer it became that to understand it and practice it, more was needed than the ability to wield a sword, fire a gun, fly an aircraft, or launch a missile.

Acknowledging this fact, the most advanced armed forces started building impressive education systems which, in some ways, have no equivalents in the civilian world. First, during the years around 1740, came military academies for training subalterns. They were followed by staff colleges—around 1780—and war colleges (from the beginning of the twentieth century on).[2] And even this list does not include all sorts of other courses young officers often go through before they join their arms of service.

In general, the more advanced the course, and the more high-ranking the officers attending it, the greater its theoretical content—as is its tendency to encompass other fields such as politics, economics, sociology, technology, culture, and what not. The objectives were a.) to make the students assimilate the distilled experience both of their own forces and of others; and b.) provide them with tools that would enable them to proceed on their own when confronted with new and unexpected challenges. As the growing presence of civilian students shows, especially at the higher levels, such study does not necessarily require previous military experience.

Furthermore, it should not be overlooked that, of all human organizations, the military is not only one of the most total but also the most hierarchical and most disciplined. Often, too, it is surrounded by considerable barriers that separate it from society at large. Such organizations are essential for waging war. Without them, doing so would be utterly impossible. On the other hand, spending too much time in the organizations in question, to the exclusion of all the rest, can easily cause originality to be suppressed and innovation to be stifled.

The outcomes are pedantry, conformism, and groupthink—also, not seldom, a certain combination of hard-to-define extreme professionalism and narrowmindedness. It even has a popular name: "coning." Not even the very best personnel and the best armies are necessarily exempt. In some cases, quite the contrary. As someone has said of the Israel Air Force, an elite force that is admired the world over: It takes in boys at the age of eighteen, only to release them twenty years later at the same age.

I can only hope that having spent almost all my life in Israel with all its wars has provided me with better opportunities to observe and study the subject than are available to many others, Westerners in particular. It is also my hope that not having served, while not without its own problems, has helped me avoid some of the above pitfalls. Doing so, no doubt I have fallen into others. But that is for readers to decide.

PUSSYCATS

Introduction: The Record of Failure

During the last days of the Western Roman Empire and throughout the Middle Ages, Western Europe was threatened, and often invaded, by outsiders. First came the Huns, then the Arabs, then the Magyars, then the Vikings, then the Mongols, and then the Turks. Each in turn, they were described as ferocious warriors none could withstand. Each in turn, their hordes inflicted immense bloodshed, destruction, and suffering on a continent rendered almost defenseless by the prevailing socio-economic-political structures and the internecine struggles to which it led.

On several occasions—Châlons sur Marne in AD 451, Poitiers in 732, Lechfeld in 955, Liegnitz in 1241, and Vienna in 1529—the fate of Western civilization seemed to hang in the balance. A different decision by a commander-in-chief on either side, or a fortuitous change in the weather, could have led to a very different outcome indeed. For want of a nail, the battle might have been lost. As late as 1683 the Ottoman Grand Vizier, Kara (Black) Mustafa, marched from Istanbul to Austria. Picking up troops on the way until he had somewhere between 90,000 and 300,000 men, he laid siege to the imperial capital of Vienna. Next he demanded the city's surrender, threatening to "enslave the children" if it did not.[1]

Yet by that time the pendulum had long started swinging in the other direction. The first permanent European stronghold in Africa was Ceuta, a city on the north African coast, which the Portuguese captured in 1415. In 1492 the last Muslim kingdom in the Iberian Peninsula ceased to exist. In 1571 the Battle of Lepanto marked the beginning of a centuries-long period, sometimes known as the "Colombian" period, during which no one so much as tried to match European fleets. Europe's military superiority—propelled by political, economic, social, scientific, technological, and possibly cultural developments to

1

which the inhabitants of other continents simply did not have an answer—grew and grew.[2] Driven by their greed, their dream of spreading "the true" religion, various strategic considerations—and not least, sheer lust for adventure—small parties of European men advanced.

Among the first and most audacious of the parties in question were the ones headed by Hernán Cortés and Francisco Pizarro. They and many of their successors took to the sea, often sailing for weeks or months to reach unknown, usually roadless continents thousands of miles from their home countries. With only small, fragile, wind-driven boats to link them with those countries, they were hardly in a position to communicate with their sponsors, let alone ask for and receive reinforcements in an emergency. Cortés at one point went so far as to burn his ships, forcing his men to choose between victory and death. Exposed to every kind of disease, known and unknown, fighting incomparably larger numbers of natives, they took heavy losses. Like Magellan who lost his life fighting in the Philippines, and Captain Cook who was killed in Hawaii, many never returned.

None of this prevented them from pushing forward with a determination and ruthlessness that, in retrospect, appear almost superhuman. The largest, stormiest oceans on earth could not stop them. Nor could the immense empty spaces of North America and Siberia, the jungles of Latin America, Southeast Asia and Africa, and the mountains of Afghanistan (though the savage tribes of the last-named country eventually did). In the words of the famous nineteenth-century explorer Henry Stanley, himself not the least of their number: "Where the civilized white is found, a difficulty must vanish."[3] Scant wonder that wherever he and the others went, they inspired terror and respect. Or, perhaps most often, both.

Whether, in all these centuries, trade followed the flag, or the other way around, is moot. Be that as it may, within five hundred years after the occupation of Ceuta about eighty percent of the world's landmass, and practically all of its water area, were ruled by just five European empires: Britain, Russia, France, Germany, and Italy. To them were added two (the US and Japan) that either were directly descended from Europe or had succeeded in copying the latter's ways and joining it on the road to expansion and dominion. The only two major exceptions were Latin America and China. The former was the all-but exclusive stamping ground of the US, and officially declared by the Monroe Doctrine to be just that. The latter had already lost vast territories to Russia and, to a lesser extent, the remaining powers. Standing on the verge of being dismantled, it was only saved by the divisions among those powers as well as its own sheer size and teeming population.

The "West"—a term which, from this point on, will refer to the countries of Western Europe and North America while excluding Russia and Japan—reached the peak of its power just before 1914. Later, owing partly to the casualties sustained in World War I and partly to a loss of self-confidence, it found that its rule over subject peoples became harder and harder to sustain. During the interwar period several colonial countries in the Middle East including Egypt, Iraq, and Jordan, gained at least nominal independence. Translating that into real independence took longer; but by the second half of the 1950s that, too, had been achieved.

Here we are concerned with the strategic aspect of the matter, not the moral one. Still staying in the interwar period, struggles such as the one against the Rif of Morocco—when some 250,000 well-equipped, highly trained French and Spanish troops took several years to defeat a loose coalition of mostly barefoot, mostly illiterate, Moroccan tribesmen—pointed to the direction in which things were moving.[4] By 1939 many colonial peoples around the world were preparing to challenge their masters—although it took World War II, in which those masters tore each other to pieces, to set the stage for the conflagrations that followed.

Since then, almost the only time Western countries gained a clear military victory over their non-Western opponents was during the First Gulf War. In 1991 NATO, as the most powerful military alliance in history, had just emerged triumphant from the forty-five-year struggle known as the Cold War. But its members had not yet begun to dismantle their armed forces as the European ones, in particular, were to do later on. As a result, they were free as never before or since to send those forces to any spot they wanted, to wage any war they wanted, against any opponent they wanted. Though few people realized it at the time,[5] in retrospect to challenge NATO, reinforced by several other countries, with a conventional army, as Iraqi dictator Saddam Hussein did, represented the height of folly. Even so, the US and its allies did not complete the job. With good reason, as it later turned out.

This episode apart, practically every time the West, or some country that was part of it, fought the rest, it was defeated. Conversely, the wars in question, and the people who waged them and fought in them, succeeded in liberating— whatever that might mean—entire continents with populations numbering in the hundreds of millions. The British failed first in Palestine and then in Malaysia, where their self-proclaimed "triumph" did not save them from having to grant the country independence and evacuating it. They went on to fail and withdraw in Kenya, Cyprus, and Aden. Thereupon they gave up what little remained of their empire, which until 1946-47 had been the largest in history, more or less without a struggle. The French failed in Indo-China and Algeria. In the latter, they did so in spite of having deployed as many as 230,000 troops (November 1955) and the largest force of helicopters in history until then, all to no avail.

Smaller colonial powers such as the Netherlands and Portugal fared no better. In 1949 the former was forced to surrender Indonesia. Twenty-six years later the latter, exhausted after decades of struggle, gave up Angola and Mozambique. One could indeed argue that in the two decades after 1945, the only European countries to escape defeat were those which were lucky enough to have lost their colonies during World War I— or better still, had never possessed any in the first place.

Looking at the Europeans' trials, many Americans took it for granted that their allies had become soft and decadent.[6] Secure in their self-confidence and often eager to go, they took over the Western man's burden (to misuse Rudyard Kipling). As then-former Israeli chief of staff General Moshe Dayan, visiting Washington in 1966, noted: What they seemed to tell both enemies and friends was, here comes the A team—the brightest, the richest, the best organized, and the most powerful in history. Nothing and no one could stop them.[7]

The outcome was the Vietnam War. Judging by the amount of ordnance expended or dropped, and the number of people killed, no colonial war in the whole of history had ever been waged with greater ferocity. All to subdue an opponent whose leader looked like a poor relation of Santa Klaus, wore black pajamas and sandals made of old tires, subsisted on the proverbial handful of rice, and operated an electric grid so small that even destroying eighty-seven percent of it made no difference.[8]

A quarter-century later the Americans, encouraged by the aforementioned victory over Saddam (as well as the much smaller one over poor little Serbia in Kosovo), compounded their error by invading first Afghanistan and then Iraq. Neither country was in any condition to fight back. The former, indeed, hardly deserved to be called a country at all. Both were overrun quickly and at very low cost. Yet the wars in question, far from producing quick and easy victories as President George W. Bush, Secretary of Defense Donald Rumsfeld, and their advisers had confidently expected, became protracted. Before they were over they produced tens of thousands of casualties, and while most Western troops have been withdrawn an end may not be in sight. The financial cost, including that of looking after wounded veterans and replenishing the depleted forces, is said to have been anything between 4 to 6 trillion dollars.[9] So heavy is the burden that it is most unlikely ever to be fully paid. All for no gains anyone could discover.

Within a decade of being called a "colossus" bestriding the globe,[10] the US was perceived as a country in full retreat. With it went what one author called "The New American Militarism."[11] Come the second decade of the twenty-first century, Americans were anything but "seduced by war." Instead they had come to see armed conflict, and even more so the casualties to which it might lead, as something to be avoided at almost any cost. To the extent that the US intervened in any wars at all, it did so almost exclusively by using aircraft, cruise missiles, and drones against which the chosen opponent had no defense.

If anything, America's NATO allies became even more dispirited than the US. Throughout the Cold War their military spending, as measured by its share of GDP, had been considerably lower than its US equivalent. Once that conflict had ended most of them reduced that outlay to levels where they barely *had* armed forces any more.[12] Orders of battle were cut to the bone. Equipment was neglected to the point where much of it was outdated and/or no longer operable.[13] Judging by all this, the claim made long ago by subsequent Israeli Prime Minister Benjamin Netanyahu that "the West can win" appears optimistic, to say the least.

To pile insult on injury, in almost all cases the victors did not consist of other regular armed forces. They did not come complete with modern equipment, training, and doctrine, not to mention official cars and smart uniforms covered with shiny, if often meaningless, decorations. Instead, from Sana to Saigon and from Kuala Lumpur to Kabul, initially at any rate, they tended to be mere ragtag irregulars. Having spent their youths scratching the earth or herding the family goats, some of the men, sometimes accompanied by a sprinkling of women who mostly performed all kinds of auxiliary tasks, were illiterate. Many others did not have proper training. That forced them to pay a very high price in blood before they finally learned how to fight.

Even fewer attended higher institutes of military education such as staff and war colleges. Nor, in truth, was there any reason why they should. After all, practically all the institutes in question were run by self-proclaimed "advanced" armed forces in self-proclaimed "advanced" countries. Their students might be assigned texts by guerrilla leaders such as T. S. Lawrence, Mao Tze Dong, Che Guevara, and Vo Nguyen Giap, but only by way of "know your enemy." Consequently, they had precious little to say about how to become an effective terrorist, guerrilla, insurgent, or for that matter, jihadist.

In appearance and behavior, the irregulars often resembled bandits and outlaws more than they did soldiers and armies. Small but flexible and nimble, they related to the latter as fleas relate to rhinoceroses. For example, as of the end of 2015 Daesh, after almost a year of fighting, was able to withstand anything the US, as the world's sole superpower, could throw at it in Iraq. So much so that it started developing into a regular state; and so much so that President Obama had to fire one of his secretaries of defense for failing to tackle the problem as he should have.

Yet Daesh, a relatively small organization numbering approximately a few tens of thousands militants,[14] did not have at its disposal anything like the territorial, demographic, economic, fiscal, organizational, and technological resources its numerous opponents commanded. Nor did it carry any of the more sophisticated weapons its Western opponents, the US in particular, were constantly inventing and throwing into the battle.

Small and decentralized as they were, the organizations in question tended to avoid strong troop concentrations. For example, throughout the struggle in Afghanistan the Taliban never put together a force larger than a battalion.

Avoiding large-scale conventional operations, they resorted to "protracted war" (Mao's term); or to non-trinitarian war (my own term); or low-intensity war, a term introduced as far back as the 1970s; or insurgency, guerrilla, terrorism, or "war among the people." The last of these terms, by emphasizing the difficulty of distinguishing between combatants and noncombatants, speaks for itself. It explains why casualties were sometimes so immense as to almost justify the term genocide.

In some ways, the very weakness of the irregulars in question helps explain their success. For too long, the West took it for granted that their troops could go wherever they had been doing for several centuries past. And doing it, what is more, in faraway countries about which most Westerners knew nothing and cared less.

Even today, given that the West is even more powerful at sea than on land, there can be no question of forces originating in other continents invading it. Should they make the attempt, long before they reach their destination they will be blasted to pieces by infinitely superior Western firepower. Taking its superiority for granted, the West neglected its defenses, especially those needed to counter the kind of opponent that is not a state and does not maintain the classic "trinitarian" separation between government, armed forces, and population—and especially those of a spiritual kind, as opposed to mere *materiel*. As it did so, it failed to see—in quite some cases, did not *want* to see—that all around it, a new world was coming into existence.[15]

What the future will bring nobody knows. However, there is reason to think that the nuclear balance of terror that has prevented first- and second-class countries from going to war against each other since 1945 will persist—even, and some would say particularly, if more countries obtain the weapons. Not that it matters. Should nuclear weapons be used, then we shall *really* find ourselves in a new world—or, perhaps, in no world at all. The likelihood is that, as has been the case since 1945, the vast majority of military campaigns in which the West will engage will be fought against irregulars, both those that operate across national borders and those who, increasingly, do so inside them.

Faced with this prospect, some of those involved in such campaigns in the past have engaged in serious soul-searching. They pointed to top-heavy, clumsy command systems; complex and confused lines of authority; bad intelligence based on insufficient acquaintance with the country, its people, its language, and its culture; and manpower systems that, failing to distribute the burden as fairly as it should and perhaps could have, led to resentment and protest. Or else to tours of duty that were either too long or too short; inadequate training; equipment more suitable for conventional warfare than for any other kind; and similar factors.

Others blamed the politicians who, they said, engaged in micromanagement and did not allow the military the free hand they needed—or else, thinking of nothing but the next elections, simply lacked the stamina and determination to carry the war through to the end. Or else it was the people who lacked those things and turned their backs on the war. Or else it was the media which, with nothing but profit in mind, kept on squirting pus and infecting both the government and the people.[16] Finally, many people in all walks of life have argued that this kind of war cannot be won by purely military means, and that the only way to resolve it is by resorting to politics. This is to ignore Mao Zedong's saying that power grows out of the barrel of a gun.[17] Short of complete annihilation, which rarely happens, the proper objective of war is very simple: namely, to wreak sufficient death and destruction to break the enemy's will, make him cease his resistance, and do what we tell him. If not completely, then at any rate in large part. If not once and for all, then at any rate for some more or less considerable time. Once that is achieved, politics will usually look after themselves.

9

Good or bad, all these explanations miss the essential point: namely that, in practically all cases, the Gooks, Hajjis, or whatever other derogatory names their opponents used to call them by, won because they were *better*. Often they lived and operated under conditions so hard that most people in developed countries cannot even imagine them. But this did not prevent them from out-propagandizing, out-mobilizing, out-organizing, out-planning, out-motivating, out-leading, out-maneuvering, out-fighting, out-lasting, out-suffering, and, yes, out-dying their opponents.

As Mark Bowden, author of *Black Hawk Down*, explains: "Civilized states [have] nonviolent ways of resolving disputes, but that depended on the willingness of everyone to *back down*. Here in the raw Third World, people had not learnt to back down, at least not until after a lot of blood had flowed."[18] As one American soldier with experience in Afghanistan put it, next to the Hajjis "the West looked like a bunch of pussies."[19] Their ability and determination to do all this was the most important advantage they had. As they themselves kept saying, often it was almost the only one. Willy-nilly, it had to be made in order to compensate for everything else.

Victory, said Nietzsche, is the best cure for the soul.[20] A glance at old newsreels showing the celebrations on V-E and V-J Day fully confirms his words. But when was the last time any Western military won a real victory? Where have they left their souls? With the mental-health workers who are looking after the various symptoms of PTSD (post-traumatic stress disorder), perhaps? Has the deadly "Western way of war," about which so much has been written, gone the way of all flesh? Have ongoing cultural changes brought about a situation where Western troops, and of course the societies that raise and maintain and deploy them, are no longer either able or ready to engage in carnage even when carnage is absolutely necessary?

How did the world's best and most ferocious soldiers, who for centuries fought and defeated anybody and everybody until they dominated the entire world, turn into pussycats? How come, whereas Stanley thought that in the presence of "civilized" white men all difficulties must vanish, now the opposite seems to be the case? And why do Western media continue to churn out any number of Rambos who, embarking on all kinds of suicidal missions in Third World countries, defeat even greater numbers of natives, whereas in reality things are turning in the other direction?

As the text known as Wu Tzu which probably dates to around 390 BC, tells us, "When the dead lay stiff and you grieve for them, you have not attained righteousness."[21] Unless you are able and willing to fight when necessary, sooner or later someone, sharp sword in hand, will come along and cut off your head. Literally so, in the case of Daesh. That is why finding an answer to the above questions is absolutely vital.

Attempting to do so, Chapter I examines some of the ways in which modern Western societies raise, or rather mis-raise young people, boys in particular—from among whom, like it or not, they will have to draw their future soldiers. Chapter II focuses on the way those societies have been doing whatever they can to defang their armed forces. Chapter III looks at the way women—or perhaps I should say the way women are being incorporated into the forces—are devastating those very forces. Chapter IV looks at the unprecedented spread of the phenomenon known as PTSD. Chapter V investigates the growing predominance of rights over duties, as well as the way war itself is being delegitimized. At the end, there are my conclusions.

One final point: Though other Western countries will not be totally neglected,[22] throughout this volume the main focus is on what is happening in the US. There are two reasons for this. First, the US is the most powerful Western power by far. Currently its military spending is, compared to that of the remaining NATO members, about two to one.[23] Second, it has often taken the initiative. Doing so, it acted as a model for its allies and, to some extent, its opponents as well. As is also the case in the civilian world, no country has more foreign officers attending its military education system. According to political scientist Joseph Nye, its armed forces wield greater "soft power" than any of the rest, and perhaps even than all the rest combined.[24] Third, if the West is to be saved at all, then the US will have to assume the lion's share of the burden.

Or else.

PUSSYCATS

Chapter I. Subduing the Young

1. A Tale of Two Childhoods

The possibility that something might be deeply, deeply wrong with the troops of "advanced" countries was first brought home to me in the summer of 1994. The occasion was a lecture about the future of war I gave to the assembled members of the Israeli General Staff. In the chair was the Chief of the General Staff, Ehud Barak, who later became prime minister. Another of those present was the then-commander of the Northern Front, a tough major-general named Yitzhak (Itzik) Mordechai. In October 1973 he had commanded paratroopers in the so-called "Chinese Farm" on the Suez Canal. Fighting what may have been the bloodiest battle of the entire war, his battalion, the famous 890th, almost ceased to exist. In 1996-99 he served as minister of defense under Benjamin Netanyahu.

At this particular meeting Mordechai complained about "those computer kids" he was commanding against the Hezbollah terrorists in southern Lebanon. "I do not know what is wrong with them," he said, throwing up his arms. Twelve years later the 2006 Second Lebanon War, in which most of the Israeli ground forces failed to come up to expectations and some all but disgraced themselves, showed that his fears had been justified. So, to a lesser extent, did Operation Protective Edge in 2014[1].

I live in an upper-middle-class neighborhood in Mevasseret Zion, a few miles west of Jerusalem. Right across the street is an "absorption center." It consists of a neighborhood made up of small, rather dilapidated houses that have seen generations of immigrants from many countries pass through. Currently this is where hundreds of Ethiopian families spend their first months in the country before they learn Hebrew, find work, and move elsewhere. For some twenty years now I have been watching their countless young children. Clearly they are much less supervised and monitored than non-Ethiopian Israeli kids of the same age are. Part of the reason is no doubt cultural. Another factor is the fact that the offspring of immigrants adjust to their new surroundings faster than their parents can. Consequently, they learn to be independent regardless of whether those parents want them to or not.

This lack of supervision—aka greater independence, greater freedom to make decisions, more responsibility—may entail some cost in the form of a relatively greater number of accidents taking place both inside the home and outside it. Perhaps because anyone who tried to compile them would quickly be labelled "racist," I have never seen any statistics on the matter. One can see the kids running about in the streets, largely left to their own devices. They climb trees and buildings. Not having safety helmets, they nevertheless ride bicycles (old and rusty ones, to be sure). They collect other people's throwaway objects and sometimes put them to unorthodox uses. They play all sorts of improvised games, some of them fairly rough. At times they fight, though I never saw a fight so serious as to make me think I should intervene and separate the parties. Briefly speaking, they do all the things kids have always enjoyed doing.

Particularly striking is the fact that older kids lead younger ones and younger kids follow older ones with few, if any, adults present to tell them what and not to do. Girls of six or seven regularly take care of toddlers, carrying them in their arms or teaching them to walk. Toddlers as young as two sometimes roam the pavements on their own—a situation which, in any developed country as well as in any other Israeli settlement, would have caused the parents to be sued and their children taken away from them.

Yet this freedom does seem to make the children enterprising and adventurous. And though it may be beside the point I wish to make, it also seems to make them happy. They do not feel vulnerable at every step, and they know how to look after themselves. Otherwise, they would hardly have survived. The contrast with mainstream Israeli children—my own grandchildren included—who are watched and guarded and chaperoned and admonished at every step, could hardly be greater. Should the two groups get involved in a fight, there can be little doubt as to who would emerge on top. In fact, something like this happened a few years ago when two boys, new immigrants from Russia, beat up some Technion students—while dozens of the latter, both male and female, stood by, not daring to interfere.

2. "They Can't Handle It"

It was not always so. By and large, the move to impose more and more restrictions on young people is a manifestation, if not to say disease, typical of modern life in general and Western life in particular. Never in the whole of history has the age in which such people started counting as adults been as high as it is today. The origins of the change are to be found during the 1820s. According to that invaluable research tool, Google Ngram, this was the time when writers suddenly started using the term "childhood" much more often than before. Sixty years later, the term "adolescence," which two anthropologists define as a period during which young people are "kept in the natal home under the authority of parents, attending school, and bedeviled by a bewildering array of occupational choices,"[2] followed suit. As of 2000 both curves were still rising, though no longer as quickly as they used to. Subsequent historians spoke of "the invention of childhood."[3] They attributed the change to rapid urbanization. It turned children from an economic asset, which was what they often were during pre-industrial times, into a burden.

No sooner had childhood been invented than attempts to provide children with all kinds of special protection got under way. The first laws regulating child labor

15

were enacted in Britain, the most urbanized and industrialized country of all, during the 1830s.[4] Other countries followed. As well as limiting the kinds of work the young were allowed to do and the conditions under which they could do it, they increased the age at which they could start doing it. No doubt many of those who helped push through the laws were philanthropists shocked by the bad conditions in the mines and factories. Acting out of the best possible motives, their objective was to protect children against exploitation and overwork, and enable them to develop and study instead.[5]

But not all the efforts were disinterested. Some of those who lobbied Parliament represented the nascent civil services. After centuries and centuries during which their main function had been to levy taxes, bureaucrats were flexing their muscles in quest for greater power. Doing so, they found childhood and education fertile fields in and on which to operate. This was carried to the point where, in all modern countries, child welfare and education have been turned into some of the largest and costliest fields of state activity. Others represented organized labor trying to keep wages as high as they could. Or else they spoke for large corporations seeking to force smaller, often family-based, competitors—who were better able to employ youngsters for low wages—out of business.

In time, almost everybody got involved in the act. Government passed all kinds of legal restrictions, and set up special agencies to ensure they were observed. Next came business, which in the US alone makes hundreds of billions a year by helping create and perpetuate a separate "youth culture." They were joined by international organizations, both state-run and others, many of which seem to consider any kind of work children may do harmful and exploitative. They were also joined by religious groups, which often accused teenagers of not having proper morals and neglecting God; as well as the media, which often presented them as lazy, self-absorbed, frivolous, oversexed, and drug-abusing.

Taking advantage of the fact that, of all groups in society, young people are least able to defend themselves, they blamed them for whatever evils society was suffering from.[6] During the last decades of the twentieth century, "developed" countries mounted an organized campaign meant to impose their own standards on "developing" ones. To make the latter kind of country feel as guilty as possible, the former—supported by any number of international organizations—have even turned the prevalence of child labor into a measuring stick for "progress."[7]

Regardless of what their motives were, all these people and organizations developed a vested interest in controlling young people. The latter had to be made to spend as large a part of their lives as possible in a state where they would be unable to work, take responsibility, and look after themselves. Here and there feeble attempts were made to put the clock back, to no avail. For example, Newt Gingrich, former House of Representatives speaker and presidential candidate, at one point dared suggest that having children contribute to the family finances might not be such a bad idea. As his reward, he was ridiculed half to death. When Senator Rand Paul, announcing his presidential candidacy, said that he had actual enjoyed doing summer jobs he risked the same fate.[8]

Again, it was not always so. Half a century has passed since the renowned child psychologist Bruno Bettelheim visited the Israeli kibbutzim. Impressed by what he saw, he praised them for making children perform some light work. Doing so, he wrote, "Enhances beyond measure the feeling of competence, of security, and well-being."[9] As long as the system of communal raising existed, it tended to produce exceptionally motivated, exceptionally high-achieving youngsters.[10] Many went on to occupy prominent positions in various parts of Israeli society including, not least, the military.

The same applies to the Amish people. As long as most of them were still engaged in agriculture, they made their children work. Children who helped with

17

the family finances felt needed. Feeling needed, they suffered from few of the problems afflicting other American youngsters, such as delinquency, drugs, and teenage pregnancy[11]—so much so that a Google Scholar search combining "Amish" with "youth delinquency" yielded hardly any hits. To this day there is no proof whatsoever that children in "developing" countries, many of whom do work, are less happy than those in "developed" ones where the law prohibits them from doing so. Judging by the percentage who are referred to psychological treatment or filled with drugs, the opposite may well be the case.

Things got to the point where, in much if not all of the West, almost the only place where youngsters could still do any productive work was the family farm. Even that was only possible because, since they did not get paid, the authorities were not informed or turned a blind eye. Elsewhere they were limited to low-paying jobs that did not demand any kind of training and which, consequently, did little or nothing to develop their minds. The best-known ones are babysitting, cleaning cars, light yard work, serving customers at fast-food restaurants, running errands, and the like. In the US they also included delivering newspapers. In folklore if perhaps not in reality, the last-named used to be the archetypical work *par excellence* for boys.

All other kinds of work were prohibited. That applied even if the jobs in question were pleasant, well within the young people's abilities, and contributed to their well-being, as some at least clearly did.[12] And this applied even if, as is the case in many fields, they demanded the kind of skills best acquired by means of an apprenticeship, especially those involving various kinds of manual crafts. In fact, it was apprenticeships rather than school that, throughout history, enabled countless people to make the first step toward success.

Driven by these forces, by the 1970s the effort to exclude the young from any kind of remunerative work was virtually complete. But that did not mean they were allowed to spend their time as they pleased or simply remain idle. Rather, increasingly they were required to volunteer so as to improve their chances of getting into some elite university.[13] What most adults will only do for pay, their offspring are supposed to do without it. A more unfair system would be hard to devise.

And yet, as Freud wrote, there is nothing like work to give those who do it "a secure place in a portion of reality in the human community." Not only does it enable them to sublimate "a large amount of libidinal components, whether narcissistic, aggressive or even erotic," Freud added, but it is "indispensable to the preservation and justification to existence in society."[14] Conversely, to prevent young people from engaging in it is cruel and can be dangerous. Insofar as it excludes them from what is normally the most important adult activity of all, it also goes a long way to prevent them from growing up.

Nor are the restrictions limited to child work only. In all "advanced" countries, probably not a day passes without some new law or regulation specifically aimed at the young being enacted. Ostensibly the goal is to help the people in question. In fact, they often hamper them in all kinds of ways. Anything to prevent them from doing as their elders do as a matter of course. And anything to prevent them from competing with those elders and, by doing so, taking over some of the latter's resources and increasing their own independence. No wonder that, apart from gangs, they seldom organize and engage in activities of their own.

Starting in the 1960s, the introduction of "the pill" and the spread of feminism reinforced the process and accelerated it. The pill "liberated" women by enabling them to have sex to their hearts' contents without fear of conception. Feminists suggested, even demanded, that they leave the home and have careers. That, incidentally, applied even if those careers involved little but taking care of other people's children, as in kindergarten, the classroom, or as child-psychologists, social workers, and the like—an irony if ever there was one. *Arbeit macht frei*

19

seems to be the motto. The way Betty Friedan, Simone de Beauvoir, and many other leading feminists saw it, women who did not work hardly deserved to live.[15]

These twin developments go a long way to explain the sharp rise that took place both in the age at which people marry and the one at which they have their first children. At the beginning of the twenty-first century, both figures are the highest in history.[16] The fact that older parents tend to be more cautious and less inclined to risk-taking than younger ones hardly requires mentioning. Claiming to act for the children's own good, they have subjected their offspring to a vast number of controls and prohibitions. Many were of the kind that, had they been applied to adults without a warrant, would have led to lawsuits, riots, and worse.

Children's hair dress and clothing are controlled. They can be "grounded," i.e., sent to their rooms and forbidden to leave it. They can have their privacy violated. They can have their property searched and confiscated. They can have their allowance reduced or cut off. They can have their driving privileges taken away. They can have their use of the telephone, television, and/or Internet monitored and/or restricted or even denied. They may be told whom they can, and cannot, associate with. They can be forced to exercise and/or participate in other activities and to undergo medical treatment against their will. Until recently in most countries, children could even be physically assaulted. In some places, that is still the case.

To protect them against themselves, youngsters are prohibited from using the social media.[17] To protect them against gaining weighty, they are prohibited from consuming soft drinks as well as many kinds of food including, one is not surprised to learn, some of those they like best. To make sure these restrictions can be enforced they are also prevented, as far as possible, from watching the relevant advertising material.[18] The right of young women to have an abortion without parental consent is being curtailed. That, of course, is but a natural consequence of sexual activity among consenting minors being demonized and banned. The expression "puppy love" speaks for itself. Having taken off around 1900 and remaining in frequent use today, its purpose is to trivialize the emotions of the young by implying that they are incapable of experiencing the most important emotion of all.

Yet it is thought that God's own choice for giving birth to His son, Mary, was probably no more than thirteen or fourteen years old. Shakespeare's Juliet was thirteen, and Romeo was not much older. Nor should this come as a surprise. It is primarily biology, meaning the age of sexual maturity which dictates when young women should start take an interest in men, and young men in them. Most preindustrial societies tolerated sex among adolescents. Many even expected them to engage in it. Women married when aged fourteen or fifteen, and men when they reached their late teens.[19] It was only in Western Europe, and then only during the Renaissance, that the age of marriage started rising, until around 1900, it reached nineteen or twenty for women and the mid- or even late twenties for men. Seen against the historical background, so unusual was the ensuing pattern that it even acquired a name: the European Pattern of Marriage.

The rising age at which Westerners got married led to a situation in which as many as one third of all these young brides went to the altar while already pregnant.[20] The rest could expect to have their first child in less than a year. The contrast with modern Western societies, most of which do whatever they can to discourage or prohibit young people from having sex, could hardly be greater. All the above-mentioned restrictions, and many others like them, are being imposed on a daily basis without any kind of judicial review. Yet that review is precisely the thing which, in the world adults inhabit, is considered *the* paramount guarantee of freedom, independence, and the pursuit of happiness.

One outcome has been the phenomenon known as "helicopter parents."[21] So popular is the term, which first came into use shortly before 2000, that the graph showing its rise is almost vertical. Most helicopter parents are middle-class. Their first concern is to ensure that their offspring do not stray from the straight and the narrow. Next comes the drive to give them a "good education." By that they mean sending them to the best available schools and making sure they get the highest possible grades. Many parents also feel guilty in the face of perfect parenthood as presented in the media.[22] Accordingly they keep hovering over the children, put pressure on them, and above all, control them. All of this is done on a twenty-four-hour-per-day basis, because even bad dreams are supposed to be indicators of trouble.

Some of the prohibitions, and some of the pressure, are exercised face to face. However, both parents are likely to work—in large part, because raising children in a modern urban environment has become horrendously expensive. Normally they do so full-time. Hence much of their monitoring is done by telephone and other modern means of communication. Some devices allow parents to control their offspring's use of cell phones from afar. Others are installed in cars or sewn into clothing. No doubt they will soon be implanted into bodies as well, as is already the case with some criminals, older people who have lost their minds to Alzheimer, and dogs. Orson Scott Card's vision in *Ender's Game*, where the boy hero has a device implanted in his neck so that the officers responsible for turning him into a fighting machine can see the world just as he does, may yet come true—if indeed, it has not done so already.

But all this only forms half of the story. Even as parents do all these things, they are determined to endow their offspring with "self-esteem." Rather than provide them with knowledge and skills, which is not easy and is certain to result in the occasional failure, they keep telling them how wonderful and how unique they are, even though they do not have such skills and such knowledge. They never correct them, for fear of holding them back, offending them, or "traumatizing" them. However insufferable they are and however bad their behavior, God forbid that anyone should say a cross word to them, let alone restrain them in any way.

In *The Slap*, the Commonwealth Prize-winning novel by the Australian author Christos Tsiolkas, just such an incident leads to a lawsuit. Ultimately the judge, a woman, acquits the person who has delivered the slap and apologizes to the person in question in the name of the law. But not before a struggle with many unexpected twists and turns tears the social group to which both accuser and accused belong apart, and brings out the ugly consequences of the situation to the full.

Coming together, the two kinds of pressure produce the kind of child who, at the age of ten, is convinced of his self-importance and genius and will suffer a mental crisis each time he is criticized, but who still cannot wash himself and depends on his parents to give him a bath. They are like hot-air balloons that need to be constantly re-inflated. Yet they do not succeed in taking off. And how can they?

Superficially the two parenting styles—the one concerned with overprotecting children, and the other with smoothing over any problems and pushing them forward at almost any cost—appear contradictory. In fact, they go hand in hand. Both originate in the idea that, whatever "it" may mean, young people cannot handle "it." That in turn obliges parents to put in almost superhuman effort, foresight, supervision, and moralizing. In the US, the same role is later played by the colleges. They act, and are expected to act, *in loco parentis*. The objective is to make the world that young people inhabit predictable, safe, and secure against sadness, pain and, perhaps most important of all, failure. Not to mention secure against every kind of terrible danger, from being scratched by the neighbor's cat to being kidnapped by a stranger who may be out there waiting for them.[23] Both are methods used, whether inadvertently or on purpose, to prevent them from growing up.

Focusing on "advanced" countries, so numerous and comprehensive are the prohibitions that preventing youngsters from evading or violating those prohibitions has grown into a not-so-minor industry in itself. Many firms, as well as armies of salesmen, consultants, and lobbyists, promise to sell parents "tools" to make such violations difficult or impossible. Should the children prove recalcitrant, then parents have the right to make them undergo all sorts of therapy. Other parents commit their offspring to so-called "Gulag Schools." There they are kept against their will, and treated more or less as prisoners and military recruits are. Whether the schools in question are good or bad for their wards is very much disputed. By definition, though, one thing they cannot do is to teach them how to become independent.[24]

3. Prohibit and Censor

Nor are parents and Gulags alone in treating teenagers as if they were some kind of wild animals which must be caged, restrained, hamstrung, and at the same time, protected against all sorts of danger and injury. All around, anti-smoking and drinking laws are being tightened. Even as this was being written, California was considering raising the minimal age for smoking from eighteen to twenty-one. Several cities already have enacted laws to that effect.[25] Young people, it appears, are deemed sufficiently mature to participate in elections. But deciding whether or not to light a cigarette is more than they can responsibly do.

But smoking is the least of it. The town of Hilliard, Florida, is but one of many which have ruled that "No person under the age of eighteen years shall loiter, idle, wander, stroll or play in or on the public streets, other public places, places of amusement or entertainment, vacant lots or other *unsupervised* [my emphasis] places, between the hours of 12:00 midnight and 6:00 a.m. of the following day, official City time."[26] At least one major city, Dallas, also prohibits them from being on the streets during daily school hours.[27]

The law can, and often does, deprive young people of the right to drive on their own to wherever they want. The same applies to their right to drive at all hours of day and night. These prohibitions are said to be motivated as much by the need to protect them as by the desire to minimize traffic jams at those times and places adults want to use the roads.[28] Teenagers may be prevented from entering public amusement places including pool halls, dance halls, and the like. They may not watch such and such movies, play such and such computer games, or buy such and such erotic material. They are also barred from watching television violence. Notwithstanding that definite evidence for its harmful effect on behavior is lacking—perhaps, even, to the contrary.[29] By one account they are almost twenty times as likely to be subject to such restrictions on freedom as adults are. In some respects, they have fewer rights than either soldiers or prisoners do.[30]

Some of the restrictions on children can only be called bizarre. Take, for example, when laws enacted in parts of Germany and some Italian towns prohibited them from building sand castles.[31] British children have been punished for wearing coats in school, wearing and trying to sell armbands in memory of a classmate who died of cancer, and a great many other things.[32] In the US schools have cut shop classes, dances, after-hours sports, and even games as innocuous as tag. Just to be on the safe side, some forty percent of schools are said to have ended recesses entirely.[33] All this, in an effort to "protect" children against themselves. And all in disregard of the fact that youth has always been, and should remain, a time in which to try and experiment. Rather than allowing them some elbow-room to do so, modern society seems determined to prevent them from growing up and looking after their own lives.

One of the most affected fields is mobility. Unlike so many others, it can be quantified. In one 2011 study, seventy percent of mothers said that, when they were young, they used to play outside the house. But only less than half of them—thirty-one percent—said their own children did the same.[34] Back in 1969, eighty-nine percent of American children who lived within a mile of school walked or rode a bicycle. Forty years later the figure had gone down to just thirty-five percent. In 1971, eighty-six percent of British children walked or rode to school. In 2013, the figure stood at just twenty-five percent.[35] These figures do not include after-school activities, many of which force so many parents to drive that "mum's taxi" has become proverbial. In Britain, a relatively small and crowded country, the average mum is said to drive her children about 1,284 miles each year. So great has the loss of independence been that some British men and women expect their parents to drive them even at the age of thirty and higher.[36]

Several factors explain parents' decisions to drive their children instead of allowing them to move on their own. One is suburbanization. In the US it accounts for two-thirds of the population, greatly increasing the distances that must be covered in order to get anywhere. A vicious cycle is created. The more parents drive their children the more traffic increases; the greater, therefore, the risk to those who still choose to walk or bike.[37] True, there is no law to determine the minimum age at which, and the distance to which, an unaccompanied young person can travel on foot, by bicycle, or by public transportation. In some ways, however, that fact only makes the situation worse. Parents may be prosecuted, or have their children taken away from them without trial, not because they have violated the law but for having acted "irresponsibly." As if adults doing the same never make a mistake or suffer an accident!

But getting to school (and home again) is only the beginning. The very idea on which school rests—namely that to prepare students for "life," it is necessary for them to spend more and more years in institutions that isolate them from it—

can only be described as bizarre. The more so because they are made to spend much, perhaps most, of their time in class studying subjects that bear hardly any relationship to the job market they will one day have to enter. As one German high-school student wrote: "I am almost eighteen years old and have no idea of taxes, rent, or insurance. But I can analyze a poem in four languages."[38] Unless she takes good care, when she graduates from a university after four years of study her situation will not be any better. No wonder her few, simple words raised a storm of indignation on one hand and approval on the other.

Worst of all, school goes far in depriving students of freedom. As in all other "total" institutions, initiative, responsibility, and the ability to cope with events as they come are thrown overboard. Students know this and behave accordingly. Many years ago I wrote an article on the fact that so many of them call their schools "cages," "barracks," "prisons," and, in Israel, "ghettoes." And with good reason, for increasingly prisons are just what they look and feel like. Complete with bars, metal detectors and even armed guards. I wrote this article in the mid-1970s when my first wife was working as a secretary at a high school. Coming to work one morning, her boss showed her the piece and angrily asked whether it had been she who told me about the school being nicknamed "The Prison." She had not; I was referring to another school. Since then, judging by the way schools in the countries I have visited look, things have only become worse.

Perhaps because supervising many is harder than controlling a few, children's lives and activities inside the buildings are even more restricted than at home. Let's not dwell on the problems caused by a system that compels youngsters to sit still at their desks for hours every day, often to the point where they cannot even go to the bathroom—certainly not without asking for permission first—or properly eat their meals.[39] It also denies them sufficient physical exercise and forces them to listen to teachers, many of whom are boring and talk about topics that are often irrelevant to their charges' lives. All the while threatening them with punishment and offering no rewards, except for purely symbolic ones in the form of grades, which no adult would accept for any length of time.

No aspect of school life, however trivial, remains unregulated. That includes whom they may and may not bring to proms and the like.[40] Many schools have rules against piercings, earrings, tattoos, perfumes, and even body sprays that adults in modern life use, and are often encouraged to use, as a matter of course. Others have dozens of video cameras that constantly monitor students (even in dressing rooms and toilets, on the assumption that those are the most likely places where "crimes" are committed). Anything to make sure they should not seize the initiative and make decisions on their own. Which, heaven forbid.

In supposedly free societies, to protect children's bodies against "unhealthy" food, they are prevented from eating popcorn, crisps, sweets, chocolate, fruit winders, fizzy drinks, hot rolls, webs, and chips.[41] To protect their tender souls and prevent them from getting "false" ideas, censorship is applied to reading materials. The list of authors whose works have been cut or banned from American school libraries reads like a Who's Who of world and American literature. It includes Aristophanes, Geoffrey Chaucer, William Shakespeare, Herman Melville, Mark Twain, Jack London, F. Scott Fitzgerald, William Faulkner, Margaret Mitchell, John Steinbeck, Ernest Hemingway, J. D. Salinger, Ray Bradbury, and Joseph Heller. The first of these was banned because it referred to "offensive" themes such as the power of women. The last, because it several times refers to "whores."[42]

Similar restrictions are applied to movies, TV programs, and computer games. Given such policies, how can youngsters ever learn to decide for themselves what is and is not good and true? And how, in the words of famed education critic Ken Roberts, can they find their own element and develop it to the limit of their abilities?[43] Not to mention the fact that bans are often counterproductive. As the Bible puts it, "stolen waters are sweet." For centuries on end, the best way to make an author famous was to put his works on the Index of Prohibited Books. The same is even more true in the age of the Internet, which many of our children can use as well as, if not better than, their parents and teachers can.

Both in the US and abroad, the latest trend is to prohibit students from bringing cell phones, music players, and even some calculators to school. The rationale is that they can be used to cheat in exams, take inappropriate photos, organize gang rendezvous, and similar offenses. All of this is true enough. But it ignores the plain fact that adults can and do use them to do all these bad things and then some.[44]

Starting school at the beginning of the year, almost the first thing students are confronted with are booklets that list all the things they are not allowed to do and the penalties attached to each. Some are dozens of pages long and contain enough paragraphs, written in legalese, to make even lawyers despair of understanding them. With computers as ubiquitous as they are, even the slightest transgression is written down. Once it is, it can be neither forgiven nor forgotten.

With little room left for what the Germans call *Jugendsuende*, "the sins of youth," young people can no longer be what they should be and have always been, i.e., the source of daring, change, and innovation. Too much is at stake. Instead they are forced to step carefully, all the while watching every single step lest it turn into a misstep. The outcome, to use the title of one 2014 bestseller, is "excellent sheep."[45] Youngsters of both sexes, each for their own reasons, timidly follow the paths their elders have prescribed for them. Asked to give their reasons, they say that their actions are controlled by outside forces rather than by themselves.[46] Typically, their response to whatever adults say is "whatever." So much so that, in both the US and Britain, there now exist a whole series of educational programs with the word "whatever" in their titles.

Even that is not the end of the matter. Apparently no government or private employer has been obliged to take on office workers who suffer from attention deficit hyperactivity disorder (ADHD); or dyslectic lawyers; or dysnumeric (people who cannot do math) accountants; or dysnomic (people who cannot remember names) lobbyists; or shy salespersons; or similar people who are unable to do the jobs they want and that will "fulfill" them, as the saying goes. Instead, they expect their employees to perform. Prodded by necessity, most of the time "perform" is what most of them do.

With the young, the situation is entirely different. Among them, what counts is neither achievement nor results. It is displaying goodwill and trying one's best. Often simply coasting along without making too many waves suffices to see one through, more or less. The first reason for this is that parents insist on it. The second is that, since parents insist on it, governments have gone ahead and mandated it.

4. Becoming Infantilized

The idea that every child is born to become a Rembrandt, a Mozart, or an Einstein is one of the greatest lies of our times. By fostering illusions and preventing the truly able from standing out, it is also one of the most harmful. Yet everybody believes in it, pretends to believe in it, or is forced to believe in it. Whoever is in any way in charge of the young and publicly proclaims his or her dissent risks being reprimanded, disciplined, fired, or tried for failing to provide "equal opportunity."

Both students and teachers have internalized the new rules. Those rules cause those who do *not* perform to get the most attention and the greatest privileges. Cases are on record when, to obtain them, students or their parents paid a psychiatrist or psychologist to certify them as suffering from ADHD and other syndromes.[47] Pressed by administrators, who in turn are being pressed by their superiors, some teachers have developed into a fine art the pretense that slow students are as good as the rest.

For example, shy students may be excused from having to speak up in class, or may be given written examinations instead of oral ones. Dyslectic students may be allowed to take oral examinations instead of the written ones everybody else takes. Slow students may be provided with additional coaching or more time to do their assignments and submit their exams. To make this look as if it never happened, another *1984*-like euphemism, "flexible hours," has been introduced. Based on the assumption that substituting other people's work for one's own requires a certain amount of intelligence, some students are permitted, even encouraged, to do exactly that.[48]

The most problematic cases are being referred to institutions that cater to students with "special needs." In Canada, this group numbers about four percent of the total. The German figure is five percent, while the American one is ten percent.[49] Possibly the last-named figure has something to do with the huge number of psychotherapists and social workers of every kind, all of whom have to justify their existence by first labeling students and then working with them. Contrary to what one might think, though, the term "special" does not mean that these students are not supposed to reach the same academic standards, and pass the same tests, as everybody else. To the contrary, they *must* do so. Should they fail, then the schools they attend may be taken to account.

Thus the creators of the bundle of programs broadly known as "No Child Left Behind" have a lot to answer for. On one hand, the general levelling process, by raising the average grade, makes it harder for those who are truly excellent to stand out and be properly rewarded. On the other, it betrays its weaker charges by failing to make them aware of their limitations and steering them in directions that are suitable for them. Instead of doing so, it raises their expectations to what are often unrealistic levels and thus preparing them for future failure.

Originally the system was only applied in kindergartens and elementary schools. Gradually, though, it started working its way upwards all the way into the colleges. As long ago as 1995 it was claimed that about fifty thousand substandard students, forming nearly three percent of all new entrants, were entering US colleges each year.[50] If any more recent statistics exist, I have been unable to locate them. I am told that even graduate schools in such elite institutions as Oxford and Cambridge are no longer immune. Faculty and administrators are exhorted to provide "adjustments," such as the possibility of "flexible work hours and other accommodations" to those suffering from LDs (learning disabilities).[51]

Taking it upon themselves to act *in loco parentis*, many institutes of higher learning have come to treat their students as if they were still in high school or lower. Regulations concerning proper behavior on and off campus are everywhere. They include many that limit freedom of speech, the one thing which it should be the first task of any educational system to protect. Coming complete with the usual lists of punishments, these regulations must be assiduously studied. As if to emphasize the extent to which the system prevents students from growing up and becoming independent, their grades are regularly sent for their parents to scrutinize.

During the rise of universal education in the second half of the nineteenth century, at first elementary school was supposed to provide students with sufficient knowledge and skills to function as citizens and hold a job. Then junior high school (an oxymoron if ever one there was) was added; then high school, which soon ceased to be particularly high; then college; then graduate school. Each additional layer did little but "prepare"—whatever *that* may mean— students for the next layer. Each time a layer was added it tended to devalue those that were under it, much as printing additional money devalues that which is already in circulation.

Together these developments keep postponing the moment students finally hatch, so to speak, and enter real life. Especially since the beginning of the economic crisis that overtook the West in 2008, for many of them it is too late. Having spent the best part of two decades bravely attending school in the hope of getting if not to the very top, at any rate to a comfortable position in the middle, they end up by finding themselves unemployable at the bottom.[52]

As society becomes more peaceful—in the absence of major war, never in history have Westerners been less likely to die a violent death[53]—people, men in particular, tend to become less willing to take risks, are less robust, and are less resilient. Both in law and in practice, countless problems that used to be settled by the antagonists themselves now require the intervention of social services, police, the courts, or some combination of all three.

Linguistic evidence confirms the abovementioned trends. Earlier on we noted the rise to prominence of "childhood" and "adolescence." Later they were joined by "youngster," which reached the peak of its popularity during the 1950s. In the 1940s the word "teenager" with is various connotations—including "lack of potency and understanding"—entered the race. Whether in spite or, which is more likely, because of its connotation, "lack of potency and understanding,"[54] it was destined to have the most spectacular career of all.

From 1840 to 1920 males enrolled in institutes of higher learning were known as "college men." The interwar period saw the emergence of "college kids," a term which refers to people of both sexes. Rising steeply, by 2000 it had overtaken "college men" and "college women," both of which seem to be heading towards obsolescence. There even is something called "college child." Traditionally almost unknown, the expression started coming into use in 1960 or so; albeit it has still not overtaken the others.

Or take "violence," a word that entered English around 1300. It used to mean "physical force used to inflict injury or damage." Another definition was "rough or injurious physical force, action, or treatment."[55] However, as physical violence receded it assumed new meanings. By one list it can equally well be verbal, cultural, symbolical, emotional, psychological, or structural (that is strange: how can a structure, which by definition denotes something fixed, be violent?).[56] Examples of such "violence" are said to be "elitism, ethnocentrism, classism, racism, sexism adultism, nationalism, heterosexism and ageism."[57] Briefly any kind of language, spoken or written, that acknowledges the fact that not all people are identical and that differences among them do exist.

Similarly "trauma," from the Greek "wound," used to mean a physical injury. Only after 1945 did it extend into the field of psychology as well. There was a time when "oppression" used to mean "unjust or cruel exercise of authority of power"[58] and was almost always backed up by violence. But now we also have verbal oppression, emotional oppression, psychological oppression, and cultural oppression. With every passing day oppression seems to be spreading to additional domains. Even a person whose dog has died may feel "oppressed" (by whom?)[59] God save that anybody should be "upset," let alone "offended," in any way.

Conversely, anybody who *is* "offended" and *is* "upset" immediately becomes a "victim." The implication is that he, and even more so she, is helpless in front or either bad luck or bad people and cannot defend himself or herself. That in turn has given to three new terms, "victimization," "victimology" and "victimhood." The first two took off during the 1960s; the third followed in the 1980s. Since then, it has embarked on an even more spectacular career than its older relatives did. Other words that have moved in the same direction are "abuse" and "survivor." Combining the two, there is even a book about "verbal abuse survivors" who dare to speak out.[60]

Perhaps strangest of all is the fate of the term "courage." Courage has always been the one quality without which the conduct of war is impossible. It meant the willingness to take risks—specifically including the greatest risk of all, that of being stabbed or shot or torn or crushed or blasted to pieces on behalf of a cause, or else other people, whose lives one values more than one does one's own. That is precisely why it was seen as the most admirable quality of all. A good example is a fireman who enters a burning house in order to save its inhabitants. Conversely, a person who saves himself by jumping out of the window of the same house is not necessarily courageous. He may, indeed, simply be in a panic.

However, the last few decades have witnessed the term expanding into all kinds of other directions. Like the rest, as it did so it was watered down and devalued. As has been said,[61] any "celebrity" who gets sick and doesn't spend every day crying about it is praised for his or her "courageous battle" with chronic fatigue syndrome, or a love affair that went wrong, or depression, or even "food addiction." People are called "courageous" because they came out about being gay, or having been abused during their childhood thirty years ago, or whatever. Some even fight "courageous" battles with the kind of stress caused, of all things, by playing cricket![62] Surely all these things do require courage of a certain kind. But what risk does an anorexia patient take, and whom but herself does she benefit by fighting her disease?

5. "From Austria Came a Man"

If it is true, as has been said, that adolescence means "novelty seeking, social engagement, increased emotional intensity, and creative exploration,"[63] then modern Western societies seem determined to prevent all four. Do-gooders, both real and false—corporations, trade unions, NGOs, "advanced" countries, parents, the law, schools, and colleges—all act as if they were engaged in a vast conspiracy to shield the young against everything, not least of all themselves. Nor is there any shortage of demands to subject them to even more restrictions, such as making under-eighteens (or twenty-ones, or twenty-fives—check the appropriate rubric) undergo "gender-appropriate bag searches/pat-downs" whenever they want to enter a "public" event.[64] All this is to ignore the fact that, in the past, the desire to "protect" children has led to some of the worst crimes of all; *vide* the execution of Socrates in 399 BC.

Scant wonder that a great many young people no longer know how to cope with anything, let alone match non-Westerners on the battlefield. Two main forces drive the process. First, as we saw, there is the wish of many adults to prevent or delay competition for as long as they can. The more so because, in a rapidly changing world, they have everything to fear from young people. After all, the latter find it easier to adjust. They learn faster, retain a greater part of what they have learned, and are better at using every kind of new technology from cell phones and their applications on up. Also because, as life-expectancy keeps rising, more and more elderly people desperately try to avoid retirement and the loss of status and income it so often brings. By so doing, they block the road to those who follow them.[65]

Second, there is the danger of liability in case youngsters either get hurt or hurt others. That this liability also has the effect of opening the door to every kind of greed hardly requires saying. The overall objective is to prevent young people from growing up. It is done by first creating the idea of adolescence and then using almost any available means to force those who reach it to remain in it for as long as possible.[66] Some people and organizations with a stake in the matter have extended it until it reaches into the mid-twenties. A few have gone so far as to include persons well into their thirties.[67]

Nor is the US the only country where things are changing. In Britain, "child psychologists" are getting new instructions concerning their young patients— "young" meaning, in this case, up to twenty-five years of age. The official objective is to prevent them from contracting an inferiority complex (why the young, with all their energy and originality, should contract such a complex more often than their elders is left unsaid; is it because those elders do everything in their power to prevent them from developing those qualities?).[68] The less official one: to allow the psychologists in question to expand their practice by treating them as well. In Italy some years ago, a court decided that a person in his mid-thirties has a legal right to be supported by his parents until he found a job that "fits his aspirations." As it happened, he was studying law.[69]

To achieve the objective, people and organizations resort to two main methods running in parallel. One consists of surrounding the young with so many prohibitions that they can hardly lift a finger without breaking one or more of them. The other is to encourage their "self-esteem" by artificially lowering or removing any hurdle they have to pass. Starting in infancy, where doing so is appropriate up to a point, it has been steadily extended. By now it has made itself noticeable even in many postgraduate programs. Back in 1940, A's only formed fifteen percent of all grades awarded in college. Now, at forty-five percent, they have become the most common grade of all.[70] Professors find themselves caught in a dilemma. Going along with the trend, they punish high achievers, foster illusions, and encourage mediocrity. Trying to resist it, they punish the students who take their classes rather than those of others. Either way, they make it harder for some of their best charges to get ahead.

Perhaps worst of all, any attempt by young people to resist the pressure brought to bear on them is seen not as a sign of maturity, let alone originality and "spunk," but as some sort of pathology. The outcome, a call for treatment, is causing the punitive and medical systems to become almost interchangeable. As they do so, both appear in a lurid light.[71] The figures speak for themselves. Intuitively one would expect the young, assiduously protected against anything that might possibly hurt their fragile egos and not yet subjected to the full pressures of adult life, to be the healthiest sector of society. In fact, in 2007 alone almost forty percent of American children aged twelve to seventeen were treated for depression and/or other psychological disturbances.[72] Six years later "an astounding 19 percent of high school-age boys—ages 14 to 17—in the US [had] been diagnosed with ADHD and about 10 percent [were] taking medication for it."[73] The cost of psychopharma youths are made to take exceeds that of all other drugs they receive combined.[74]

The situation in Germany, where six times as many children were diagnosed as suffering from depression in 2014 as in 2000, is not so very different.[75] The fact that, there as in all countries, many of the diagnoses may turn out to be false only rubs salt into the open wounds. In the US in 2014 about one in five schoolchildren were taking Ritalin, a drug that differs from cocaine mainly in that it is legally manufactured by leading pharmaceutical companies at an enormous profit to themselves. Never mind that the list of side effects it causes, some of which are classified as "serious"—including slowing down growth, seizures, and blurred vision—is much too long to be cited here.[76]

Ritalin is prescribed about three times as often to boys as to girls. One possibility is that the former's biology makes them less obedient and less submissive on the average. Another possibility is, those higher energy levels make it harder for them to sit still for hours on end, as school life increasingly demands. Yet another, that teachers and other educational personnel, the great majority of whom are female and many of whom are feminists, have declared war on them. In the words of one author, "boys are scolded even for their violent fantasies—for the violent stories they want to hear, the violent books they want to read, the violent games they want to play. [These qualities] are punished, pathologized, and stigmatized from cradle to campus. Even the good guys are treated like bad guys for ganging up, for being 'xenophobic,' patriotic, or too exclusive. Videogames, fighting sports, and movies are decried for being 'too violent.'"[77] Either the boys must include girls, whose natural inclinations are quite different, in their activities, or those activities must be brought to a halt.

Yet it is boys who have always provided armed forces with the vast majority of their soldiers. Forty years after the feminization of those forces got under way during the 1970s, they continue to form practically all combat troops. This is especially true on the ground, where most of the "new wars"—to speak with political scientist Mary Kaldor—take place and almost all the casualties are incurred.[78] That is why, during the so-called "Global War on Terror," fewer than three percent of US troops killed in battle were female.[79] These calculations exclude private military contractors, practically all of whom are male and many of whom perform tasks similar to those in which soldiers engage. Hence even the figure of three percent exaggerates the contribution of women and understates that of men. Probably, as we shall see later, on purpose.

In the words of the famous German Field Manual (HDv 300) of 1936, war demands "the *independent* [my emphasis] commitment of all spiritual, intellectual and physical faculties" from all soldiers, from the highest to the lowest.[80] Given all the above factors, is it any wonder that the age of senior commanders in particular has been going nowhere but up? Gone are the days when Alexander, aged eighteen, commanded the most important force in his father's army at the battle of Chaeronea in 338 BC and went on to conquer the world. Or when Scipio, twenty-five years old and not yet known as Africanus, took over the defeated Roman Army in Spain and led it to victory against Carthage. Or when Pompey, later to be nicknamed "the Great," was granted his first triumph at the age of twenty-five. Or when Octavian, nineteen years old and not yet known as Augustus, took over the armies of his maternal great-uncle, Julius Caesar, in 44 BC. Or when Salahuddin Ayubi ("Saladin") became commander in chief at the age of twenty-nine. Or when Jeanne d'Arc, aged eighteen, inspired the French to victory.

PUSSYCATS

At the Escorial, the somber palace Philip II of Spain built for himself north of Madrid, there is a crypt where some members of the Habsburg family are buried. One of the graves carries the words, "from Austria came a man." The "man" in question was Don John of Austria, illegitimate son of Emperor Charles V and thus Philip's half-brother. Aged twenty-four, he commanded at Lepanto, dealing the Ottomans a blow from which their navy never recovered. Another of Philip II's most successful generals, Alessandro Farnese, was thirty-three years old when he took over the eighty thousand men forming the Spanish Army of the Netherlands, then the most powerful army in existence anywhere in Europe. Sweden's Charles XII was just eighteen when his country came under attack by a coalition made up of Denmark-Norway, Saxony-Poland-Lithuania, and Russia. Did he break down? Was he traumatized? Did he need psychological treatment by child experts? No. Always cool under fire, first he put himself at the head of a force of eight thousand men and forty-three ships and knocked the Danes out of the war. Next, taking on a Russian army four times the size of his own, he beat them in the Battle of Narva. Two years later, fighting the Poles, he inflicted such a crushing defeat on them that he was able to put his own candidate on the Polish throne.

Frederick II of Prussia was twenty-eight when he launched his first campaign against the Austrians (he almost lost). Napoleon, or rather General Bonaparte as he then was, was twenty-six when he assumed command over the Army of Italy and led it to some of the most spectacular victories in history. Much later he wrote that "once a man reaches the age of 35"—his own age at the start of the 1805 Austerlitz campaign, the most brilliant of his entire career—"his military abilities start withering. Nobody ever loved his bed more than I did." Compare this to the situation in today's Western armed forces where thirty-five-year-olds are just entering staff college and, until they graduate, are not yet considered fit to command even a battalion!

Israel's *de facto* commander-in-chief during the country's War of Independence in 1948, Yigael Yadin, was thirty-one years old. His most successful subordinate, General, Yigal Allon, was the same age. Allon started the war by beating the Arabs in the north of the country, then in the center. Next, commanding a division against the Egyptians, he drove them from the Negev into the Sinai. Had he been given a free hand, he would have annihilated the Egyptian Army. At the time Yitzhak Rabin commanded a brigade during the desperate fighting for Jerusalem in April-May 1948, he had just turned twenty-six. Most of his men, serving in the elite Palmach ("Shock-Troops"), were between eighteen and twenty-two years old.[81] Many had not finished high school before enlisting. Some had run away from home. Lack of experience and equipment, as well as the fact that Palmach had long been forced to operate in a clandestine manner under the British Mandate, often prevented them from being properly trained. However, as their heavy losses show, they certainly knew how to fight and die; over a twelve-month period, one third of their number were killed.

To quote a famous Hebrew poem, in their death they formed the "silver tray" on which the State of Israel was established. Conversely, had modern Western countries deliberately tried to design an education system for neutering the young and turning them into pussycats—the kind of pussycats who, whenever and wherever they are sent to fight in the Third World, are invariably defeated—they could hardly have done a better job.

Chapter II. Defanging the Troops

1. "To Horse, to Horse!"

In the early 1970s the US, sobered by the Vietnam experience, did away with the draft. Instead it reverted to armed forces made up of long-service, professional volunteers, a model it had used during most of its history.[1] Since then, almost all other Western countries have done the same. So, somewhat later, did NATO's newly acquired East European members.

As the forces shrunk, one outcome was a vast increase in the relative number of senior officers. In 2015, in proportion to the number of troops, the Bundeswehr had four times as many generals as the Wehrmacht , widely acclaimed as one of the most effective armed forces of all time, did in 1939-45.[2] Insofar as the change reflected the need to make the generals accept ongoing cuts in the defense budget, it would be true to say that those generals preferred their own interests to those of the forces as a whole.

The situation in the US is worse still. In World War II the army had one colonel per 672 enlisted men. At the time of Vietnam, the figure reached 163.[3] Between March 1942 and April 1945 there was just one four-star general per two million men in the army and air corps. In 2015 there was one for every 37,000 soldiers and airmen, a fifty-four-fold increase.[4] Costs, consisting not just of salaries but of retirement benefits, pensions, and all kinds of perks, rose in proportion.

Yet money was only part of the price paid and probably not the most important one. The Pentagon has been blasting the Obama administration, especially National Security Adviser Susan Rice, for trying to micromanage the military.[5] The accusation rings true; but it is equally true that, in all Western countries, rank-inflation has caused any number of decisions that used to be made by one-star generals to be referred to those who have two or three. Not to mention entire hierarchies of senior officers using their helicopters to fly over the battlefield supervising the hapless subaltern on the ground. Commanders, take the beam out of your eye! The sheer number of generals all but guarantees that they will get in each other's way. And so, too, further down the ladder. That in turn helps account for some of the phenomena that the present chapter will review.

Another problem is the way civilian attitudes have been spreading into the military. The fewer and less serious the wars, the more likely they are to do so. Ever since 1945 the vast majority of Western troops have been spending most of their time at home. Even during the Vietnam War, the largest armed conflict any Western country has waged since 1945, only about twenty-seven percent of all the GIs who went through the forces were actually sent to Southeast Asia.[6] That peace is a blessing, almost the greatest blessing there is, none can dispute. Too, one would not want to live in a society where civilians and soldiers are so far apart as to form separate worlds and where, as a result, the latter may represent a danger to democracy. Nevertheless, there should be limits. But for its own values, such as hierarchy, discipline, and certain other things, no fighting organization can exist, let alone operate, for very long.

Let us start with what military service used to be and what, in recent decades, it has become. Throughout history, people recognized that war is a deadly, if sometimes absolutely necessary, business. Throughout history they also understood that those who fight in it and die in it on behalf of the community to which they belong must be allowed to enjoy some liberties others do not have, the more so because of the deprivations they had suffered and which made them hungry for life. Thus Spartan troops used to sacrifice to the love-goddess Aphrodite before entering battle (just what they did is not clear; however, *aphrodiazein* means "to indulge one's lust").[7]

While outlining his imaginary totalitarian society in which *everybody's* sexual behavior was strictly controlled, Plato suggested that men who had distinguished themselves in war be given more opportunities to mate.[8] Caesar, his biographer Suetonius says, "neither noticed all [the soldiers'] transgressions nor punished them according to strict rule.... Sometimes, after a great battle ending in victory, he would grant them a relaxation from all kinds of duty and leave them to revel at pleasure. Being used to boast, 'my soldiers fought nothing worse for being well oiled.'" Celebrating a triumph, his troops were even allowed to sing bawdy songs about him (imagine that!).[9]

Early sixteenth-century Spanish commanders in Southern Italy and elsewhere habitually permitted their troops certain comforts and privileges not normally available to stay-at-home civilians.[10] So did Napoleon in respect to his Imperial Guard. Meeting them at Fontainebleau in 1814, a British painter, Benjamin Haydon, wrote that "more dreadful looking fellows... I have never seen. They had the look of thoroughbred, veteran, disciplined banditti. Depravity, recklessness, and bloodthirstiness were burned into their faces... Black moustaches, gigantic bearskins, and a ferocious expression were their characteristics."[11] The Emperor, a born leader, knew how to take good care of them. That included showing his affection by closing an eye to certain liberties they took. All these were elite troops. Each in turn, in their own time, were famous for their discipline—on the battlefield, not when on leave—and exhibited endurance, courage, and, above all, determination to conquer or die. So much so, in fact, that when the Guard started retreating at the Battle of Waterloo in 1815 people at first refused to believe their eyes.

Such troops have always formed the backbone of armies and will continue to do so until the Day of Judgment. Nobody put the idea better than Friedrich Schiller in *The Cavalry Song* (1797). It is a great piece of poetry, which is why it is quoted in its entirety here:

PUSSYCATS

Huzza! O my comrades! To horse! To horse!
In the field still can freedom be wrested,
For there in the battle is proved manhood's force
In the field our hearts will be tested!
None can another's place supply,
Each standeth alone—on himself must rely.

Now freedom appears from the world to have flown,
None but lords and their vassals one traces;
While falsehood and cunning are ruling alone
O'er the living cowardly races.
The man who can look upon death without fear—
The soldier—is now the sole freeman left here.
The cares of this life, he casts them away,
Untroubled by fear or by sorrow;
He rides to his fate with a countenance gay,
And finds it to-day or to-morrow;
And if 'tis to-morrow, to-day we'll employ
To drink full deep of the goblet of joy.
The skies over him shower his lot filled with mirth.
He gains, without toil, its full measure;
The peasant, who grubs in the womb of the earth,
Believes that he'll find there the treasure.
Through lifetime he shovels and digs like a slave,
And digs—till at length he has dug his own grave.

The horseman, as well as his swift-footed beast,

Are guests by whom all are affrighted.

When glimmer the lamps at the wedding feast,

In the banquet he joins uninvited;

He woos not long, and with gold he ne'er buys,

But carries by storm love's blissful prize.

Why weepest, my maiden? Why grievest thou so?

Let me hence, let me hence, girl, I pray thee!

The soldier on earth no sure quarters can know;

With constancy never repay thee.

Fate hurries him onward with fury blind,

Nor peace nor rest is it his to find.

Away then, my comrades, our chargers let's mount!

Our hearts in the battle bound tightly!

Youth's foam effervesces in life's bubbling fount.

Away! While the spirit glows brightly!

Unless you have courage your life to stake,

Of life's true worth you will never partake.

2. The War on Men

As the fact that the "maiden" weeps at his departure indicates, Schiller's cavalryman is not simply a lout. He must have seduced her, not raped her. But neither is he a sissy or a prig. He knows how to take his pleasure where he finds it and does so in full measure. Nor does it sound as if he will stand for attempts to prevent him from doing just that. Yet who can blame him? For him there is no tomorrow. Today he is feasting. By the time the sun goes down tomorrow it may well find him lying on the battlefield, badly injured or dead.

All this is a far cry from today's Western militaries. As the size of the wars in which they engage declines and the number of casualties they suffer falls, increasingly they insist on treating their troops as if they were rowdies, and/or babies unable to look after themselves, and/or pussycats. Worse still, they do so precisely at a time when, owing to the shift from conscription to all-volunteer forces, the average age of the troops has been rising.[12] Among officers, the growth of life expectancy and the cost of paying pensions have initiated a similar trend. Presumably the older the officers, the more inclined they are to treat their subordinates in the manner just described.

For fear of friction with the surrounding civilian population, the tens of thousands of US Service personnel stationed at Yokosuka, Japan, are not supposed to go to a bar on their own. They are required to be home at 2300 hours, and while at home they may not drink after 2200 hours.[13] Touring the area during the evenings in June 2014, I was surprised to see how few of them were out and about as soldiers, their duty having ended, are likely to be. Let alone seemingly under the influence of alcohol. What I did not know at the time was that they were more or less under curfew. The lower their rank, the more likely this is to be the case.[14] Much the same applies in Korea. As one GI wrote, in some respects the troops have fewer rights than their teenager offspring do.[15] The list could be extended at will.

For fear of standing out in a crowd and drawing the attention of terrorists, US troops in Europe have been prohibited from wearing uniform off base.[16] So have several others. One cannot help but wonder: Did Roman troops stationed in Palestine and seeking to avoid the dagger-carrying "terrorists" known as *sicarii* discard their armor?[17] To use another and perhaps more relevant example: Should the Wehrmacht troops in occupied Paris have worn civvies, so that the *Résistance* would be unable to spot them? Since when do troops assert themselves by such means? Supposing such directives had been issued, how would those troops have felt about them? Isn't it true that, throughout the ages, one reason why troops were made to wear military attire was precisely to separate them from the civilian world, increase their cohesion, and make them feel proud of themselves?[18] Nobody denies that military life does and should entail some restrictions in respect to lifestyle, behavior, and mobility. But do these restrictions have to be as humiliating and as dishonorable as the above policies are?

The way the military academies are run is, if anything, even worse. As one long-time instructor at the Naval Academy in Annapolis wrote, the central paradox of the service academies is that they attract "alpha" types. They represent the flower of the nation with the greatest ambition and the greatest drive.[19] However, once they have proven their worth, these charges are put through the ultimate nanny state. Students must live on base where all their movements are supervised and controlled to the last button and the last salute. They are told when to study, when to work, when to exercise, and when to sleep. The regulations also tell them whom they can and cannot date, when they can and cannot wear civilian clothes, at what point in their studies they can buy a car, and so on. All must go to football games and cheer. All must attend various cultural events which are generally held during the evenings. By that time, following a hard day's work and exercise, they tend to be so tired that many simply fall asleep.

As in the case of the young, one very important reason behind all this is fear of liability, in case anything happens to anybody. As the above instructor wrote, that is why much of what is going on in the academies is make-believe. It may impress visiting dignitaries, but it achieves little else. The students, or cadets as they are called in other countries that maintain similar institutions, tend to be highly intelligent and eager to master their future profession. Yet most of them are not really academic types whose objective is to gain knowledge and understanding. They do not want to sit at desks, study, take exams, and write papers. In fact, a desk-bound life is just what, by entering the academies, many of them hope to avoid. Otherwise, putting economics—the fact that they have their four years' worth of education in what are often considered elite institutions funded by the government—aside, they might as well have attended some civilian college.

As if to add offense to injury, it is more than doubtful whether subalterns on their first tours of duty really need much of the theoretical knowledge the academies keep filling them with. Instead, what they require is hands-on training that will enable them to do anything as well as, if not better than, those they command, as well as some management and leadership skills. Most of the rest can and should be provided later during their careers, as is the practice in a few other modern militaries around the world. However, acquiring that training and those skills only occupies a relatively small part of the various curricula.

Treating the troops as if they were babies incapable of proper behavior or looking after themselves, the military have also been putting restrictions on what they may and may not say and think. Some of the restrictions are official, other unofficial. Insofar as the latter do not make it crystal-clear what is permitted and what is not, they are worse than the former. Historically, troops have always called their enemies by all kinds of names. The Greeks called non-Greeks—not just soldiers but all of them—"*barbaroi*," meaning that, unable to speak properly as sensible human beings do, they only emitted noises: *bar-bar*. Other examples are "*Boches*," "Krauts," "Japs," "Nips" and "Nippers," and, as late as Vietnam during the 1960s, "Gooks."

But by no means were all the names contemptuous. Some, such as "Tommy," as the Germans called their British opponents—and "Jerry," as the British, returning the compliment, did—had respectful, almost affectionate, overtones. So, up to a point, did "Ivan" and "Ami," words the Germans in World War II used to describe their Russian and American opposite numbers respectively. Another term US troops used in Vietnam was Charlie. Originally it was an Americanization of VC (Viet Cong).[20] Later, though, it came to be used in ways that did not necessarily imply either disgust or hatred.

In today's politically correct world it is no longer enough to kill those who would kill you. Nor are you allowed to take souvenirs, or take a selfie while standing in triumph over your enemy, or set up monuments showing that enemy at the moment of his defeat, as used to be the case during most of history.[21] No, the folks at home—most of whom have never had a shot fired at them—in their wisdom have decreed that you've got to keep in mind that he, too, is human and pay him due respect[22]—even when he is committing unspeakable atrocities, as many, especially those waging Jihad against the West, are doing all the time.

Such policies probably affect the troops in two opposite ways. First, there is reason to think that complimentary epithets would not have come into the world if they had not helped those who invented them cope with war—the hardest test there is. Second, and working in the opposite way, derogatory ones makes it easier to kill the enemy as ordered. "Dehumanization," is the phrase modern psychologists have coined for this.[23] Yet trying to resist the trend does not only constitute crying in the wilderness—quite often, it can lead to one being put out there. So strong is the pressure in this direction that the words "to kill" themselves have become more or less taboo. Rather than call what the military are doing, and are supposed to be doing, by its proper name, one is expected to say "neutralizing" or "taking out"—as if one were playing some innocuous computer game.

As one would expect, many if not most of the prohibitions are meant to regulate, read reduce, the troops' interest in pornography and sex. Nowhere is that more true than in the US, but the militaries of many other Western countries are not far behind. The principal objective is to help create a female-friendly working environment and prevent servicewomen from being "offended." The military's official definition of pornography is too long to be cited in its entirety here.[24] It consists of "materials that are grossly offensive to modesty, decency, or propriety, or shock the moral senses because of its vulgar, filthy, or disgusting nature, or its tendency to incite lustful thoughts, which violates community standards.... They appear [sic] to the prurient interests of a reasonable person," including, but not limited to, "nudity of a person, actual, simulated or animated." Even if the figures shown did not engage in any kind of sexual activity.

By that standard much of the world's greatest art should be, and for all I know is, prohibited. That includes both the Venus of Milo and Polycleitus' fifth-century BC *Doryphoros* (the Spear-Carrier). The latter may well be the greatest statue of a warrior made by any artist, in any country, at any time. Not to mention numerous statues, both ancient and Renaissance, of nude wrestlers deliberately shaped in such a way as to titillate by bearing a mixed combative and homoerotic character. Millions of people of many different cultures, both male and female, both young and old, come to see the statues each year. Those of them who like such things buy them, or copies of them, and display them in their homes. Yet doing so does not seem to make them feel offended or cause them any special psychological problems.

Claiming that pornography negatively affects the troops' effectiveness, one US divisional commander in Iraq threatened to court-martial his troops for watching it.[25] Whether he succeeded, and if so to what effect, is anything but clear. Had similar rules existed during World Wars I and II, then much of the so-called, often quite magnificent, "nose art" aircrew used to express their affection for the machines in which they flew and on which their lives depended would also have to be banned. That, in fact, was precisely what did happen when US Air Force officers searching bases for "inappropriate" material found "more than 200" examples of such art and confiscated them.[26] The total number of "unprofessional/offensive" items this particular sweep uncovered "at 97 active duty installations and offices worldwide" was 27,598, no less.

Interestingly, "the majority of 631 items deemed pornographic were found at the Air Education and Training Command." By that criterion, it does not seem to fulfill its mission of imbuing personnel with the "appropriate" values and skills very well. Even more interesting is the fact that the exact definition of what comprises "vulgar, filthy, or disgusting" material was left to the commanders in charge—few of whom, one supposes, have attended art school. Some seem to have interpreted their instructions rather broadly. They confiscated not only *Playboy* but the *Sports Illustrated* swimsuit edition as well as *Maxim*. Is it necessary to remind readers that neither magazine publishes nude, let alone lewd, photographs?

The consequences of disregarding other aspects of the prevailing climate of opinion can be much more serious—even if it is done inadvertently. That was what happened to Captain Owen Honors in 2011. Honors' efficiency reports must have been good enough for his superiors to appoint him commander of an aircraft carrier. Built some years ago at a cost of perhaps $5 billion, it is home to eighty to ninety aircraft which probably cost about the same. Some of them were nuclear-capable. In a navy which, with a surplus of senior officers on its hands, is always ready to drop them at the drop of a hat, obtaining the job was no mean achievement.[27]

Honors' misdeed was to allow some members of his five-thousand-strong crew to screen a video without first making sure that nobody, but nobody, would be offended by it. Later it transpired that he himself had appeared in the video, which had been made years before. When news about its "raunchy" contents leaked out he was relieved almost on the spot. Though he was ultimately allowed to remain in the Navy, his career was clearly over.[28]

One officer, Gregory McWherter, who was former commander of the Blue Angels, the Navy's elite aerobatic team, lost his job for painting a blue and gold penis so large that it could be seen from space (and from nowhere else).[29] Nor is it merely a question of speaking no evil. In the US as elsewhere, determined efforts are being made to turn soldiers into eunuchs. That includes a ban on adultery which, though not explicitly prohibited by the Uniform Code of Military Justice, does fall under the rather flexible category of "inappropriate" conduct. So wide does the Code cast its net that even single persons can be, and have been, accused of adultery![30] But that is not all. As of 2013 oral and anal intercourse were still listed as crimes. Apparently the military remain stuck in the world of Richard von Krafft-Ebbing, the well-known German author of *Psychopathia Sexualis* (1886). "Every expression [of the sexual instinct]," he wrote, "that does not correspond with the purpose of nature, i.e. propagation, must be regarded as perverse."[31]

Returning to the Navy, the 1991 Tailhook "scandal" alone caused dozens of highly qualified personnel to lose their jobs. Many were pilots whose training costs are in the millions of dollars.[32] It also brought down two senior admirals and probably contributed to the suicide of a third, Chief of Naval Operations Jeremy Boorda. It has been described, quite correctly, as the greatest defeat the US Navy has suffered since Pearl Harbor.[33] All because of dubious claims by a female officer who said she had been fondled by her comrades during a wild party in Las Vegas. As her reward, not only did President George Bush, Sr. invite her to the White House "for tea," but she went on to make millions out of her accusations.[34] She even had a movie made about her.

As of 2014 the US military was said to have had more sexual assault response coordinators (SARCs) than it had recruiters.[35] If only because all those coordinators had to either show results or be assigned to some other, perhaps less congenial task, the problem grew and grew. One estimate is that, between 2005 and 2013, almost one third of all officers fired lost their jobs because of sex-related offenses such as adultery and "improper" relationships. And no wonder, given the extended nature of sea-duty and the cramped quarters where men and women live and work. In 2010 alone the US Navy got rid of forty officers accused of sexual misconduct of some kind.[36] Many never got a hearing, let alone an opportunity to put their case to a proper court. Instead, they were simply presumed to be guilty and pressed to resign.

The best-known case was that of David Petraeus. Petraeus was a four-star Marine Corps general widely believed to have distinguished himself like no other American commander in Iraq and Afghanistan. He was accused of exchanging "sexually charged" messages with a former female assistant, Paula Broadwell. However, it was only after he had doffed his uniform and taken over as head of the CIA that their relationship became physical, and it was then that he was forced to resign. Never mind that the two had known each other for decades. Never mind, too, that Ms. Broadwell was a reserve US lieutenant colonel. Qualified to command a battalion or equivalent, presumably she was well able to look after herself. Nor did anybody doubt she did.

So prevalent is the problem as to have acquired not one name but two: "the Bathsheba Syndrome," after the biblical Bathsheba whom King David took and slept with; and "zipper failure." As in all modern countries and institutions, fear of liability plays a large role. To avoid it, even many relationships clearly based on consent between adults are banned. Casting their net wider still, some military authorities have been trying to bar the troops from visiting prostitutes (in other words, pay for sex).[37] By this standard many past commanders would have been fired long before they ever took up their posts, let alone won the victories for which they have remained famous.

For example, the young David was already married when he took up first with Abigail, who was herself married, and then with the aforementioned Bathsheba.

Julius Caesar slept with any number of women, preferably married ones. So promiscuous was he that he was said to be "the husband of all women and the wife of all men."[38] Maurice de Saxe, who saved France's fortunes during the War of the Austrian Succession, slept with anything that moved. Marshal André Masséna, whom Napoleon called "the brightest star in my military empire," was a notorious fornicator. Nor was Napoleon himself far behind. While on campaign he employed the Grand Marshal of the Palace, General Duroc, to make sure a woman, properly prepared for her duties, would be waiting for him at his quarters each night.[39]

The list goes on and on. Admiral Nelson was a married man when he started his scandalous relationship with Emma Hamilton, the wife of the British ambassador in Naples. Eisenhower supposedly made out with his British chauffeur, Kay Summersby, and Patton with his niece Jean Gordon. He may have been boasting; in the eyes of one historian, that was sufficient to question his mental health.[40] Douglas McArthur had a film actress named Isabel Rosario Cooper. When the story leaked, it almost wrecked his career—not because they had sex, but because she was Eurasian.[41] All three, of course, were married. So was Moshe Dayan, probably the greatest soldier Israel has ever produced. With his one eye he attracted more women than most men do with two.

As Homer noted, and as has since been confirmed billions of times over, Mars and Venus have always gone together rather well. He needs her encouragement and also to relax after the terrible things he has seen and done. She admires him for those things—see Desdemona's attraction to Othello.[42] Even more important, she needs him to defend her against other men. No less a feminist than Simone de Beauvoir wrote that, as soon as the Wehrmacht had entered Paris in June 1940, the German troops were surrounded by French women, both professional and amateur.[43] Campaigning in France in the summer of 1944, US troops, "over paid, over sexed, and over here," as the saying went, were similarly besieged.[44] To say nothing of their subsequent experience in occupied Germany as recorded, among other things, by various obscene variations on the famous song "Lili Marlene."[45]

Chris Hedges, Pulitzer-Prize winner for journalism, has noted:[46]

> There is [in war] a kind of breathless abandon... those who in peacetime would lead conservative and sheltered lives give themselves over to wanton carnal relationships.... There is, in these encounters, a frenetic lust that seeks, on some level, to replicate or augment the drug of war.... Casual encounters are charged with a raw, high-voltage sexual energy that smacks of the self-destructive lust of war itself. The erotic in war is like the rush of battle. It overwhelms the participants. Women who might not otherwise be hailed as beauties are endowed with the charms of Helen. Men endowed with little more than the power to kill are lionized and desired. Sex in war is another variant of the drug of war. Soldiers want nothing but have sex; women find a strong attraction in uniforms, particularly in wartime. Neither linguistic barriers, nor cultural divides can prevent the sexes from going after each other. In the soldier lies absolute power, protection, and possibly escape. The woman's appeal lies in the gentleness that is absent in war. Each finds in the other attributes that war wipes out—tenderness or security....

That rape, sexual abuse and sexual harassment do exist in the military as they do everywhere else, nobody denies. There is, however, some reason to think that interested parties have vastly exaggerated the number of alleged incidents in the US Forces.[47] Whatever the correct figures, the impact on military life is multiplied many times over. Entering on their careers, soldiers are made to undergo "sexual harassment" courses. They are given to understand that, simply by virtue of having a penis, they are all potential rapists and are going to be treated accordingly. Need anybody be surprised that they find the experience humiliating?[48]

Next, they are ordered to snitch on one another and report any offenses they learn of. Had it not been for such snitching, the vast majority of "victimless crimes" committed by consenting adults would never have been discovered, let alone led to disciplinary proceedings or trials. As it is, the system invites blackmail of every sort. In the words of one retired American officer with experience in the matter, that applies "whether the unit was living in tents in the Arabian desert or at an Army post somewhere in the United States."[49] It discards honor in favor of siding up with superiors, and shreds to pieces precisely the kind of artificial family without which no fighting force can exist, let alone operate. Least of all, a modern force whose mode of fighting is dispersed so that commanders are unable to use coercion as they did, say, from the time of the Greek phalanx to the machine-like armies of Frederick the Great. Even the Petraeus affair may have been linked to a turf battle within the US intelligence establishment, some of whose members resented his appointment as head of the CIA.[50]

Many service personnel who claim to have been subjected to sexual harassment or assault do not have what it takes to stand up and testify in court[51]—let alone, one supposes, to take up a gun and fight for their country. Conversely, so bad have things become that many servicemen are more afraid of being falsely accused of harassment than of the enemy.[52] And with good reason; the number of cases reported each year is incomparably larger than that of troops killed in action.

As we shall see later in this volume, some of the pressure against many, if not most, expressions of sexuality in the services is applied by female soldiers, some of whom have their own objectives in mind. But much, probably most, of it did not originate within the military. Instead it was imposed on them from outside by a world gone soft in the head, with the kind of political correctness that has been preventing people from calling a spade a spade.[53] It also seems that certain groups have been trying to use the issue in order to further defang the military.

A typical organization involved in the effort is named, perhaps with unconscious irony, "Protect Our Defenders." The latter's "human right" is "to work and live in a safe and respectful environment"—as if they were not tough, grown-up warriors earmarked to fight "respectful" organizations such as Daesh but little children who need to have their eyes covered and their ears stopped, lest they learn that the world also contains some ugly and cruel things! Never mind, incidentally, that, at countless times and places throughout history, the prevailing morality as well as cramped living arrangements caused even little children to watch not only nudity but sexual activity among their parents and relatives as a matter of course. And to do so, what is more, without suffering any apparent psychological damage.

The moving spirit behind the organization is a lady by the name of Nancy Parrish. As well as "protecting" the tender souls of her country's soldiers, she is involved in all kinds of human-rights work both in the US and abroad.[54] She is constantly hunting for "violent"—another unconscious irony, perhaps— "pornographic" and "misogynistic" material, all to have it removed from government computers and other places where soldiers may be exposed to it.

Among Ms. Parrish's prime targets are two publications carrying the title, *Fighter Pilot Songbook/Combat Songbooks* and *The Fighter Pilot's Handbook*.[55] The name "books" is much too grandiose for them. In reality they are mere pamphlets. That the titles "did not match any products" on Amazon.com hardly requires saying.[56] Prior to Ms. Parrish's threat to make them the subject of a federal lawsuit few people had heard of them. Much of the material is both incredibly filthy and very violent. "Back your ass against the wall, here I come balls and all" is one of the less "offensive" lines they contain. Many others are much, much worse.

However, two points need to be made. First, to reverse one of Nietzsche's best-known aphorisms, thus spoke the iron to the magnet: I hate you most of all, because you attract me and I am powerless to resist you.[57] It is precisely men's love of women, combined with their inability to resist the charms of the females of the species, which feeds many of their fantasies. Fantasies, because 99.99 percent of the time that is what they are and that is what they remain. In that respect they are not too different from the ones described in that great literary work, E. L. James' *Fifty Shades of Grey*, which countless women have been lapping up.

Second, as with Schiller's cavalryman, the personnel in question must always be ready to look death in the face. Infantilized and protected against everything, including themselves, they are unlikely to be willing to do so. The anonymous editor of the *Fighters Pilots' Handbook*, borrowing and somewhat modifying a World War I soldiers' drinking song, does not put it quite as poetically as Schiller does. But the point he makes is the very same:[58]

> As we stand near the ringing rafters
> The walls around us are bare
> As we echo our peals of laughter
> It seems as though the dead are still there.
> So stand by your glasses ready.
> Let not tears fill your eye.
> Here's to the dead already
> And Hurrah for the next to die!

Is it necessary to remind the reader that, but for the readiness to be "the next to die" if necessary, no armed force ever has, nor ever will, win a war?

3. A Government of Lawyers

To say that the Petraeus affair shook the country would be going too far. Still, it was deemed sufficiently important for President Obama to take a hand. So did other members of the White House Staff, the Secretary of Defense, the head of the National Security Council, the Attorney General, the chief of national intelligence, the heads of the CIA and FBI, and several members of the US Congress. None of these people, it appears, had anything more important to do with their precious time than to find out whether or not the correspondence between the general and his lady friend did or did not contain some sexual content.

Judging by the vast number of media headlines that keep exposing "sexual misconduct" in the military, it is safe to say that voyeurism, Puritanism, and sheer prurience all play a large role. But that is only part of the story and perhaps not even the most important one. Probing deeper, we find that what is lacking is *trust*. As political scientist Francis Fukuyama pointed out, the breakdown of trust is one of the outstanding characteristics of many if not most modern societies. As so often, the US heads the list.[59]

Many causes contribute to the phenomenon. First, there is the kind of suburbanization that has vastly increased the average distance between houses. To be sure, American houses are no longer the largest in the world. That record is now held by Australia. However, as the lower number of inhabitants per square mile of city land shows, lots are still so.[60] The outcome is to prevent people from getting to know their neighbors as they used to. Often to arrange a meeting, it is first necessary to use the telephone and drive. Had FDR been president today, he would have to recognize the fact that many garden hoses are simply not long enough to reach the neighbors and help them put out a fire.

Coming next, there is geographical mobility. About one in six Americans move home each year. That is two times the British figure, four times the German one, and almost five times the Chinese one.[61] What is more, the average distance to which they move is increasing, causing whatever social ties existed to be cut. Turnover at work is also much higher.[62] People are constantly coming and going without bonding or even trying to do so. Such is the breakdown of trust that a would-be Good Samaritan is much more likely to be sued for providing the wrong kind of assistance than to be rewarded for his or her efforts.[63]

Another important factor in the equation is the government-mandated move toward "diversity." Diversity has come to mean that people are admitted, employed, rewarded, or promoted not by merit but by the color of their skin or the sex to which they belong. Whether it really does much by the way of achieving equity and fairness is moot. That it forces people coming from different backgrounds to work together, even against their will, is clear. Coming as they do from different backgrounds, they may well find it much harder to understand each other or build up mutual trust.

All these problems go some way to explain the difficulty the US has in trying to compete with some other countries, especially those of the Far East. In those societies, and the corporations that they spawn, "rugged individualism" is muted. Instead, personal acquaintanceships are allowed to play their natural role as the grease that makes it easier for the wheels to turn. People are also likely to be more committed to the companies for which they work.

Where trust is in short supply, lawyers are needed. At the turn of the millennium the number of lawyers in America was estimated at 750,000. That works out to one for every 373 members of the population, far more than in any other country except tiny Israel.[64] In the US as well as other Western countries, quite a few lawyers make a living by advising other lawyers. The outcome is to create opaque hierarchies and even more opaque networks.[65] Between them they are more than ready to serve every conceivable cause, interest, and pocket.[66]

If only because they keep moving house even more often than civilians, the military too suffers from these problems.[67] Soldiers' "core business," as the saying goes, is or ought to be to defend the country by fighting for it and, if necessary, dying for it. Insofar as the US in particular has scarcely fought a war anywhere near its borders for over a century and a half, doing so often takes the troops to places as remote and as underdeveloped as the Halls of Montezuma and the Shores of Tripoli. This fact, as well as the Forces' traditional reputation as "no-nonsense" organizations that hold scribblers in contempt, would lead one to expect that, proportionally, the number of military lawyers would be smaller than in civilian society.

In Afghanistan and other places, surely shooters are in greater demand than pen-pushers. Nevertheless, back in 1998 the US Army had 4,438 active-duty lawyers.[68] During the same year the number of men and women wearing the green uniform stood at 440,000.[69] Even when we subtract the one quarter of the general population who are under eighteen and presumably not in need of legal assistance, proportionally the Army had almost three times as many lawyers per person as civilian society does. To be sure, the military contains a disproportionate number of young men, precisely the group most likely to break the law and be disciplined or put on trial for doing so. On the other hand, unlike the general population, those who want to join the military are screened for their criminal record first. Focusing on the Army, in 2006 the number of lawyers was ten percent larger than it had been when the Cold War ended in 1991. This was the same decade and a half which saw the number of troops going down by thirty-one percent.

The expansion was used to justify an attempt to provide the Judge Advocate General (JAG) head with three stars instead of two. Had the move succeeded, it would have led to many of his subordinates being promoted as well. One participant in the discussion told the *Washington Post* that "National security was subordinated to the JAG's self-interest."[70] Other Western militaries do not seem to have suffered that much, but clearly they are moving in the same direction. Back in 1999 the British military counted 130 uniformed lawyers. Fourteen years later the figure stood at 190, civilians and all kinds of legal assistants not included.[71] During the same period the total number of uniformed personnel fell from 208,000 to 173,000. Thus the proportion of lawyers had gone up from 1 in 1,600 to 1 in 1,094. Clearly the British Forces, rooted as they are in a very different military tradition, have so many fewer lawyers than their American colleagues that it is no contest. Yet the same factors are at work, causing the armed forces of both countries to move in the same direction.

Coming on top of the loss of trust and the consequent overregulation is the ongoing shift from regular warfare to counterinsurgency, counter-guerrilla, and counterterrorism. In all of them the opponent is not a recognized state entitled to use violence, nor does he obey the law of war by wearing uniform and carrying arms openly. The outcome is numerous ambiguous situations involving non-combatants. Many have the potential to be understood as violations of the rules of engagement or even as war crimes. How do you know the man or woman approaching the roadblock is or is not a bomb-carrying terrorist? And how about the kid standing in the corner over there? Is he acting as a messenger? Or just playing around?

Ambiguity, in turn, results in proceedings, whether disciplinary or legal. Their purpose is to establish what really happened and, in case violations did take place, punish those responsible. Things got to the point where, each time a member of the local population was killed during the campaign in Afghanistan, the

American officer in charge had to fill out a five-page form. It detailed everything from the dead person's posture and dress to the ambient temperature.[72] Looking over his shoulder stood lawyers, word-processors at the ready, waiting to pounce on every word and every letter. That the commanders in question did everything possible to avoid trouble, if necessary by telling lies, hardly needs to be said. Some wit has even claimed that the well-known acronym LIC, which stands for low intensity conflict, is a misnomer. Its real meaning is "lawyer-infested conflict."

The other face of the coin is the skyrocketing number of lawsuits directed by the troops *against* the forces in which they serve or have served. In 2005 365 British soldiers made personal injury claims. By 2011-12 that figure had increased more than twentyfold and was rising still. Some of the lawsuits are very serious, involving as they do the loss of, or severe damage to, body parts. Others are frivolous. In just one year, 2012-13, the bill went up by one quarter, with no limit in sight. The total paid since 2005 is said to stand at 340 million pounds.[73]

A vicious cycle is created. The forces have no choice but to defend themselves against the troops. The troops have to evade, as far as they can, the often humiliating, often foolish restrictions the forces, often acting in the name of political correctness and against their own will but too cowardly to admit that fact, impose on them. But that is not all. The troops, assisted by specialized law firms that ask for no fee but expect to receive a percentage of any damages awarded, have a powerful incentive to sue as often as they can for as large a sum as they can. With a little luck they can hit the jackpot. In all three situations, it is the lawyers who benefit.

There used to be a time when lawyers were called the envoys of the devil. Now films and novels such as "*A Few Good Men*" (1992) and *The Night Crew* (2015) lionize uniformed ones at the expense of fighters. True, no large organization can exist without lawyers. As to what lawyers actually do, take a look at the great nineteenth-century English author Charles Dickens in his seven-hundred-page novel, *Bleak House*. Lawyers, he says, bring with them "trickery," "evasion," "procrastination," "spoliation," and "botheration." Not to mention "depositor[ies']", affidavits, repetition[s], prolixit[ie]s, filing[s], cross-filing[s], sealing[s], motioning[s], and referring[s]. "Everybody must have copies, over and over again, of everything that has been accumulated," creating "cartloads of paper." It is, he concludes, as if "the sky rained potatoes."[74]

Let the reader decide whether anything has changed since then.

4. The de-Militarized Military

Back in 1991-92, I had the good fortune to spend a year in Quantico, Virginia, living on base and teaching at the Marine Corps Staff College. This being shortly after the First Gulf War, on one occasion I asked my students, about two hundred in number and almost all of them men, whether they had been there. Practically every hand went up. Next I asked "How many of you would have missed it for your lives?" In response, every single hand in the hall went down.

That war is the most terrible of all activities we humans engage in, none can or will deny. However, for good and ill it can also be the source of great joy—perhaps indeed, the greatest joy of all. Not only Schiller but many others, including some of the most important war resisters such as the British poets Wilfred Owen and Siegfried Sassoon, acknowledged that fact.[75] Here is what one American former soldier had to say about the matter:[76]

> War is hell, but that is not the half of it, because war is also mystery
> and terror and adventure and courage and discovery and holiness
> and pity and despair and longing and love. War is nasty; war is fun.

War is thrilling; war is drudgery. War makes you a man; war makes you dead.

The truths are contradictory. It can be argued, for instance, that war is grotesque. But in truth war is also beauty. For all its horror you cannot help but gape at the awful majesty of combat. You stare out at tracer rounds unwinding through the dark like brilliant red ribbons. You crouch in ambush as a cool, impassive moon rises over the nighttime paddies. You admire the fluid symmetries of troops on the move, the harmonies of shape and proportion, the great sheets of metal-fire streaming down from a gunship, the illumination rounds, the white phosphorus, the purply orange glow of napalm, the rocket's red glare. It is not pretty, exactly. It is astonishing. You hate it, yes, but your eyes do not. Like a killer forest fire, like cancer under a microscope, any battle or bombing raid or artillery barrage has the aesthetic purity of absolute moral indifference—a powerful, implacable beauty—and a true war story will tell the truth about this, though the truth be ugly....

At its core, perhaps, war is just another name for death, and yet any soldier will tell you, if he tells the truth, that proximity to death brings with it a corresponding proximity to life. After a fire-fight, there is always the immense pleasure of aliveness... You are never more alive than when you are almost dead. You recognize what is valuable. Freshly, as if for the first time, you love what is best in yourself and the world, all that might be lost.... You are filled with a hard aching love for how the world could be and always should be, but now is not.

In the prevailing climate of political correctness, to write like this invites attack. That is why, had I asked the same question under similar circumstances today, almost certainly the vast majority of hands would have stayed up. Any member of the armed forces who publicly dares to say he or she enjoyed war—even a war against a mass murderer such as Saddam Hussein, who deserved to be overthrown if not killed—can expect to be quickly silenced if he is lucky and fired if he is not.

That is just what happened to two legendary American warriors. Not accidentally both were Marines—by tradition the toughest and, by the numbers, the most male of the services. Their careers must have carried them through the very room (Breckenridge Hall) where I raised my question. They were Marine Corps commander General James Amos and Central Command commander General James Mattis. Amos resigned after forty-four years of service because, as he said, he was "just sick of dealing with these savages in the press and in Congress. They keep asking me questions about snipers pissing on people, Nazi flags, and other crap." "I figure," he added, that Jim [Mattis] will certainly know how to handle them."[77] That proved not to be the case. For saying that shooting some people, especially those who, like the Taliban, slapped women, was "a hell of a lot of fun," Mattis was "counseled" to shut up.[78]

In every field of human endeavor, be it art or science or economic life or whatever, it is those who enjoy what they do who are most likely to succeed. Has there ever been a good carpenter, or an outstanding musician, to whom this did *not* apply? Conversely, those who cannot, or are prohibited from, doing so are almost certain to fail in whatever they undertake. If only for that reason, those who are good at what they do should have the right to be proud of their success. Nowhere is this truer than in the military. With them, failure must be paid for by the harshest of all penalties. That is why, as Frederick the Great once said, the one thing that can make men march into the muzzles of the cannons trained at them is pride.

To adduce just one out of any number of examples of what this meant, take the World-War I poem, "The Superman." Written by a World War I British soldier, Robert Grant, it was published in the United States as the latter entered the conflict in 1917:[79]

Relentless, savage, hot and grim the infuriate columns press

Where terror simulates disdain and danger is largess

Where greedy youth claims death for bride and agony seems bliss.

It is the cause, the cause, my soul! Which sanctifies all this.

Ride, Cossacks, ride! Charge, Turcos, charge! The fateful hour has come.

Let all the guns of Britain roar or be forever dumb.

It is more doggerel than poetry, but that is beside the point. The point is that, had it been written today, both the "infuriate columns" and the versifiers who praised them would have been publicly crucified as trigger-happy, murderous monsters. So would the riding Cossacks, the charging Turcos, and the roaring guns of Britain. Fighting for one's country and risking one's life for it is no longer enough. Assuming one has survived the ordeal, one also has to display one's sensitivity by putting on record one's suffering (and the enemy's!)—both while it lasted and, even more so, in retrospect.

One symptom of the problem may be seen in the changing fortunes of the terms "hero" and "heroism." In ancient Greece "heroes" were men whose prowess was so great as to appear almost divine. Quite a few heroes, in fact, *were* semi-divine, having been begotten by a god on a human female or, less often, by a human male on a goddess. As, for example, Achilles was. Quite some others were deified after their death and had temples and cults established for them, paid for out of the public purse.[80] Society permitted, even encouraged, heroes to feel proud themselves. In Homer, whenever two heroes meet on the battlefield they immediately start boasting about their ancestry and deeds. The same was true in Anglo-Saxon England and Samurai Japan—in fact, wherever tribal or feudal warriors confronted each other.[81]

It may be true, as the philosopher Ernest Becher wrote in *The Denial of Death* (1973), that heroism is a method we humans use to overcome the limits of our physical existence. We do so by identifying with, and if necessarily dying for, something we consider greater, better, nobler, longer-lasting, than ourselves. Heroism, in other words, is a way to gain immortality. If so, then it is interesting that in English, the use of the word peaked around 1900, precisely the time when Western power peaked. Since then it has gone into a slow, uneven decline. This has reached the point where, very often, it refers to trivia, as when a woman complains about her alleged harassers or a gay person publicly admits his or her inclinations. Trivialization in turn has led to irony and caused the term to be put in quotation marks. Often soldiers to whom it is applied are expected to be apologetic about it. In calling his memoirs *It Doesn't Take a Hero*, General Norman Schwarzkopf, who led the coalition forces to victory over Iraq in 1991, understood this very well. Albeit that, if (as he says) his objective was to emphasize his pride in the achievement of the troops he commanded rather than his own, he did not succeed very well. Too many people thought all he did was display false modesty.

An acquaintance of mine, a retired Marine Corps Colonel, told me how, as a young officer, at the San Francisco airport on his way to Vietnam, he was met by a young girl (this was before "girl" became a term of abuse). She gave him a flower and told me she hoped he would not come back alive. Since then, so reluctant has American society become to look the troops whom it sends into harm's way in the eye that the media are no longer allowed to film homecoming coffins. Neither America's Vietnam veterans, nor those of Afghanistan and Iraq, were ever given a proper welcome in the form of the traditional tickertape parade.[82] Some European ones of the two last-named conflicts actually had to slink away and hide from an indifferent, even hostile, public that did not want to hear anything about them or their deeds. Visiting military museums in Western Europe, I cannot remember the last time I saw schoolteachers leading their flock.

The one word that best sums up all the bad things the military are supposed to stand for is "militarism." Originally the term, which goes back to the 1880s, meant no more than the belief or desire of a government or people that their country should honor their military. It also carried the conviction that they should maintain a strong military capability and be prepared to use it, if necessary, for waging war on the country's behalf. So understood, not so long ago almost all Western governments and peoples were militarists—even enthusiastic ones.

Writing between the world wars, the English historian Arnold Toynbee once called militarism "by far the commonest cause of the breakdown of civilizations."[83] Opening Google, the very first thing we learn is that militarism is a "noun, derogatory." In particular, what gave the term its bad odor was its association with Japan and Germany before 1945. Notwithstanding that Hitler himself, well aware that many of his senior officers in particular did not like him very much, tended to avoid meeting them in any but official capacities. And notwithstanding that, throughout the twelve years of the Third Reich, the only serious organized attempt to overthrow him was made by dyed-in-the wool Prussian officers such as Henning von Tresckow and Claus von Stauffenberg.

Definitions of militarism vary. Some understand it as the idea, which they consider mistaken, that armed forces may have something positive to contribute to society that goes beyond their obvious function of waging war and, all too often, allowing themselves to be shot to pieces on its behalf. Or else they understand it to mean that they should serve as the school of the nation, an idea that used to be common before the cancellation of the draft put an end to it. Or else it meant that military personnel should play a leading role in politics and society. It is often said to be associated with negative qualities such as the inability to tolerate ambiguity, rigidity, conservatism, authoritarianism, and dogmatism[84]—not to mention aggression, imperialism, and that dreadful thing, anti-feminism.

Militarism, in short, is the worst of all bad things. In the Israel where I grew up during the 1950s and 1960s, "military" stood for efficient, effective, and even heroic. Both in Israel and in the West in general, nowadays it is more likely to mean second-rate—as in military cooking, military art, military music, and the like. There even exists a certain class of wits who claim that "military intelligence" is an oxymoron. As if waging war did not require the highest intellectual qualities and then some besides! According to Merriam Webster, a militarist is "one who urges or attempts to cause a war." Synonyms and related words are said to be "hawk, jingo jingoist, war-hawk, agitator, firebrand, fomenter, instigator, rabble-rouser, belligerent, combatant, militant and chauvinist." Antonyms and near antonyms include "peacemaker, peacekeeper, dove, pacifist and peacenik."

The fact is that most military works of art, both good and bad, represent society's way of thanking those who risked their lives on its behalf. As such, surely they deserve to be treated if not with admiration then at least with respect. Carping critics to the contrary, military art has produced some of the most magnificent works of all times. Starting, say, with ancient Egyptian paintings that show pharaohs firing arrows from their chariots. Passing through Greece and Rome, where the kind of beauty that is acquired through mutilation was considered the highest of all;[85] and so on through Renaissance statues of warriors all the way to Le Brun's Galerie des Batailles at Versailles.[86]

Some, such as Alfred Vagts whose *History of Militarism* (1937) is still the best on the subject, have tried to separate "the military way" from "militarism." The former, they explain, is necessary for creating and maintaining military effectiveness; the latter, a devotion to what I have called the culture of war for its own sake.[87] On the way, they ran into insuperable difficulties. That is because, in such things, ends and means are very hard, probably impossible, to keep apart.[88] What commander has ever told his troops that the reason why he wanted them to salute the flag was to make them maintain and raise their fighting spirit? Suppose he had done so: Wouldn't he have been met with derision?

Battle is the most atavistic environment on earth. Filled with terror, it sets back evolution a million years and creates a situation where the only thing that matters is getting out alive. Paradoxically, that is just why the culture of war is as vital as it is. Any attempt to tamper with it, even if laudable in terms of a progressive country's instincts, is dangerous and should only be undertaken with the greatest caution. What has been demolished can never be restored. A good army that does not have a powerful cultural tradition, one that can act as a kind of corset and hold it together through thick and thin—especially thin—is impossible.

Nor is militarism necessarily incompatible with a peaceful foreign policy. Thucydides in *The Peloponnesian War* commented on Sparta's conservatism and its reluctance to go to war.[89] Later it was the only city-state that did not join Alexander in his campaign against Persia. Throughout his early years in power Hitler repeatedly complained about the reluctance of his generals, those in charge of the army in particular, to go to war. He actually called them by the German equivalent of pussycats.[90] As recently as 2014 the Swiss people, one of the very few that have fought no war for a long, long time past, in a referendum decided to keep the draft.

To the extent that the world today enjoys peace, that peace is brought about very largely by the kind of deterrence only soldiers and their weapons are able to create and maintain. Almost all "peacekeepers"—i.e., men and some women who take a certain amount of risk, not to mention all kinds of physical and emotional deprivations, in order to help others in faraway countries—are military personnel. Who else could do it? Who has the necessary manpower, ready to follow orders and deploy? Who has the training? Who has the equipment? Or does anyone really believe that, to stop or at least mitigate some of those ferocious wars that seem to be constantly breaking out in large parts of the rest of the world, all we need are a few starry-eyed conflict-resolvers?

None of this has prevented many Westerners, especially but not only in Europe, from demonizing both their armed forces and, even more so, the "militarist" traditions in which the existence of those forces is rooted. Listening to some of those who do the demonizing, one would almost think that preparing to defend one's country, and being proud of doing so, is a crime.

5. Soldiers into Mercenaries

As many of their titles show, for millennia the most important function of rulers was to lead their forces in war and combat. To do so they had to receive the appropriate training as Greek *strategoi*, Roman consuls, and medieval rulers such as dukes, counts, and earls all did. As late as 1535 Emperor Charles V, campaigning in Tunis, had several horses killed under him. Even after crowned heads ceased to fight and command in person—a shift that began in mid-sixteenth-century Europe—they were still expected to engage in a close study of military matters. Clausewitz himself spent some of his career tutoring the princes of Prussia, the subsequent King Frederick William IV and Emperor William I, in the subject. Most hereditary rulers continued to receive such an education right down through the last decades of the nineteenth century. Many non-hereditary rulers, having been drafted and spent some time in the forces, gained at least some experience of what the latter are all about.

Starting in the late 1960s, things changed. As one Western country after another abolished the draft, the number of citizens who still had any kind of military experience started declining. Increasingly ministers, state secretaries, civil servants, members of parliament, and others in the upper echelons of government saw themselves making what were sometimes life-and-death decisions in fields, and on topics, without first acquiring the necessary understanding of what Clausewitz calls "the grammar" of war.[91] In Britain, one analyst came up with the idea that "defense is no longer about lining up soldiers against each other to do battle." Consequently, she argued, senior politicians and defense-officials no longer needed some kind of "military service experience."[92]

Especially but not exclusively in Europe, not a few of these people themselves are pussycats. Not in their wildest dreams would they do, or even train to do, what, when war breaks out, they send others to do. In most cases they would not even permit their sons, let alone their daughters, to join the military and go out to fight. So what is the alternative? Sweden's foreign minister, Margot Wallström, thinks she has a solution. President Putin's "macho aggression" in the Ukraine, she said, would be met by a "feminist foreign policy."

Such a policy would not rely force or the threat of force, heaven forbid. Instead it would be built on representation, resources, and respect.[93] How those nice things would prevent Russian submarines from prowling around Sweden's shores, and Russian combat aircraft, including some that are nuclear-capable, from violating Swedish airspace she didn't say. Unless what she really meant was that she was making ready to kiss the rod he was holding to beat her country with, in case it dared intervene in the conflict. If such was indeed her intention she was hardly alone. To quote German minister of defense Ursula von der

Leyen: Is there anything NATO could do to stop "Russia's gigantic military machine"?[94]

Scant wonder that, in all Western countries, the willingness to serve has been declining for decades. The outcome has been to make military manpower scarce and often hard to find. Even though the population has been growing, and even though, as conscription has ended, it is now possible to recruit not just eighteen- and nineteen-year-olds but older people as well. And even though, in theory, opening the ranks to women has slightly more than doubled the manpower pool on which the forces can draw. To be sure, enlistment is not uniform. Periods of full employment causes fewer recruits to join, whereas during periods of low employment the opposite is the case.[95] However, the long-term trend is unmistakable.

In the US, the rates at which people of different segments of the population enlist correlate negatively with college-educated parents, high grades, and plans to go to college. They correlate positively with African and Hispanic origin.[96] So great is the shortage of suitable candidates that the US, following the ancient Roman example, has taken to non-citizens to fill the ranks. Among the benefits on offer are easy access to naturalization representatives at the military personnel section at their base and reduced processing time. After 9/11, which greatly increased Uncle Sam's demand for cannon-fodder, a waiver of naturalization fees was added.[97] As of late 2014, that meant a savings of almost $1,000, exclusive of any family members.

Other incentives are designed to make them re-enlist at the end of their first period of service. The system seems to be working. In 2012 non-citizens made up 2.2 percent of the US population of prime military age (18-29). The figure in the military was almost twice as high. Thanks partly to their ethnic diversity— which for all its disadvantages may come in handy when the troops are deployed overseas—and partly to their willingness to take greater risks in order to gain citizenship, they are said to be excellent soldiers. [98]

Not only the world's most powerful country but some of the smallest Western ones also allow foreigners to serve. In Denmark they can do so either under the same conditions as Danish nationals or by signing longer-term contracts and undergoing specialist training. The latter two prerequisites demonstrate just how unpopular service has become among citizens. Even having a "special connection" with Denmark, whatever that may mean, suffices for an application to be considered.[99] Switzerland, the one European country in which the link between citizenship and conscription has always been the strongest, at one point considered a similar system.[100] Switzerland has a higher per capita income and lower unemployment than most. Proportionally it also has more foreign residents than any other European country. Thus instituting the reform would make perfect sense—except that the Swiss people, to their very great credit, would have none of it.

Other Western countries that enable, not to say beg, non-nationals to enlist and serve are Belgium, Britain, Canada, France, Ireland, Luxembourg, Norway, and Spain.[101] Of these, three—Britain, France, and Spain—maintain elite units whose rank and file are made up exclusively of foreigners. In practice if not in theory, the lives of those who serve in the units in question are regarded as more expendable than the rest. As a result, whenever there is military work to be done they are always the first to be called upon. They are, in other words, an instrument that enables the military of which they form a part to be re-fanged, at least to some extent.

Another very important innovation pointing in the same direction is the growing number, size, and importance of private military corporations. In other words, of mercenaries, or "mercs" as they are sometimes called.[102] At the time of the 1991 Gulf War one in fifty US troops was a mercenary. Not long after, during the wars in the former Yugoslavia, the number of mercenaries involved was estimated at about one in ten of all the troops. When the so-called "Coalition of the Willing" invaded Iraq in 2003 they formed the second largest force after the US military. Between 2000 and 2005 alone US spending on them doubled from $134 to $270 billion. Relative to the size of the country and that of its armed forces, developments in Britain have been even more dramatic.[103]

Like so many others, the industry is highly concentrated. Most of the big Western players are American, British, and French corporations. The founders/owners/managers tend to be retired generals and admirals. With them comes a sprinkling of former secret service personnel as well as the usual bean-counters. They recruit their troops, most of whom are also retired military, where they can find them. Expertise and cost come first, national origins often a fairly distant second. Depending on their age, former rank, and experience the men—there appear to be few if any women among them—can earn several times as much as their regular opposite numbers. In return they neither expect nor receive many kinds of benefits, such as housing, health plans, and retirement plans, which can double or triple the cost of a soldier serving in a regular state-run force.[104]

Some of the firms in question own heavy, if rarely the most recent, weapons and weapon systems. They buy them on the cheap on the international market from arms dealers who specialize in second-hand equipment. The work they make their troops do, especially when campaigning in the Third World, in many ways resembles that of their defanged regular colleagues. They fly aircraft and helicopters. They drive armored vehicles. They set up communications networks, organize and secure supply lines, guard bases, and escort VIPs. Operating with or without permission, when necessary and opportune they blast whoever stands in their way to pieces.

Mercenaries are not, and never have been, pure and tender souls. But at any rate they do enjoy the inestimable advantage of not being bound by the usual, often senseless and often humiliating, conventions modern politicians and public opinion have imposed on the regular forces—including those conventions which caused Petraeus, Amos, Mattis, and countless other more or less outstanding soldiers so many difficulties that some had to go and others resign "of their own free will." In other words, they enjoy the advantages of being able and willing to do what, in a dangerous and often rather nasty world, has to be done.

Chapter III. Feminizing the Forces

1. In Pursuit of Equality

Currently Western countries are embarked on a social experiment that has no precedent in history. I am referring to the feminization of the armed forces. Except insofar as feminists are pushing women into roles and places for which they are not suited, it is not the women's fault. Many, probably most, of them are doing their best. What is at fault is the way they are inducted into, and treated inside, the forces. That way is one cardinal reason why those forces are not nearly as effective as they ought to be. Should the process continue, then it has the potential to make them even less capable of fighting and winning than they already are. That is why it must be discussed in some detail.

The feminization of the forces appears to be a near-exclusive Western phenomenon. To be sure, some non-Western forces also have some female soldiers or, much more often, images of female soldiers. That even applies to a few Muslim countries. However, they do not seem to take them very seriously. The late King Hussein of Jordan at one point set up a woman's corps with one of his own daughters, Aisha, as commander in chief. However, but little has been heard from it since. The principal task of the ladies that formed Colonel Gadhafi's female bodyguards was to put his power and eccentricity on show. After he had been killed they themselves, perhaps fearing reprisals, claimed that they were used to amuse him and his henchmen.[1] The pink uniforms worn on parade by some Chinese female soldiers, who seem to be specially selected for their outstanding good looks, speak for themselves. So do the Ms. Armed Forces competitions held in Russia, allegedly with the objective of attracting more women to serve.[2] Not to mention the fact that neither the Russian troops who occupied the Crimea and fought in the Ukraine in 2014 nor their Ukrainian opponents, as far as may be determined, included a single woman.

The history of women in war is long and fascinating.[3] Many pre-modern armies had a handful of women who served in them, whether openly or in disguise. In tribal and feudal societies, they sometimes took the place of their dead or absent male relatives and exercised command. But even then they did not fight in person, as most male commanders were expected to do until 1550 or so. Such cases were entirely exceptional. Where women *did* make their presence felt was as camp followers: foragers, sutlers, laundresses, cooks, nurses, and of course, prostitutes. Cases are recorded when they and their children actually outnumbered the troops.

As manpower shortages developed during World War I, first the British and then the Americans allowed women to volunteer for the forces. To prevent what, at that time, was known as "moral corruption" and is now known as "sexual harassment," they served in their own separate corps. They could neither be sent abroad against their will nor serve in combat. Most worked in administration or as nurses. As volunteers they could leave the service as any moment. All of which meant that, in reality, they were only half-soldiers. It also explains why very few were killed or injured by the enemy.

The situation in World War II was broadly similar. In both Britain and the US, the range of MOS (military occupation specialties) open to women grew. So did the number of those who served. As one would expect, there were quite some love affairs between service personnel of both sexes. Since women served in their own separate corps and were not under the authority of men, though, there were few complications and few people who objected. Men wanted women and women men—especially men who, should the liaison become permanent, had something to offer. Such is the way of the world.

As in World War I, the various women's corps were seen as temporary experiments. That is why, in 1948, the US Congress held hearings as to whether women should be allowed to join the military during peacetime. The upshot, Public Law 625, authorized the US Armed Services to take in women on a permanent basis for the first time.[4] The objective was to create a nucleus of female personnel that could be expanded in case another total war broke out and made mobilization necessary.

The way it was done was governed by two different, even opposed, propositions. First, as had also been the case during both World Wars, Congress wanted to protect military women. The latter were seen as too weak to stand up for themselves against their male comrades-in-arms. To do so, it ruled that they should continue to serve in their own corps under their own female commanders. Second, since it was taken for granted that the purpose of the Forces was to fight and that only men could do so, it wanted to retain the essentially male character of the military. Thus military women were subjected to strict limits. The way the Forces interpreted the Law, those limits became stricter still.

The number of women in the Forces was capped at two percent of strength. They were barred from combat, including both sea duty (there were to be no women aboard any naval vessel except transports and hospital ships) as well as flying aircraft engaged in combat missions. Similar restrictions also prevented them from entering any number of MOS. No military woman was to carry any rank higher than colonel (Navy Captain) and allowed to command men. All this, as well as the fact that they were not accepted into the service academies, meant that their prospects of being promoted were rather limited. Women were also subjected to a whole series of petty restrictions that discriminated against them. For example, they could claim dependent husbands and/or children only if they could prove that these family members were in fact dependent on them for "chief support."

Women trained in their own bases. They got sufficient physical exercise to keep them fit and trim, but no weapon training at all. The vast majority, ninety-three percent, worked either as secretaries or in the medical field.[5] Judging by recruitment posters, one might think that female soldiers were born with typewriters chained to their necks. Very great emphasis was put on external appearances. The Air Force, for example, demanded that each applicant submit no fewer than four pictures of herself, each taken from a different angle. To guarantee "lady-like behavior" women had to take classes in comportment, the application of makeup, and so forth.[6] Marine Corps women were even required to wear lipstick and nail polish while on duty.

Whether because the limits in which military women were allowed to operate were so narrow or for other reasons, few decided to join. During the Korean War George Marshall, now serving as Secretary of Defense, tried to increase recruitment by setting up DACOWITS, the Defense Advisory Committee for Women in the Services, to conduct propaganda on behalf of the services. To no avail, since the original target figure of two percent was never met. Up to the late 1960s women only formed 1.2 percent of the Forces. Like their predecessors in both World Wars, they were in reality only half-soldiers. Surrounded by every kind of restriction which prevented them from playing a more important role, when it came to discipline and the like they were treated with kid gloves.

What started changing the situation was the War in Vietnam. Hard-pressed to fill their insatiable demand for manpower without mobilizing the reserves, in 1967 the Forces decided to turn to women as a partial solution to their problems.[7] The two-percent cap was removed and the first female general officer got her star. Between 1973 and 1976 alone, women's share in the Forces more than doubled from three to seven percent. The percentage of MOS open to women also more than doubled from thirty-five to eighty.[8] Much of the change was due to the shortage of qualified men. In the words of Lawrence Korb, a professor of government and management who served as undersecretary for manpower during the first Reagan Administration: "No way [would we] ever leave a spot vacant rather than take a woman."[9]

The second factor behind the process was the growth of feminism, especially the kind known as "liberal" or "equity" feminism, from the mid-1960s on; the third, the growing shift, all over the West, away from conscription toward all-volunteer forces. The last-named, in particular, played into women's hands. It enabled them to continue their drive for equality—in reality, as we shall see presently, privilege—without having to fear the possibility that they would be drafted as men had been for so long.[10]

Especially during the early days, many of the reforms had to be carried out in the teeth of male soldiers, both officers and enlisted, determined to maintain their position.[11] At the time the process got under way, scarcely anybody thought of using women in combat. On the contrary: The idea was to see which military posts could be occupied by women so that men, such men as were to be had, could be sent into combat units. Women, in other words, were considered very much a second-rate substitute. A whole series of elaborate calculations were made and summed up in a Brookings Institute study of the subject.[12] Some of the so-called "nontraditional" fields that were now opened to women involved work in science and engineering and were highly prestigious. Many others, though also "nontraditional," merely gave uniformed women the right to join men in performing blue-collar work in maintenance, logistics, housekeeping, etc.

To expand women's roles in the military it was necessary to lift a whole series of restrictions on the things they could, and could not, do. Thus, by order of the Naval Chief of Operations Admiral Elmo Zumwalt, women were allowed aboard ships, though not combat ships.[13] Women were allowed to pilot aircraft, though not combat aircraft. Later they were allowed to pilot combat aircraft too, but only on missions behind the front such as ferrying aircraft, testing them, and teaching other pilots to fly them. For the first time women began to receive at least some weapons training, although what they received was not very serious.

Women maintained aircraft, launched missiles, and operated computers. They also ran construction equipment, refueled tanks, and controlled air, land, and sea traffic. As if to prove that they could do whatever men did, some women even drove forklifts around ammunition dumps.[14] At the time that was considered something of a marvel and a great advance for women's liberation. In 1972 the separate officer training courses for women were abolished and women were taken into Reserve Officer Training Corps (ROTC) at civilian universities. In 1976, against much opposition, Congress forced the military academies to open their doors to women. Four years later, the first coed class graduated.

Under President Carter's undersecretary for manpower, Clifford Alexander, Jr., the shift toward this kind of equality accelerated.[15] In 1978 the position of commander, women's corps, was abolished. Women were incorporated into the normal military chain of command, with the result that men could command women and women, men.[16] Women's separate bases were also closed and women's living quarters integrated with those of men. As a result, instead of being largely segregated, members of the two sexes now often occupied separate floors in the same building. The aim was to create a unisex military, even to the point where unisex uniforms were tried. In the end they turned out to fit neither men nor women, causing the experiment to be quietly dropped. As of early 2015, though, fresh trials in the same direction were under way.[17]

By 1981 the number of servicewomen had grown to 8.5 percent of the total. However, since the forces had been designed very much with male soldiers in mind, women's growing presence led to all kinds of problems. To quote Korb again, the issue of women—who, at the time he spoke, formed about eleven percent of the forces—took up more of his time than any other.[18] Some of the regulations which discriminated against them were quietly dropped. Others led to much controversy. They only disappeared after lawyers, representing female soldiers, took the military to court or threatened to do so.

For example, *Frontiero v. Richardson* (1971) struck at the rule which did not allow female soldiers to claim dependent pay unless they could prove they were the family's "main breadwinner." *Cushman v. Crawford* (1976) enabled pregnant women to remain in the service and return to it after giving birth—a privilege, incidentally, neither required by American labor law nor by any means granted by all of America's civilian employers. Next, *Owens v. Brown* (1978) forced the Navy to open additional ships to women.[19]

In these and other cases the military, claiming to act in the name of national defense, tried to block the reforms. In fact, almost all the dozens of witnesses invited to testify during the hearings held by the Presidential Commission on the Assignment of Women in the Services in 1991-92 opposed them.[20] To no avail: In the aforementioned cases and others, invariably the courts accepted the arguments in favor of granting women equality. So much so that, when four former servicewomen threatened to sue the military so as to make them remove the remaining restrictions on participating in ground combat, Secretary of Defense Leon Panetta promptly rolled over. He granted their demands without even trying to fight.[21] So did his immediate subordinates. No claim made on behalf of "gender equality" is too foolish to use. Not even the one made by the Chairman of the Joint Chiefs of Staff General Martin Dempsey, who said that having women in combat units would reduce the incidence of sexual assault![22]

By and large the armed forces of other Western countries—including those of Belgium, Britain, Canada, France, Greece, Sweden and the Netherlands—followed the US lead. Several, switching from conscription to voluntary service, found that they could not obtain enough men, especially the kind of highly qualified men they needed most. All tried to fill at least part of the gap by taking in additional women. All also busily conducted experiments, many of them superfluous because all they did was to duplicate the American results to see what could, and could not, be done with them.

As in the US, this led to limited female penetration of a very large variety of "nontraditional" MOS, ranging from technical and scientific work (France) to limited sea-duty (the Netherlands).[23] As in the US, servicewomen were sometimes compelled to resort to the courts in order to obtain what they regarded as their rights. Usually it was a question of opening additional MOS to women. In other cases, the issue was putting them on equal basis with men in respect to pay, admission to service schools, promotion, and so on.

Starting in 1988 America's wars, each in its own way, have assisted military women's drive toward equality. That includes the ones in Panama, the Gulf, Bosnia, Kosovo, Afghanistan, and Iraq. In all Western Forces one may now find women doing the kind of work, and occupying the kind of rank and position, that would have been inconceivable even as late as the 1990s. Many women are still occupied in administration, communication, medical work, and food supply. Others perform engineering and technical work though hardly, as far as may be determined, of the harder, dirtier, and more dangerous kind. Women fly combat aircraft. Others "man" naval vessels and even command them.

Several Western Armed Forces are blessed with female generals. Back in 2011 it was a female general, Margaret Woodward, who coordinated NATO's air attacks against Libya.[24] Later—how typical—the Air Force put her in charge of fighting sexual assault in the service. Germany's Ursula von der Leyen has vowed to increase the number of female generals.[25] How this will help solve the Bundeswehr's problems, the result of years of neglect, she did not say.

As Panetta's decision in particular shows, officially at any rate the last remaining barriers are crumbling. To make this possible, hardly a year passes without the regulations being rewritten and the meaning of "combat" redefined. However, as the vast surplus of male casualties *inter alia* shows, the achievement of near-complete equality has not solved all problems as feminists believed or claimed to believe. Instead it gave rise to any number of new ones; and it is to these that we must now turn our attention.

2. *Amazones Antianeirai*

Speaking of the *Amazones*, Homer calls them *antianeirai*, "equivalent to men."[26] In the whole of ancient Greek literature the Amazons, to use the modern spelling, are the only noun to which this epithet is applied. And *antianeirai* they had to be; or else they would hardly have been able to match men in the kind of close combat with edged weapons and heavy metal armor that formed the standard way in which Greek troops fought. The difficulty is that, whatever feminists may claim and the statute books may say, women and men are only equal in certain respects but not in others. Hence, the attempt to treat them as if they were was bound to cause as many problems as it solved. And so it proved.

Let us ignore the enormous, but largely inconclusive, body of research on the mental and emotional differences between people of both sexes. Doing so we are left with two principal physical differences, both of them well-known to every man and woman who ever lived. The first involves bodily strength, aerobic capacity, endurance, ability to run and throw objects, robustness, and resistance to the kind of conditions, such as dirt, that are likely to be found in the field. Contrary to what many people believe or pretend to believe, it affects not only ground combat but many kinds of flying and shipboard duty as well as heavy maintenance work. The other, pregnancy—and, by extension, motherhood—will be discussed in the next section.

Thanks precisely to the attempts to integrate women into the Forces, concerning the first difference a vast amount of data has been gathered and is readily available in books, articles, and on the Internet. Studies found that the average US female Army recruit was twelve centimeters shorter and 14.3 kilograms lighter than the average male one. She also had 16.9 fewer kilograms of muscle and 2.6 more kilograms more of fat.[27] Upper-body strength stood at fifty-five percent of that of men, lower body strength at seventy-two percent. Since fat mass is inversely related to aerobic capacity and heat tolerance, women are also at a significant disadvantage when performing aerobic activities such as marching with heavy loads and working in the heat. At high altitudes, so great is the women's handicap that it may affect their ability to reproduce.[28]

Even when the experiments were controlled for height, women only had eighty percent of the strength of men. Overall, only the upper twenty percent of women can do as well, physically, as the lower twenty percent of men. One biologist claims that, if the hundred strongest individuals were to be selected out of a random group consisting of one hundred men and one hundred women, then ninety three would be male and only seven female.[29] Another has calculated that only the upper five percent of women are as strong as the median male.[30] Thanks to the "superior ability of men to add muscle to their bodies,"[31] intensive training, far from diminishing the physical differences between the sexes, tends to increase them still further.[32]

Morphologically, too, women are less well adapted to war. Thinner skulls, lighter bone ridges, and weaker jawbones provide them with less protection against blows.[33] Shorter arms make it harder for women to draw weapons from their scabbards, stab with them, and throw them. To say nothing of the possibility that a different brain structure may render them less adept at guiding or intercepting projectiles.[34] Women's legs are shorter and set at a different angle from those of men. The outcome is to make them less suitable both for sprinting and for running long distances.[35]

All the above-mentioned tests have been made on young, childless women. Once a woman has given birth, the difference in pelvic structure becomes even more noticeable. Many also develop large, pendulous breasts that can get in the way of strenuous physical activity.[36] The only relevant physical advantages women possess is that they are apparently less subject to altitude sickness. Since they have proportionally more body fat, they also endure cold better.

Given these limitations, very few women have been able to participate equally in military training and combat. "To strike down an enemy, to mount guard... to endure winter's cold and summer's heat with equal patience, to sleep on the bare ground and to work hard on an empty stomach," as the Roman writer Sallust, quoting the great commander Marius, put it two millennia ago.[37]

Time after time, attempts to ignore these problems have led to disastrous results. Some standard training devices, notably monkey bars, proved too dangerous for women who did not have the requisite upper-body strength and had to be taken off them.[38] Women lagged behind on road marches and dropped out of group runs, so that some of the latter had to be abolished. They failed to negotiate obstacle courses (later modified to make them easier) and could not climb a rope. Nor could women throw a hand grenade, that weapon *par excellence* of future urban warfare, to the minimum distance necessary so that they would not be blown to pieces. Consequently, training with it either had to be canceled or was turned into a meaningless charade.

In the US Army, enlisted women lost their periods for months on end.[39] At West Point during the early eighties, women suffered ten times as many stress fractures as did men. One study found that women were more than twice as likely to suffer leg injuries and nearly five times as likely to suffer fractures as men. Injury also caused women to sustain five times as many days of limited duty as did men.[40] Women at the Air Force Academy visited doctors' clinics four times as often as men did. They suffered nine times as many shin splints, five times as many stress fractures, and more than five times as many cases of tendonitis.[41]

89

The very first American servicewoman who officially participated in combat was Captain Linda Bray of Operation Just Cause (Panama, 1988) fame. A small, rather fragile- looking woman, by her own account she carried so much equipment that she ended up with broken hips. Later, having returned to civilian life, she explained that she couldn't run, jump, or even go grocery shopping because doing so hurt too much.[42] In Canada, only *one percent* of women who entered the standard infantryman's training graduated. No wonder the Canadian authorities have been reluctant to release the number of women who actually took part in combat.[43] Of the two US Marine Corps women who volunteered for an infantry officer course in Quantico, one washed out on the first day. The other, perhaps less wisely, kept going for two weeks until medical problems forced her to leave.[44] While Israel is not a Western country as defined in this volume, IDF data point in the same direction.[45]

The greater vulnerability of women both to orthopedic trouble and to amenorrhea, which in case it persists can lead to sterility and osteoporosis, is recognized.[46] Other health experts have emphasized the connection between women's participation in many different kinds of competitive sport and eating disorders, such as anorexia and bulimia.[47] The list of diseases ends with infections of the urinary and reproductive tract that result from rough living in the field as well as a hundred percent increase in the miscarriage rate for female sailors serving at sea.[48] A new report, issued by the British Ministry of Defense in December 2014, confirms all these facts and more.[49]

Living in Israel as I do has provided me with some opportunities to watch the problem firsthand. During coed pre-military training in the hills near Jerusalem, female runners regularly lagged so far behind their male comrades that the two groups could not even see each other. This could present a threat to the women's safety. In case anything went wrong, it could lead to lawsuits. Solving the problem by making everybody run together meant slowing down the men to the point that they hardly got any training at all. Giving the women a head start could be construed as sexual harassment, especially if they were also used as bait to make the men run faster.

The same reasons—i.e., lack of physical strength on the one hand and fear of harassment on the other—prevented the women from either carrying stretchers or being carried on them. Yet those were the days when the Israelis were still occupying a security strip in southern Lebanon; teaching the trainees how to carry a wounded comrade was among the objectives of the exercise. Briefly, whenever the group included more than a few women, and whenever those women were treated as anything other than a fifth wheel in a cart, the entire course began falling apart. Making women measure up to the same standard as men will also lead to a massive waste of resources, as a high proportion of women sustain injuries and/or drop out.[50]

One "solution" to these problems has been to put men and women through separate courses while requiring different physical performance from each sex. At Britain's Sandhurst Military Academy a compromise was adopted. Vainly trying to disguise the fact that women have an easier time of it, instructors made male and female cadets begin and end their training runs at the same locations but follow a different course in between. To no avail: For simply putting three Royal Air Force women on parade side by side with their male comrades, thereby forcing them to take longer strides than usual, the Ministry of Defense had to pay them $150,000 each. Never mind that many injured combat veterans received less. And never mind that the "injuries," if that is the appropriate term, did not prove permanent. They certainly did not prevent the women from recovering completely and having successful careers in the civilian world.[51]

Another method is known as "gender norming." A visitor coming from Mars might think that what gender-norming is about is making men and women meet the same norms so as to enable them to work together and take each other's place as, given war's lethal nature, may well be required. In reality, as the system is practiced both in the US military and in other Western countries, the opposite is the case.[52] It is defined as "the practice of judging female military applicants or recruits, or female employees or job applicants in the civilian workforce, by less stringent standards than their male counterparts."[53] Another definition is a general lowering of standards so that women can meet them along with men, as for example lifting such and such a weight, running such and such a distance with or without pack, doing so many pushups and pull-ups, and the like.[54] In some cases standards have been not only lowered but abolished. For example, no sooner were the Marines forced to "integrate" basic training than women were excused from doing as many pullups as men (if any at all).[55]

If men and women are held to the same standards the former will not be challenged, so that part of their training is wasted. If not they will say, as they almost always do when they think nobody is listening, that women are allowed to graduate from all kinds of courses, take up all kinds of assignments, and receive all kinds of promotions and benefits. All without having proven their ability to meet the same standards as they themselves are held to.[56] Apparently where women are concerned, what counts is not achievement but displaying goodwill and effort. To that extent, what we see here is another example of the way the infantilization process is creeping up from the world of children into the military.

Much more serious: Either the training soldiers about to deploy receive is good enough for them to be enable them to participate in combat with a reasonable chance of doing their job and getting out alive, or it is not. If it is, then everybody should be held to the same standard. If it is not, then those who go through it should neither be permitted nor obliged to fight. Either way the men, or the women, or both, are betrayed and have their lives put at excessive risk by the unwillingness, or inability, of the organizations they serve to prepare them as they should.

3. Retaining Privilege

From ancient times on, no organizations have been more hierarchical, more disciplined, more unequal, than armies. Some are field marshals, others privates. Generally, the stronger the hierarchy the better the army. Thucydides says that the large number of officers in the Spartan army enabled orders to be transmitted quickly from the top to the bottom.[57] The Roman army was famous for its discipline. When a unit had shown cowardice in battle the troops were lined up. Lots were used to select one man out of every ten. Those who drew the wrong number were stoned or bludgeoned to death by their comrades.[58] All this was done to ensure that there should be no confusion as to who issued orders, and who obeyed them and carried them out.

However, as the use of lots shows, there is another face to the matter. If men forming a group or organization are to put their lives in jeopardy, it is essential that they be treated fairly. Fair treatment implies equality, at least of a certain kind. Good times and bad, hardship and danger, must be equally shared by all. Men must forget their individuality, respond to the same orders in the same predictable way, and become as interchangeable as possible. They must be prepared to take each other's place at a moment's notice. Rewards and punishments must be distributed equitably according to performance rather than owing to some innate qualities the men possess. There can be no favoritism, no preference given to one man over another. Or else dissatisfaction, intrigues, and even mutiny are likely to result.

As German soldiers used to say at the time their country still had an army worthy of the name: "Today it's you, tomorrow it's me." Without equal treatment, unit cohesion is inconceivable. Cohesion, the ability to stick together and stay together even when—particularly when—things go disastrously wrong, is the most important quality any military formation must have.[59] Where it is absent, such a formation is but a loose gathering of men. They will be incapable of coordinated action, easily scattered, and of little or no military use. As Clausewitz says, they are best stationed way behind the front where they can amuse themselves.

However, *esprit de corps*, to use an expression that has become much less common than it used to be, does not appear spontaneously. Instead it must be deliberately fostered by commanders who know what they are doing, working through organizations designed for the purpose. Take the example of the US Marine Corps. The first thing fresh recruits know is that their civilian clothes are taken away from them and replaced by uniforms. They also have their hairs cut and beards and moustaches trimmed until they fit the regulations. Briefly, they have their previous identity demolished in order that they may be provided with a new one. So much so that their own family members coming to visit them for the first time are often unable to recognize them. They rise together, wash together, eat together, exercise together, chant together, and go to sleep together. Beds are made to a uniform pattern. Everybody's shoes are lined up at exactly so and so many centimeters from their beds.

Even eyeglasses are collected and replaced by government-issued, standard ones. Indeed, armies have been known to try and make their troops look as ugly as possible so as to force them to face ridicule and stick together. Another way to maintain equality is to make everybody share everything with everybody else. That is why, during the first weeks, neither letters nor phone calls are permitted. Even later, food packages reaching the men from outside are scrutinized. There must be enough for everybody to go around, or else they will be confiscated by the base personnel.

The duty, and the right, to share includes not just material possessions but joy, hardship, suffering, pain, and sorrow as well. Much later, many of those involved will look back in nostalgia to the time when they were all equal. A "happy... band of brothers," as Shakespeare's King Henry V put it and as Admiral Nelson, quoting him, reminded his chief subordinates on the eve of the Battle of Trafalgar, in which he himself was killed. They meet, they reminiscence, they drink, they slap each other's shoulders, they visit the places where they fought, and they pay tribute to fallen comrades. As long as the occasion lasts, any social differences that separate them are temporarily forgotten.

The problem is that, since men and women are *not* identical, treating them as if they were is unfair. But treating them as if they were not is also unfair, though in a different way. Sticking to our topic, the military sphere, throughout history the most important difference in the way men and women have been treated has been that the former were often obliged to serve, whereas the later almost never were. Now, fighting is a question of life and death from which many who enter it do not return. Hence, in the whole of social life a no greater privilege has ever existed nor, as long as armed conflict remains, is likely to exist.

Western countries' decisions to end the draft notwithstanding, echoes of the problem still persist. Back in 1981, the US Supreme Court, in *Rostker v. Goldberg,* was called upon to rule on the question as to whether the Government had the right to register men, but not women, for the possible reintroduction of the draft. With a majority of six to three, it voted that doing so was, in fact, constitutional. To justify its decision, the Court argued that the purpose of any future draft would be to provide *combat* troops. Since women were excluded from combat they would not have to register either. By using this piece of casuistry the Court, well aware of political realities in general and feminist pressures in particular, made sure that one privilege women enjoy would lead to another.

Never mind that, should war in fact break out, the military will almost certainly be as short of noncombat personnel—i.e., specialists of every kind—as of front-line fighters. It was precisely this shortage which, in 2006, made the army raise its maximum enlistment age from thirty-five to forty-two years. For example, the forty-one-year-old grandmother who joined in 2010 was trained to be a clerk, not a sharpshooter or artillerywoman.[60] And she was not the only one.

Never mind, too, that women have long since started participating in many forms of combat, so that exempting them on this ground has ceased to make sense. Yet these facts did not prevent the Presidential Commission of 1991-92 from reassuring women that any policy changes it might recommend would not cause them to register, let alone don uniform and serve against their will.[61] Nor does President Obama, heading as he does the administration most attentive to feminists' demands in the whole of US history, seem eager to revive the issue. It might, after all, explode in his face.

As of the second decade of the twenty-first century several other Western countries were experiencing, or at any rate trying to deny the existence of, similar problems. Among them is Greece, where men are obliged to serve whereas women do so only as volunteers. To repeat, in no country is the link between citizenship and conscription as strong as in Switzerland. That was one very important reason why Swiss women only got the vote in 1976, over half a century later than their American and most European sisters did. Yet now that the Swiss have decided to retain the draft, Swiss women still remain exempt. They are likely to remain so until the Day of Judgment.

Much more important than Greece and Switzerland combined is Germany. When the German Bundeswehr was established in the mid-1950s conscription too was reintroduced. To avoid any noxious comparisons with the Third Reich, however, the authorities also set up a Zivildienst, Civil Service Organization. Its purpose was to enable conscientious objectors to serve their country for a similar period, and for similar pay, as conscripts were made to do. Most of the men who took this alternative were employed in such jobs as assisting the sick, the handicapped, the very young, the very old, those who are addicted to drugs, and the like. Work, in other words, most of which had traditionally been done by women.

It goes without saying that women, not being subject to conscription, were never required to do civil service either. Even more significant, the authorities often found themselves facing a surplus of presumptive *Zivildienstleister* (civil-service employees). That meant some of them had to wait, which in turn meant that they were not allowed to enter the universities and start on their studies. In this way, women enjoyed not one privilege but two.

In no Western country where the issue was debated were women obliged to serve as men did. To the contrary: Faced with the possibility, even a remote one, that the courts, in the name of equality, would order the authorities to make women perform civil service as men do, those authorities preferred to abolish conscription rather than face the issue head on. That, for example, was what happened in Austria.[62] The one country that took a somewhat different road was Norway. In 2013 the Norwegian Parliament decided not only to retain the draft, as Switzerland had done, but to extend it to women. However, no sooner had the decision been made than the announcement was made that it was "not expected to force women to serve against their will." All it would do was "improve gender balance."[63] To which one can only say, Amen.

Whether or not they did or did not have conscription, all Western Forces that did take in women and expanded their role quickly discovered another problem in the form of pregnancy. Since practically all servicewomen are between about eighteen and forty-five years old that fact should hardly come as a surprise. There is no question that pregnancy makes the vast majority of women less able to do work. Especially heavy work, and especially if it has to be done under the difficult, often unhygienic, conditions soldiers are likely to meet in the field. The problems will persist for several weeks after delivery and as long as the women continue to nurse. They themselves, by demanding all kinds of privileges, keep saying as much.

During World War II, in all countries that allowed women to volunteer for the military, those who became pregnant were discharged. Later, when women's roles in the services started expanding during the 1970s, the authorities took a similar line without, apparently, spending too much thought on the matter. That, for example, was what the British Forces did between 1978 and 1990, only to discover that discharging pregnant personnel was against European Law. The upshot was that 4,100 women, some retired, some still serving, went to the courts and demanded compensation. Some 2,400 women got their way and received sums that ranged as high as $600,000. The average settlement cost the taxpayer $10,000.

Some of the women even got paid for allegedly suffering "emotional damage"—not because they could no longer bear but because, not wanting to leave the military, they had postponed pregnancy and used contraceptives instead.[64] All this took place at a time when, following the First Gulf War, budgets were falling very rapidly and the forces were cut to the bone. Even so, the problems did not end. During one six-year period when the Army was deployed in Afghanistan and Iraq some two hundred pregnant British servicewomen had to be evacuated. Some were flown out on aircraft reserved for the use of the wounded.[65]

In the US things were no different. Partly because they recognized the medical implications of pregnancy, partly because they found it impossible to stand up to feminist pressure, and partly because of the usual fear of liability, the Forces have granted pregnant servicewomen a whole series of privileges. So and so many weeks having passed since conception, they may not be deployed overseas or aboard ship. They have the right to be separated from the Services (not always granted); the right to receive maternity care for six weeks after separation (provided certain conditions are met); exemption from the physical readiness program both during pregnancy itself and for six months following delivery; permission to wear tennis shoes rather than standard-issue ones; and convalescent leave after giving birth.[66]

Like all forms of privilege, the rules and regulations in question are open to abuse. In some cases, it has been claimed, women got pregnant *in order* to be sent home.[67] It is, indeed, quite possible that servicewomen's wishes to avoid deployment to undesirable places such as Afghanistan and Iraq is at least partly responsible for the rise in the number of (allegedly) accidental pregnancies—notwithstanding the issue of free contraceptives, and notwithstanding that the women surveyed said that they were easy to obtain. As of 2008 the number of such pregnancies was proportionally twice as high as in the civilian world.[68] So bad did the situation become that the same US general who had threatened to punish soldiers for watching pornography threatened to do the same to pregnant servicewomen, and to the servicemen who impregnated them. However, the rules in question did not survive "fierce criticism" by Democratic lawgivers and had to be rescinded.[69]

There seem to be only two possibilities. The first is that the women did not know about contraception. That seems rather unlikely. After all, one of the first things they and their male colleagues are made to do during basic training is to attend obligatory classes on sex, reproduction, contraception, and every form of sexual abuse from harassment to rape. To the point, indeed, that less time was left for training. The second is that they were simply not speaking the truth. Privacy concerns make it impossible to determine which is which. Still it is worth noting that many male soldiers—who, since they live and work in close proximity to the women, are better placed to know than anybody else—believe the latter.

Severe injuries apart, as long as the campaigns in the hellholes known as Iraq and Afghanistan lasted, pregnancy, intentional or not, was the fastest way to get back home. But even this is only a small part of the story. Having started taking in women during the nineteen-seventies, the Greek Armed Forces provided them with better quarters and less harassment.[70] Belgian female soldiers were barred by law from doing dangerous and insalubrious jobs such as trench-digging, handling lead-containing dies, and working in pressure chambers.[71] In Switzerland, they had to do considerably less service in order to gain promotion.[72] The list goes on and on.

To return to the US, servicewomen, but not servicemen, may keep their hair and wear some jewelry. To protect their hair, female officers are also allowed to carry umbrellas.[73] In all the Services except the Marines—who are forward-deployed, and always the first to engage—proportionally more women than men carry commissioned rank. And that, *nota bene*, in a military whose official *raison d'etre* is to engage precisely in the kind of activity (i.e., combat) which women have yet to fully enter.[74]

In some ways it has become much easier for a military woman to gain fame and money than for a military man. Hardly a day passes without the media putting "the first" woman to do this or that into the limelight, with all the benefits that such publicity brings. So much so that an Iraqi physician who treated Jessica Lynch, the US servicewoman who was captured in Iraq in 1991, sought out American troops and told them where she could be found. And so much so that the Americans set up a special rescue mission to retake her from her captors' hands.[75] Later her heroic experience as a prisoner of war was made into both a book and a movie. In January 2015, a quarter-century after the event, her name still brought 420,000 hits on Google.com. As if to dot the i's and cross the t's, the headlines remind us of the "Grim Toll of Military Women Killed in War."[76] Never mind that the male dead outnumber female ones by about fifty to one.

In sum, military women's demand for "equality" runs at cross-purposes with their demand for all kinds of privileges in several fields. The most critical of the privileges in question is the fact that, in countries that still have conscription, women are not obliged to serve or spend time in some civilian organization instead. Second come policies pertaining to pregnancy and childbirth; and third, preferred promotion to commissioned rank. All this, on top of gender-norming. The last-named is simply a politically correct term for lowering standards for some, often all, soldiers so that women should be able to meet them. As General Dempsey put it, it is now up to the military to prove that any standard women cannot meet is, indeed, required for operational effectiveness.[77] Either that or it will be quickly abolished, perhaps with interesting consequences for those who devised it or upheld it.

It is as if, in a coed football game, female pass receivers had been allowed to take up a position half the distance to the goal behind the defensive's team line. Or as if, competing with them in the hundred-meter dash, they had been given a ten-meter head start. That has not happened yet. Could it be that, in the US and other Western countries, people are taking sports more seriously than they do war? If so, it would not be surprising. After all, for them war has become something that takes place far, far away. Often in countries nobody has ever heard of, let alone cared about. Not so sports, which is watched by countless millions as if their lives depended on it.

Contrary to some popular images, ninety percent of war consists of hard, often dirty and not seldom dangerous, work. People become positively retarded with exhaustion. Already during the First Gulf War, male troops complained that their female comrades were not up to the work involved. As, for example, in setting up tents or loading and unloading artillery ammunition. This increased the burden they themselves had to shoulder, and sometimes slowed down the pace of operations.[78] So unable to look after themselves were many servicewomen in Afghanistan and Iraq that, according to one source, seventy-one percent were sexually assaulted, and thirty percent raped. At night they even had to be escorted to the toilets—by men who had better things to do with their periods of rest![79] Could it be that previous generations which, for fear of women being "harassed" at work as well as well in the military, used to segregate the sexes, knew what they were doing?[80]

Should women really participate in ground combat on an equal basis with men—as they are supposed to start doing from 2016 onward in the US Forces—then as sure as night follows day their inadequate physiques and inability to keep up will make them into even more a liability than many of them, deployed in the field, already are. The outcome will be, and most probably already is, reduced performance and increased casualties both among the women and among the men who have to look after them.

In truth, men and women are *not* interchangeable. Nor are they at all likely to become so before a.) Their physiques are no longer distinct; and b.) Men start giving birth and/or women cease doing so. Not being interchangeable, they cannot be treated as if they were. One man who understood this very well was President Wilson's Secretary of the Navy, Josephus Daniels. A highly successful newspaper proprietor, Daniels was a longtime supporter of the suffragette cause. Just before the US entered World War I he became the first official in American history who, using a legal loophole, allowed women to volunteer and wear uniform. No sooner had Daniels done so than he had to confront the resulting dilemmas. As he told his subordinates, he took "a dim view" of any attempt to court-martial women—in other words, treat them as offending soldiers have always been treated. "One cannot," he insisted, "deal with women as with men."[81] Presumably the prospect of being subject to strict military discipline would have deterred many women, particularly the well-educated middle-class ones the Navy wanted most, from stepping forward. Nor would public opinion have stood for it.

In practice if perhaps not in theory, Daniels' view has persisted. Both during the world wars and afterward, Western servicewomen who broke the rules were much more likely to be separated, instead of punished, than men were.[82] That even applied to the Soviet Union which, though not "Western," was famous for its extensive use of women in the military. For all the talk about equality, nobody puts a stronger emphasis on the need to give women every kind of privilege than feminists do. In particular DACOWITS, originally designed to attract women to the military, at one point developed into a fearsome watchdog with the self-imposed mission of protecting them and furthering their interests in every possible way. So it has been since some bold apes first left the forest, started living on the savannah, and slowly evolved into humans. And so, we may safely assume, it will remain as long as human we remain.

4. In the Land of Doublethink

There is nothing new about society allowing women to enjoy any number of privileges men do not, and perhaps should not, have.[83] Indeed one could argue that, but for those privileges, most women—being physically weaker and perhaps less aggressive and less competitive than men on the average—could never conceive, bear, deliver, nurse, and raise children. Men are aware of these facts, or else they would hardly have allowed the situation whereby they have always carried and still carry the lion's share of feeding and defending women and children to persist.

Two things are new. First, there is the extent to which lawyers and lawsuits are involved. When servicewomen women feel they are not being treated equally, they sue. When they feel that equal treatment leads to problems, they also sue. As, for example, happened when one British female soldier, Tilern DeBique, sued the Forces for ordering her to present herself on parade at any hour regardless of the fact that she had a baby to feed. Having been dismissed, she demanded $1,600,000 in compensation from the service. In the end the sum was reduced to just $25,000. Not much, some would say, but her lawyer did get the court to rule that the services had erred, thus opening the way for other women to demand similar privileges in the future.[84]

Second, service personnel are prohibited from saying that such privileges do exist. Should anyone attempt to do so—in other words, point out that there are some things women cannot do as well as men and are therefore excused from doing—then the accusation of being "hostile to women" will follow almost automatically. And being brandmarked as "hostile to women" can easily bring about the end of one's career. Even if the idea is grounded in religious beliefs; even if it is uttered in private; and even if the soldier in question expressly added that, whatever his beliefs, he would still be willing to lead women in combat.[85]

Anyone who wants to know why almost all of those who testified to the Presidential Commission against having women in combat were ether retired or on the point of retiring need look no further. Unless one is a woman, of course. That explains why quite some studies that dispute women's attempts to gain equality with men in every field, including not least a couple quoted in this volume, have been written by persons of the female sex. Nowhere is the problem more serious than in the military, though certain parts of the civilian world, academia in particular, are not far behind.

How to maintain a fiction-within-a-fiction—i.e., that the mythological Amazons, though female, were indeed fighters "equal to men"—preoccupied ancient Greek artists even before the beginning of the great classical period. Their solution was to paint them in such a way that, had it not been for the lighter colors of their hands and faces as well as an occasional characteristic piece of attire such as the skin of an animal, they would have been indistinguishable from men. So how to identify them? By writing their names (e.g., Areto, Derinoe, Melousa, etc.) alongside their images. In quite some cases that is the only reason why we know those names at all.

During the first half of the fifth century BC things began to change. What factors were responsible for this we do not know. Perhaps they were the same which, somewhat later, caused a growing number of statues of nude females to be made alongside those of men. More and more often, vases and reliefs show the Amazons not as armor-clad, practically sexless, warriors but as women. Complete with long hair—by which they are often being pulled—slender upper bodies, and relatively undeveloped muscles. Often they expose one breast or even two (perhaps because it would have made them ugly to look at, there are no representations of one-breasted Amazons in art). A fact which, while no doubt titillating, hardly increases their credibility as warriors.

In other words, early on maintaining the pretense that the Amazons were fighters "equal with men" and able to fight them forced artists to conceal any sign that they were, in fact, female. Once subsequent artists started presenting them as female, though, any pretense that they were equal did not take long to disappear. By the first half of the fourth century BC the change was virtually complete. Paintings of fighting Amazons became rare. Instead we see them engaged in all kinds other, less violent, activities. They put on armor, leave for the fray, and return from battle with their dead. Others lead horses, ride or dismount from them, equip and ride chariots. Others still simply wash themselves in a fountain as their weapons lean nearby.[86] To the extent Amazons still fight, as on some Hellenistic and Roman sarcophagi, they do so mainly to be defeated.

Representations of fighting women, of which there are far more than real ones, still continue to suffer from similar problems. Present-day books, movies,

105

and TV series bristle with female heroines. In sharp contrast to those shown on the sarcophagi, though, they regularly outsnarl and outfight feckless males, finishing off entire battalions of them. Yet somehow practically all these women also manage to have well-developed, and at least partly exposed, female attributes. Think of Tarzan's Jane, in many ways the prototype of them all. Wearing her bikini in the jungle, she would have been torn apart by branches and eaten alive by mosquitoes. Or of Jane Fonda in *Barbarella* and Pamela Andersen in *Barbed Wire*; or more recently, of Brooklyn Decker in *Battleship* and Anne Hathaway as Catwoman in *Dark Knight Rises*. Or even of twelve-year old Maddy Ziegler in *Chandelier*, where she performs a dance pretending to make mincemeat of a muscular man a least twice her size and weight.

Not one of these viragoes looks as if, in real life, she could swing from trees, do heavy labor, or live through the grueling hardship ground combat in particular often involves—let alone take on an average male and defeat him in a fight. Otherwise, they would have to develop the powerful necks, shoulders, torsos, arms, and legs so characteristic of flesh-and-blood warriors. Had they done so, though, presumably not many people would have wanted to watch them either on the screen or anywhere else. The discrepancy explains why several heroines, such as Wonder Woman and Xena the Warrior Princes, came complete with all kinds of magic abilities and devices only they possessed. The same is even truer of computer games of every sort.[87] Judging by their anatomies, many of these ladies could hardly stand straight, let alone fight on equal terms with men.

Practically all these productions are aimed at males, young ones in particular. The objective is not to reflect reality but to provide entertainment: the means, a highly explosive Freudian combination of weapons and cleavage. Had the situation been reversed and men were shown killing or subduing hordes of women, then surely the outcry would have been heard all the way to the moon and back. As it is, nobody takes them very seriously so that they do little harm.

Certainly they do not make many girls try to emulate the heroines' impossible feats as boys, watching *their* heroes, sometimes do. Girls, it seems, know better.

The situation in real life is less comforting. To avoid trouble men, military men more than most, are expected to believe—or at least to conceal their disbelief in—two contradictory things. The first is that military women can serve and fight just as well as men can and that they therefore deserve the kind of equality they and their supporters are demanding. The second is that, being equal, they do not enjoy privileges of any sort. Precisely the kind of thing George Orwell in *1984* called "doublethink," involving the ability "to hold simultaneously two opinions which cancel out, knowing them to be contradictory and believing in both of them."[88]

As in *1984*, the most important device the military and their political masters use to enforce doublethink is censorship. Censorship may be active, in the sense that discussion is prohibited. Or else it is passive, in that data is not gathered or not made available to the public. As a result, except for anecdotes on the Internet—many of them posted by servicemen, or ex-servicemen, or people claiming to be such—information that might cast doubt on servicewomen's actual performance is hard, often impossible, to obtain.

Examples of both kinds abound. During the 1990s annual surveys showed that only ten percent of US Army enlisted women supported the involuntary assignment of women to combat units. Scant wonder the series was brought to a halt and has not been restarted since.[89] We know that, for men, mixed basic training is much less effective.[90] What we do not know is how much of it men have to repeat when they continue to more advanced training, and at what cost. Such is censorship that, on occasion, not only outsiders but the government itself is unable to acquire information on what its various components are doing. When the General Accounting Office asked the Army to provide a study of such training it had done back in 1982, it was told that the records in question could not be found.[91]

We know that, from the time West Point first opened its doors in 1802, graduates, unless they were declared medically unfit, would be automatically assigned to one of the combat arms. Providing the country with combat leaders was, in fact, the most important part of the Academy's official mission. As the first coed class approached graduation, though, the authorities were clear in their minds that one could not do the same with women. This caused the system to be changed and graduates to be given the opportunity to join any branch they wanted. How did the change affect both the combat arms and West Point itself? We do not know.

We know that, over time, military women are consistently less likely to extend their terms of service than military men. In the Navy the difference is no less than fifty percent.[92] Probably that has something to do with the fact that sea duty is considered the most important of all and that such duty is demanding both physically and psychologically. Not to mention the impact on family life. But how does the fact that the expertise of so many highly trained troops is lost affect the effectiveness of the forces? And what is the cost to the taxpayer? Never mind. What matters, we are told, is just one thing: namely, that more female personnel should be promoted more often and receive the benefits promotion entails.[93]

We know that, in the US and elsewhere, servicewomen do not have to meet nearly the same physical standards as men do, nor do they participate nearly as often in combat. What are the consequences of these privileges, both for the military and for the women themselves? Why, in spite of the fact that they hardly participate in the most strenuous activity of all, do American military women visit walk-in clinics fifty percent more often than men? And why do they report three times as many migraines?[94] Is it because, owing to their constitutions, they get sick and injured at a higher rate? Or because they are less willing to put up with their complaints? Or because they expect that military physicians of both sexes will be more inclined to listen to their complaints than to those of their male comrades? And if so, is that because the military, like society as a whole, take women's health much more seriously than that of men?[95] And what does all this mean in respect to their effectiveness as soldiers?

We know that, in the civilian world, female criminals and offenders are treated *much* more leniently than male ones.[96] The difference persists even after all other factors—race, class, age, the kind of crime or offense committed, and the like—are compensated for. Would it be surprising if the same were true in the military? Hardly. But trying to find information about the question is like barking at the moon.

We know how many military personnel are single parents (approximately 156,000, as of 2013).[97] The figure represents well over ten percent of active strength, with all that means in terms of availability for deployment. So serious was the problem that, in the same year, the Services decided to stop taking in single parents at all. But how many of those already inside are women? Supposing the pattern is similar to that in the civilian world, where the ratio of single mothers to fathers is 4.25:1, the answer is 131,000.[98] However, there is a catch. Military women are much more likely to be divorced than civilian women. With military men the opposite is the case.[99] Thus the real figure is almost certainly higher. Are single parents, the great majority of whom are women, really as available for deployment as other soldiers? If so, what are the consequences both for the children and for the women themselves? And who makes up the difference and carries the burden?

Why has no fresh information on the number of American servicewomen who unintentionally became pregnant been made available since 2008? Why has no fresh information on the number of British ones who had to be evacuated from theaters of war for the same reason been made available from 2009 on? Is it because the servicewomen of both nations have suddenly become much more careful in using contraceptives? Or because the data, had it been known, might have shown the impact on effectiveness and hurt the feminist push towards equality both inside the military and outside it?

At times, the published information seems deliberately designed if not to mislead, then at least to cover up. For example, one article says that from January 2003 to December 2011, 50,634 American troops were flown out of Afghanistan and Iraq for medical reasons. Among them were 44,258 men and 6,376 women. "While women have accounted for about 10% of the US forces deployed into the post-9/11 wars, they represented less than 13% of those medically evacuated." Surely whether that figure is "pretty close to their share of the force"[100] or thirty percent larger depends on one's point of view.

Moreover, the article, and presumably the Pentagon sources on which it is based, does not tell us how many soldiers of each sex were evacuated owing to injuries received in battle versus all other causes. All we know is that such injuries only form fifteen percent of the total. Since women hardly participate in combat—their share among those KIA is just two percent—clearly the figure of thirty percent for all other causes is much too low.

Back to accusations of sexual harassment, sexual abuse, and rape. All have been turned into a formidable weapon that servicewomen can and sometimes do use against servicemen. As one female American pilot put it to me some years ago: "Sexual harassment is what I decide to report to my superiors." In other words, *any* advance except those that are welcomed and taken up. Even when the accused is cleared, the damage almost always sticks. By some reports the number of false accusations made by military women is rising faster than that of genuine ones.[101] But has anybody ever been punished for making false claims? Outside the military the answer is, very few indeed.[102] As to the situation inside the military, as is so often the case there seems to be no information.

Yet one need not be a biblical scholar—remember the story of Joseph and Potiphar's wife, who accused him of attempted rape—to come up with some of the reasons that can lead, and on occasion almost certainly do lead, to such claims being made. Among them are the wish to avenge oneself for what men have, or have not, done to and for one; the wish to conceal the real reasons for failing to perform as one should; fear of being accused of, and perhaps charged with, having an "inappropriate" relationship with another soldier; fear of being accused of adultery; unintended pregnancy while a husband is stationed in some faraway country; and, last not least, simple greed.

Finally, the long wars in Afghanistan and Iraq were the first of their kind in which women were deployed in any numbers. Not accidentally, they also generated a hitherto unknown kind of casualty among the troops. Meet the newest disease: MST (military-sexual trauma). Spreading like wildfire, practically all the victims are female.[103] Yet as far as MNF-I (Multi National Force-Iraq) and ISAF (International Security Assistance Force) troops were concerned, both Afghanistan and Iraq presented lethal environments where one might easily be killed or maimed for life. What does the fact that so many military women were incapacitated or claimed to have been incapacitated by MST—which, when everything is said and done, is a much less serious problem—say about their fitness to serve, let alone fight?

Similar issues abound. Each time one is recognized as a "problem," invariably the solution is to tighten the screws on military men while giving military women even more privileges than those they already enjoy. For example, to increase female retention legislation has been passed to extend maternity leave. It is often assumed that the reason why, over extended periods of time, more women than men choose to leave the service is because they are not promoted at the same rate as the latter are. Nobody seems to contemplate the possibility that things may work in reverse, i.e., that women are not promoted because they leave. Hence invariably the proposed solution to the problem, assuming that a problem it is, is to end "discrimination" against women. At the expense of the male majority, of course.

By way of a final example, the US Senate, the media, and public opinion have all joined hands in pressing hard to make the military increase the rate of convictions for violent sexual offenses. This has been taken to the point where the Senate passed a bill, 97 to 0, aimed at taking jurisdiction over such cases away from the military and entrust it to civilian courts.[104] As of early 2015, only the House of Representatives is preventing the bill from becoming law and the military justice system from being emasculated. The law's proponents will not rest until that rate is as high as is the case with other offenses (over ninety percent).[105] Clearly any accusations servicewomen raise against servicemen must be gospel truth, or almost so.

To repeat, perhaps the worst aspect of it all is that those who probe too deeply into such issues and come up with unconventional wisdom put their careers on the line. To that extent, much of the modern Western military is based on sex, lies, and videotape. As anybody who has ever talked to soldiers—*not* to pollsters, most of whom either come up with the data they are supposed to find or simply do not ask the relevant questions—in confidence knows, the outcome is suppressed discontent. It is waiting to explode, and occasionally it does.

But there are limits to what even the strictest censorship can do. In Greek mythology the god Apollo punished King Midas by giving him an ass's ears.[106] To conceal that fact, the king put on a specially designed conical hat. Legend has it that it was the prototype of a tall type later known as "Phrygian." The only person who knew the secret was Midas' barber, whom he had sworn to silence on pain of death. But the man was unable to contain himself. One day he went out to the banks of a river, dug a hole, whispered the secret into it, covered up the hole, and went home feeling much relieved.

To no avail. The reeds picked up the message and repeated it. Soon it was being spread by the wind until everybody knew it. The rest is (mythological) history.

5. The End of Masculinity

To conclude this particular part of the story, feminizing the Forces and having women take an active part in war and combat threatens to take away one of the most important reasons, sometimes even *the* most important reason, why many men enlist and fight: namely, to prove their masculinity to themselves and to others.

As so often, it was Nietzsche who hit the nail on its head. "Man," he wrote, "is the unfruitful animal."[107] Nature, by making women conceive, bear, deliver, and nurse children, has provided them with what the great majority of them see as their most important mission in life by far. That remains as true in today's emancipated world as it has ever been—to the point, indeed, where some of them insist on their "right" *not* to know they have HIV so they can have children[108] Personally I find that the most egocentric, the most despicable, idea I have ever seen, but that is beside the point. With men the situation is different. Willy-nilly, they must create their own *raison d'etre*. If Freud and many other psychologists may be believed, another reason for this is the need to separate themselves from the mother, under whose wings they spend their early years, and set themselves up as men.[109] As to the way society treats those who, in its opinion, fail to make the transition, see Donald Trump's harsh words about Jeb Bush.[110]

From time immemorial, society's method in bringing about this separation has been to impose hardship and inflict pain, which must be withstood without flinching.[111] As carried out in countless societies around the world,[112] initiation rites start with the boys being separated from their mothers. Next, they are taken to some secret place no woman is allowed to enter. There they may have their bodies tattooed or cut, circumcision included. They must endure hunger, thirst, cold, and sleep deprivation, and may be confronted with unfamiliar noises and smeared with various unpleasant substances. Ancient Greek youths spent time undergoing military training and patrolling the borders. Far away, in Papua New Guinea, some tribes had a rite in which men climbed a tower, and were dropped upside down with a rope tied to their legs. That is said to be the origin of bungee-jumping. Very often physical punishment was accompanied by various forms of humiliation.

The purpose of initiation is precisely to reduce or remove the boys' "female substance."[113] Therefore, as long as women do not share in the rites their exact nature does not matter much. This is also evident from the fact that, at some point during the proceedings, the novices will be presented with male "secrets" they must never afterward divulge even to the women who are nearest and dearest to them.[114] Having graduated, youngsters are presented with special clothing, ornaments, and implements—including, not least, weapons—that will henceforward mark their status as men.[115]

Even so, masculinity cannot be established once and for all. It must be asserted and re-asserted throughout life—or at least until old age sets in, physical prowess declines, sexual activity diminishes, men and women become more alike, and it no longer matters much in any case. Thus certain fields, or activities, must be set aside as exclusively male and reserved for men. Assuming, as Plato did, that the sexes overlap and that no activity is inherently suited only for men or only for women,[116] these considerations probably do more to explain the existence and persistence of the sexual division of labor than any others.

Of all the activities in which we humans engage, obviously no other is nearly as suited for asserting masculinity as war is. All the rest are hedged in by more or less artificial limits on what may and may not be done. It is only in war that such restrictions do not apply. War allows, demands even, the most complete use of all man's faculties, physical as well as emotional and intellectual. The more so because it is waged against the most dangerous opponent of all: to wit, another man who is as strong, intelligent, and determined to win as oneself.

Hence it comes as no surprise that, among the ancient Hebrews described in the biblical book of Exodus, the words for "adult man" and "warrior" are interchangeable.[117] The same applies to many other tribal societies around the world. Among the Germans during the first century AD, no young man was permitted to marry ere he had killed an enemy.[118] Similar customs prevailed among many West African, East African, and Polynesian tribes almost to the present day.[119] Among some tribes in North America, Cuba, Greenland and Micronesia, so strong was the link between masculinity and war that any man who for one reason or another could not or would not fight was classified as a woman and made to wear feminine dress.[120]

The Hebrew term for heroism, *gevura*, comes from *gever*, man. That word in turn is linked to *gavar*, to conquer or overcome. The citizens of Greek and Roman city states could never praise *andreia* (courage; from *anēr*, man) and *virtus* (prowess; from *vir*, man) highly enough. Not only in militarist Sparta but even in civilized Athens, some form of military training was regarded as an indispensable prelude to manhood, citizenship, and marriage. The same applied in many other civilizations. So much so that, in both Modern Hebrew slang and ancient Greek, the same term can mean either "killing an enemy" and "having sex with a woman."[121] In fact, as the statues of many commanders that dot the squares of many American and foreign cities confirm, the idea of war as the highest proof of manhood is universal.[122]

Need it be added that, no sooner do women enter the fray in any number, then war's ability to provide such proof is lost? At all times and places, whatever men did was considered too hard for women. Whatever women could do (except, of

115

course, for giving birth) was considered too easy for men. Often, given the physical differences between the sexes, the very ones which the term "gender" was designed to conceal or abolish, with very good reason.

That is why, when the gods, fate, or a ruler wanted to humiliate men they forced them to assume the roles of women. That is why Heracles, as part of his punishment for slaying his wife and six children, was sold to Queen Omphale of Lydia. She made him perform a woman's tasks and wear a woman's dress, whereas she herself put on Heracles' own clothes. To this day, in all known cultures, the worst thing a man can be called is a "woman."

So much for fighting side by side with women. Unless the balance of forces is terribly skewed, having to fight *against* women is much worse still. As we saw, with few exceptions, men's bodies are considerably stronger and tougher than women. Men also have greater endurance. But their very superiority works against them; it explains why, should they "win" such a struggle, doing so will hardly earn them any sort of respect. It can, indeed, easily lead to the opposite. Even more surely, should they themselves be defeated they will become objects of derision in the eyes of both men and women.

The outcome, a lose/lose situation, was understood at least as far back as ancient Greece. It was one reason why the Amazons, as long as they kept fighting, had to be *antianeirai.* And why Achilles, having unwittingly killed an Amazon who was dressed as a man, felt embarrassed rather than proud. By one source he even went so far as to kill a man who suggested that he, Achilles, was sexually attracted to her.[123] Aristophanes, in *Lysistrata,* also refers to the problem. Should women participate in riding contests, he says, then men will stop taking part in them and the contests themselves come to an end.[124] All this explains why, when rumor had it that President Obama would make male Marines men wear the same hats as female ones, the outcry could be heard all the way from sea to shining sea.[125]

Other things equal, the more feminized the forces the more serious the problems. This includes the loss of prestige which, as quite some female scholars have noted, any field, profession, or organization with too many women in it *will* suffer in the eyes of men and, perhaps even more so, women.[126] With the loss of prestige comes reduced financial rewards and a diminished ability to attract first-class personnel. The outcome is to bring into being a vicious cycle such as is known in many civilian fields as well.

Some hope that the day will come when all armed forces are so feminized as to make fighting and war themselves impossible. The emphasis would have to be on "all." Or else surely, predominantly male armies will pass through predominantly female ones as red-hot pokers pass through pastry. That day, however, is still very far off if it will ever come at all. Meanwhile, can anybody say why men should be willing to put their lives on the line on behalf of societies that insist on humiliating them in this way?

Chapter IV. Constructing PTSD

1. "Seek, and You Shall Find"

"Seek and you shall find," said Jesus. Never more so, one supposes, than in our own "post-modern" age in which everything goes and virtual reality has developed to the point where it is sometimes no longer distinguishable from real reality. Countless things that were supposed to have an objective existence suddenly stand revealed as "constructed" by this group or that, in this way or that, at this time or that, for this reason or that, and for this purpose or that. Not only words, as Humpty Dumpty in *Alice in Wonderland* says, but facts and objects can mean whatever we make them to. If not completely so—in this respect Michel Foucault's most extreme followers may have gone too far—then at any rate, to a very considerable extent.

Take our chosen "thing," i.e., war. In ancient Greece and Rome war was supposed to be associated with *arête* and *virtus*. They are best understood as excellence and prowess respectively. Achilles preferred a short, heroic life to a long and dull one. Alexander, who when young studied Homer under the guidance of Aristotle, told his troops that "work, as long as it is noble, is an end in itself."[1] As one Hellenistic funeral monument put it, excellence meant exchanging life for bravery.[2]

Virgil, by common consent the greatest Roman poet, celebrated *virtus*. It was this quality that had enabled his city to conquer first Italy and then the world:[3]

> Strong from the cradle, of a sturdy brood,
> We bear our newborn infants to the flood;
> There bath'd amid the stream, our boys we hold
> With winter harden'd, and inur'd to cold.

They wake before the day to range the wood

Kill ere they eat, nor taste unconquer'd food.

No sports, but what belong to war, they know;

To break the stubborn colt, to bend the bow.

Our youth, of labor patient, earn their bread;

Hardly they work, with frugal diet fed.

From plows and arrows sent to seek renown,

They fight in fields, and storm the shaken town.

No part of life from toils of war is free,

No change in age, or difference in degree.

We plow and till in arms; our oxen feel,

Instead of goads, the spur and pointed steel;

Ev'n time, that changes all, yet changes us in vain;

The body, not the mind; nor can control

Th' immortal vigor, or abate the soul.

Our helms defend the young, disguise the gray

We live by plunder, and delight in prey.

At some point during the Middle Ages the idea of excellence was replaced by honor.[4] The two are related. Those who have excellence will be held in high honor, or so they themselves hope and others expect. Thus understood, the latter is the reward of the former.

However, as the link with chivalry shows, honor also has another meaning which its synonym, glory, does not cover. The rules of honor/chivalry dictated that fights should be fair. How different from antiquity, and also from the Chinese military tradition as exemplified by Sun Tzu, where stratagem was often seen as the preferable way to fight and preferable to a head-on clash, an indication of stupidity. In tournaments and other forms of mock warfare, the outcome was attempts to ensure that the opponents should be balanced, including the use of umpires. Again this was just the opposite from the Roman gladiatorial games. In them, combatants were deliberately given different kinds of weapons. Umpires who ruled on what was and was not allowed were not only absent but inconceivable.[5]

Honor also meant that one should respect the enemy's courage. One should not stab an opponent in the back. One should not violate truces. Oaths, even those made to the enemy and even those that result in negative consequences for oneself, were binding and should be kept. Better to fight honorably and lose, than fight dishonorably and win. Opponents who did surrender, says the late fourteenth-century chronicler Froissart, should be treated as "the law of arms" commanded.[6] Instead of being killed or enslaved, which throughout antiquity was standard procedure, they should be given an opportunity to ransom themselves. They might even be freed after having given their word, as Clausewitz, captured after the Battle of Jena in 1806, was.

Better death than disgrace. Roland, the hero of the song that bears his name, prefers being killed to the likelihood that subsequent generations will sing of him as a coward. Following his crushing defeat at Pavia in 1525, King Francis I of France is said to have exclaimed that "everything is lost, save honor." The embodiment of this ideal was Francis' contemporary Bayard, the chevalier *sans peur et sans reproche*. Such was his reputation for honorable conduct that, having been captured twice, twice he was released without having to pay the customary ransom. So conscious of honor were Spanish soldiers during the same period that they sometimes executed those of their comrades who proposed surrender.

As expressions such as "the field of honor" and "an honorable death" show, such ideas had a long future in front of them. In one way or another they also underlie many royal mottos. Including *"Dieu et mon droit"* (the English Crown), *"nemo me impune lacessit"* (the Scottish one), *ne plus ultra* (Emperor Charles

V), and "*Je maintiendrai*" (the House of Orange). Louis XIV had "*nec pluribus impar.*" The Sun King opened his memoirs by explaining that, to earn a position of honor among his fellow sovereigns, it behooved a young prince in particular to go to war.[7] Frederick the Great once said that the only thing that could make men march into the muzzles of the cannon trained on them was honor. But he did not always have it his way. In a fit of pique, he once ordered one of his subordinates to demolish the property of an enemy commander. Only to have the officer in question invoke honor and refuse.

To say that the ideas in question always made their impact felt would be a gross overstatement. Yet to claim that they were never more than a hypocritical cover for barbaric deeds—"the etiquette of atrocity," as one author puts it—and never had any influence at all would be an even greater one. They are perhaps best understood as forming the compass of war, one that had a certain impact even when warriors and organizations were travelling in the wrong direction, as they not seldom did.

From about 1740 on, the term was used less and less often. As my friend and former student Professor Yuval Harari has shown in his book, *The Ultimate Experience*, it started being replaced by the idea that war conferred some kind of secret, or superior, knowledge only available to those who had been through it.[8] The kind of which Tolstoy, in *War and Peace*, says that it "lies one step beyond that line, which is like the border dividing he living from the dead.... What is there? Who is there? No one knows, but who does not long to know?" The kind which, in the same novel, was given to Prince Andrei as he was lying, badly wounded and close to death, on the battlefield of Austerlitz. All of a sudden the sky opened up to him; what he saw reduced everything else he had ever seen, or heard, or experienced, or done, to total insignificance.[9]

Many others have provided similar descriptions, albeit rarely of as high a literary quality. Here is Siegfried Sassoon, English poet and a serving officer in World War I, writing to his family in 1916:[10]

> Last year, before the Somme, I had not known what I was in for. I knew now; and the idea was giving me emotional satisfaction! I had often read those farewell letters from second-lieutenants to their relatives which the newspapers were so fond of printing. "Never has life brought me such an abundance of noble feelings," and so on. I had always found it difficult to believe that these young men had really felt happy with death staring them in the face and I resented any sentimentalizing of infantry attacks. But here I was, working myself up into a similar mental condition as though going over the top were a species of religious experience.

Whereas excellence and honor had been reserved for upper-class warriors, experience and insight were things anyone could obtain. Among hundreds of thousands, perhaps more, who felt that way was the future commander of Auschwitz, Rudolf Hoess. Aged sixteen, he joined the army which, as it happened, sent him to serve in Mesopotamia of all places. "My horizons," he later wrote, "had widened.... I had seen and experienced a great deal. I met people from all walks of life and had seen their needs and weaknesses. The schoolboy who... trembled with fear during the first battle had become a tough, rough soldier."[11]

The shift reflected the ongoing transition from an aristocratic society toward a more bourgeois and democratic one. This dependence on external circumstances explains why it proceeded in different ways, at a different pace, in different countries, and among people belonging to different social classes. As

Cervantes' Don Quixote shows, there were always those who adhered to old ideas even as others were already discarding them, and even if they themselves were ridiculed and/or defeated as a result.

At the time Sassoon wrote, war was still supposed to generate "an abundance of noble feelings" in the breasts of those who had experienced it. The most important writer who kept the idea alive during the interwar years was a German, Ernst Jünger. Jünger was an infantry officer. Having participated in any number of battles and skirmishes, he ended by being awarded the *pour le merit*, the highest medal the Kaiser had at his disposal. The way he saw it war, precisely because it was as terrible as it was, demanded that combatants rise above their own nature. Liberated from the latter, they should enter a realm that, being purer and nobler, enabled them to do so.[12]

Here and there the idea that war's impact on the individual was not necessarily entirely negative was kept alive even after 1945, by none more so than Guy Sajer. Sajer (real name Guy Mouminoux) was a young man of French Alsatian origin. Aged sixteen, Sajer volunteered for the Wehrmacht. He fought on the Eastern front from the summer of 1942 to the end of the war. His best-selling memoirs evoke the terror of war as few other works have. Yet at one point he speaks of the "almost drunken exhilaration" that follows the most intense fear.[13]

In the long run, this became very much a minority view. The essential nature of war, if such a thing there is, remained what it had always been, a violent duel between two opponents.[14] What changed was the way it was perceived and understood. From a revelatory experience akin to a religious one—Sassoon again—it was turned into a thoroughly rotten business. It was without either virtue or honor or knowledge of any sort, merely a process whereby obtuse generals sent millions to be mechanically slaughtered—often by men, and with the aid of weapons, they never laid their eyes on. Excitement and heroism were out; unspeakable suffering was in. All, wrote the American poet Ezra Pound, "for an old bitch gone in the teeth, for a botched civilization."[15]

Throughout the interwar years famous writers such as John Dos Passos, Robert Graves, and Ernest Hemingway never stopped hammering away on this theme. So, having undergone a remarkable transformation, did Siegfried Sassoon himself. From there it was but a short step to the idea that war, far from elevating the soul and/or opening the way to a superior form of knowledge as most past generations had believed, was harmful to it. Also that, as a result, almost anybody who spent enough time fighting was bound to suffer psychological damage—of the kind, say, that is entirely absent in Jünger's numerous works, almost all of which were obsessed by the joys of war as well as its aesthetic effects. In one way or another they continued to do so until Jünger, at the age of 102, died.

2. Achilles in Vietnam

The fact that war inflicts physical injuries on those who have fought in it, some of which continue to be painful long after the event, has always been obvious. Throughout history, some of those concerned spent the rest of their lives blind, or mutilated, or invalided in some other way. A fourth-century BC inscription from the sanctuary of Asclepius in Epidaurus tells of one Gorgias of Herakleia. He "was wounded in the lung by an arrow in some battle, and for a year and six months it was festering so badly that he filled sixty-seven bowls with pus."[16] What has been much less obvious is that participating in it is likely to lead to psychological injuries *not* obviously linked to any physiological ones. Or else, to use the term people seem to like at present, trauma.

In 2014, two modern authors published an article in which they tried to trace such traumas all the way back to ancient Mesopotamia.[17] It had the good fortune of being picked up by the BBC, which spread the news—welcome news?—

through much of the world. There do in fact exist some cuneiform texts that mention persons who suffered from depression, unintelligible speech, and the like. The ancient authors, not being as knowledgeable as present-day psychologists are, made the mistake of attributing them to the influence of ghosts. However, judging by the translations as they appear in the article, not one of the texts so much as mentions war and the military. The same applies to the "evil spirit from the Lord" which, according to the Bible, troubled King Saul.[18]

Another author who sought and found is Jonathan Shay, an American psychiatrist who has worked with numerous Vietnam veterans. The title of his book, *Achilles in Vietnam*, was well chosen. It implied, first, that every American soldier was a dauntless Achilles; and second, that even an Achilles would have been traumatized by the war. However, in analyzing the great Greek hero, Shay overshot the mark. Whatever else happened to Achilles, he did *not* suffer from "lifelong disabling psychiatric symptoms."[19]

Nor, except perhaps for a couple of hours during which, following the death in battle of his friend Patroclus, when he went berserk and committed some truly terrible deeds, did war and combat "ruin [his] good character."[20] If anything, to the contrary. The episode was quickly followed by remorse. It transformed him from a petulant, quarrelsome, ruthless young ogre into an infinitely more compassionate, more mature, human being.[21] One who made his peace with the inevitability of death—which did in fact follow not long after.

Other attempts to discover ancient cases of PTSD have been no more successful. Modern scholars have sometimes identified the hero of Sophocles' play *Philoctētēs* as suffering from the syndrome.[22] In fact, it was triggered by a snakebite which developed into a stinking, festering wound, causing him to go mad. So insufferable were Philoctētēs' screams that the Greeks, making their way to Troy, dumped him on an inhabited island. Only then did they continue their voyage.

Gorgias, a pre-Socratic philosopher, in *Encomium of Helen*, says that "whenever hostile bodies put on their bronze and iron war-gear of war and defense against enemies, if the visual sense beholds this, it is troubled and it troubles the soul, so that often panic-stricken men flee future danger [as if it were] present.... Some who have seen dreadful things have lost their presence of mind in the present time; thus fear extinguishes and drives out understanding. And many fall into useless troubles and terrible diseases and incurable dementias; thus sight engraves in the mind images of things seen. And the frightening ones, many of them, remain; and those that remain are just like things said."[23]

Gorgias' topic was neither war nor the psychology of combat. It was love, the impact of which he compares to that of war in order to achieve his purpose: namely, to prove that Helene, though not forcibly abducted, was innocent. This somewhat dubious analogy apart, historians who have searched ancient Greek literature could only find one clear instance of *post*-TSD.[24] "A strange prodigy," says Herodotus,[25] "likewise happened at this fight [the battle of Marathon, in 490 BC]. Epizelus, the son of Cuphagoras, an Athenian, was in the thick of the fray, and behaving himself as a brave man should. Suddenly he was stricken with blindness, without blow of sword or dart. And this blindness continued thenceforth during the whole of his life. The following is the account which he himself, they say, gave of the matter: 'he said that a gigantic warrior, with a huge beard, which shaded all his shield, stood over against him. But the ghostly semblance passed him by, and slew the man at his side.' Such, they say, was the tale which Epizelus told."

The catch is in the words "they say" *and* "he said." They are the standard expressions Herodotus uses whenever he wants to cast doubt on his sources' veracity. In this sentence we find the verb "say" not once but twice, a highly unusual occurrence. Elsewhere in the *Histories* Herodotus says that as a historian (investigator), "it my duty to report what is said. But nothing at all obliges me to believe it."[26] Finally, had PTSD been at all widespread, surely we would have learned of some of the methods used to deal with it. As, for example, by surrounding veterans with comrades to whom they can talk; watching, or participating in, theatrical performances so as to achieve catharsis; and rites of purification and triumph. The ancient world had any number of such rites. But it did not, as far as anybody is able to make out, consciously use them for the purpose at hand. None of this is to say that many soldiers did not expect to approach battles with fear and trepidation. Of course they did. That is one reason why commanders made it standard practice to put them on parade and harangue them before the fighting got under way.[27] Music, too, was used for the purpose.

Attempts to locate instances of PTSD in Roman historical sources, which like Greek ones deal more with war than with almost any other topic, are equally problematic. As in Greece, Roman references to the inner world of combatants are rare. On the few occasions when we do get a glimpse of what veterans may have felt we find them boasting, not suffering.[28] One difference between Greek and Roman armies was that the latter remained intact for centuries and centuries on end. Inevitably this kind of continuity, which from about 100 BC on was accompanied by professionalization,[29] led to the emergence of a large and sophisticated bureaucracy far beyond anything found in the former. Forming part of the bureaucracy in question, commanders and military doctors paid attention not only to the physical ailments soldiers suffered but to their mental ones as well.[30]

Some of the known cases refer to soldiers who had tried to commit suicide but survived. Normally such attempts were treated as treason was. However, there were extenuating circumstances such as unbearable pain, illness, sorrow, weariness of life, madness, and the kind of shame produced by cowardice or defeat. That shame, *pudor,* was understood as a negative quality, not as a positive one as is so often the case today. Soldiers affected by *pudor*, instead of receiving the death penalty, were punished by a dishonorable discharge. They were brought into ill repute and deprived of the normal privileges to which veterans were entitled: a piece of land or a donation of money, citizenship, and the right to marry. The decision seems to have rested in the hands of a committee made up of a competent jurist assisted by a number of physicians. To establish the facts of the case, they must have relied on the testimonies of the soldier's closest comrades, i.e., those who had lived in the same tent with him.

During the second century AD we also start learning more and more about cases of self-mutilation. Again, the normal punishment was death. Again, however, we learn of extenuating circumstances. First introduced by the Emperor Hadrian (reigned, 117-37), they are same ones that surrounded attempted suicide. The interesting point is that, in both cases, of the six motives listed only one, "unbearable pain," refers to a purely physical ailment. Another, illness, can refer both to a bodily and a mental impairment; the remaining four are purely states of mind: to wit, sorrow, weariness of life, madness, and shame.

In both cases, too, we do not have any information about the causes that produced, or were supposed to produce, such states. Hundreds of passages prove that the ancient Roman army, like all others before and since, was acutely aware of the importance of morale. The same applies to the factors that could lead to its decline or collapse and the various methods for countering them. Yet not once do the sources mention anything like PTSD.

Modern psychologists' attempts to help patients while at the same time bolstering society's need for themselves by reading PTSD into other historical periods have not been very successful either. As any number of movies, TV series, journal articles, and printed volumes show, in today's world the million-dollar question asked of military history, raised by Westerners who have not served or experienced war in their own lives, is "What did it feel like?" Not so late-medieval and Renaissance military memoirists. Far from arguing that

PUSSYCATS

nobody who was not there will be able to understand, they assumed that there was no need to describe their experiences. That was because readers would know them or be able to imagine them for themselves. Recounting the plight of survivors who spent six days drifting at sea with nothing but salt water to drink, the early sixteenth-century Spanish explorer Álvar Nuñez Cabeza de Vaca says: "I tell this so briefly because I do not believe there is any need to recount in detail the miseries and difficulties in which we found ourselves. For... everyone can easily imagine what happened there."[31]

Cabeza de Vaca's contemporaries follow a similar pattern. Even in the rare cases when memoirists show awareness of the existential gap between them and their audience, they do not use it to buttress their authority as their modern successors regularly do. Instead, they worry lest their readers might conclude that they are lying. That is why, describing the miserable conditions in the besieged castle of Luxembourg, the Burgundian nobleman Olivier de la Marche (1426-1502), says that "none can believe it unless he had seen it." The objective was to narrate the facts of the case, not to explain how horrible, much less often marvelous, it had all been.[32]

My guide in all this is the aforementioned Professor Yuval Harari. His two books, *Renaissance Military Memoirs* and *The Ultimate Experience*, deal precisely with the topic at hand and explore it as deeply as anyone has. He told me that "there are individual cases that can be seen as something like PTSD." However, he added, "even if there was something similar, there was no political, cultural or medical awareness to it, and no legitimacy either." A more widespread phenomenon seems to have been peculiar to the Spanish Army. This was *mal de corazon*, bad feeling of the heart. It referred to soldiers who had suffered no physical injury but were debilitated by mental factors. But whether that amounts to PTSD, Harari says, is debatable.[33]

In 1688 a Swiss physician, Johannes Hofer, coined the term "nostalgia."[34] It was made up of two Greek words: *nostos*, returning home and also, at times, travel in general; and *algia*, pain or ache. The French translation was *mal du pays*, "homesickness." The first group of people to whom he applied it were Swiss mercenaries stationed abroad. However, it was not just soldiers who suffered from it. It was also said to afflict sailors, such as those who went with Thomas Cook on his voyages of exploration,[35] as well as civilians. Hence it seems to have had little to do with PTSD as we understand it today. The same is true of the cures Hofer suggested. They included leeches, warm emulsions, opium—not yet considered the terrible "addictive" drug it has since become—and a trip to the Alps. But none of these were as good as simply going home.

Not everybody was as benevolent as Hofer was. The years around 1800 witnessed a revolution in the way the mentally ill were treated. Most reformers worked towards finding more humane methods, but some conducted all kinds of bizarre experiments in the use of pain and terror.[36] At least one French doctor, Jourdan Le Cointe, suggested using similar methods to cure nostalgia. In his support he adduced the case of an anonymous Russian general. As his forces were preparing to march into Poland in 1733, he announced that the first soldier to be struck down by it would be burned alive.[37] However, I have not been able to verify either the existence either of the general or the episode in question.

As late as 1864 Benjamin Butler, a Union general, wrote to his wife: "Don't write me to come home any more. You make me so homesick, I shall have nostalgia like a Swiss soldier." And again, on the next day: "You must not write to me any more about coming home. You have made me so homesick now I am almost unfit for duty."[38] In 2011 the *Yale Herald* republished a story, often told before, that military bands during the Civil War were prohibited from playing "Home Sweet Home." That was because five thousand soldiers had been diagnosed with nostalgia, of whom seventy-four had died.[39] Again, I have not been able to verify the story, or even whether the figures referred to the Union, the Confederacy, or both together.

In sum, the evidence for PTSD before the American Civil War, on which there is more in the next section, is weak to nonexistent. To be sure, here and there contemporaries registered complaints that, in retrospect, bore a superficial similarity to it. However, they were neither limited to soldiers nor necessarily understood as the outcome of participation in combat. Nor did people understand them as mental diseases. And no wonder, since that idea itself only made its appearance during the second half of the nineteenth century when psychiatry emerged as a separate discipline. Not everybody was as tough as the anonymous Russian general was supposed to have been. On the other hand, clearly he was not alone to suspect that at least some of the afflicted were malingering—and that, if he treated them with velvet gloves, the phenomenon would spread like wildfire until it wrecked his army.

To return to Hofer, up to a point he did not see the symptoms in a negative light but in positive one. To him, what their existence proved was that his countrymen, however long they might have been abroad, nevertheless remained patriotic a heart!

3. From Soldiers' Heart to Combat Fatigue

In the literature, the real starting-point of PTSD is usually said to be the American Civil War (1861-65). One name it was given was Soldiers' Heart. Another, Da Costa Syndrome, after a well-known physician of the time called Jacob Mendez Da Costa. The symptoms were fatigue, shortness of breath, palpitation, and sweating. It was as if patients were suffering from heart attacks—except that, as far as Da Costa and others could see, their hearts appeared to be fine.[40] Much later, they were classified as part of an "anxiety syndrome."

But why the Civil War in particular? By way of an answer, take just one article on the subject, which will have to do duty for all the rest.[41] Unfortunately almost everything the author says is wrong. Surely it is true that, during the War, more soldiers died of disease than of bullets. But that had always been the case and remained the case until the early years of the twentieth century. In any case, it is not clear why the prospect of a miserable death by sickness is worse than that of a violent one by force of arms. Surely it is true that many of the wounded became invalids and, unable to work, faced the prospect of becoming destitute. But that, too, had always been the case and, in developing countries, often remains the case to the present day. Though opinions concerning the Confederates are divided, Federal troops during the war were not short of food. They were, in fact, the best-nourished in history until then.[42]

Some American PoW (prisoner of war) camps were bad indeed. But they were certainly no worse than many others at many other times and places. Just think of the fate of the seven thousand Athenian soldiers captured in Syracuse in 415 BC. For ten weeks they were held in stone quarries without so much as a roof over their heads. Some were sold as slaves, the rest left to die slowly of disease and starvation.[43] During the War of American Independence more colonists died in British prison ships—rotten, dark, stinking hulks no longer in commission—than in any battle.[44]

It is true that many Civil War units were established on a local basis, and that therefore heavy casualties could lead to demoralization. On the other hand, local recruitment has its advantages. Both before and after the middle of the nineteenth century it has often been used to raise fighting power. Putting "brother against brother," civil war is indeed bad—the worst thing in the world, Plato says.[45] But there is no evidence that it has produced more psychological casualties among combatants than any other kind.

As the author of the abovementioned article herself says, "psychological warfare has been a vital part of combat for thousands of years." It remains so today; in this respect as in others, whether the Civil War really introduced an element so novel as to explain the sudden emergence of the various syndromes is questionable. Many of the wounded have always screamed in agony (on other occasions, though, they have been strangely silent, presumably owing to shock and/or loss of blood). By the time of the Civil War hand-to-hand combat, far from being exceptionally prevalent, was well on its way to oblivion.

All these factors were adduced in an attempt to explain why the War was more terrible than any of its predecessors, leading to what, much later, became known as PTSD. However, on closer examination every single one of them falls apart. The more so because, according to not one but two late-twentieth-century medical texts, Da Costa's Syndrome "is found commonly, but not exclusively, in women"![46]

The sufferers brought the problems to the attention of physicians who did their best to help. With what success remains unknown. Strangely enough, the symptoms resembled those associated with another illness popularly known as "railway brain."[47] Nowadays the very term will make most people smile. However, between about 1870 and 1914 many doctors on both sides of the Atlantic took it very seriously indeed. Railway brain attacked some, but by no means all, passengers who had been involved in serious railway accidents. It did so either immediately after the event or, in some cases, later on. Some of the symptoms were very similar to those just listed. But they also included headaches, sleeplessness, nightmares, indifference, taciturnity, and what we today would call depression.

Railway brain merged into neurasthenia, literally "weakness of the nerves." Neurasthenia was discovered in 1888 by an American physician, George Miller Beard, who believed that it was caused by overwork as well as the pressures of modern life. It soon became immensely popular among doctors and patients alike. Often it was assimilated into yet another popular disease of the time, hysteria. Martin Charcot, widely respected as the top expert on every form of mental disease and the teacher, among others, of Sigmund Freud, used to speak of "*histèro-neuroasthénie*."[48] Both neurasthenia and hysteria were predominantly associated with women of the middle and upper classes. Proving—if proof were needed—that they had nothing to do with war at all.

All these diseases, and similar ones associated with them, resembled Da Costa Syndrome in that nobody could identify the physical damage in which they were rooted. That was why some doctors, well aware that railway brain in particular could be and was used to make the companies pay, doubted whether they existed at all. The opposite also took place. Trying to make their claims stick, people made strenuous attempts to trace them as far into history as possible in order to prove that they were, in fact, real.

Initially both neurasthenia and hysteria were seen as near-exclusive female, particularly upper- and middle-class female, complaints.[49] Men, whose bodies and minds were more robust, were supposed to be more or less immune. Imagine the surprise of the military authorities when early in World War I the healthiest males of all, i.e., young ones specifically examined and declared fit for service, suddenly started developing similar symptoms. The number of the afflicted was very large. By one estimate, 613,047 German soldiers became psychiatric casualties.[50] That was almost one in twenty of all those who served. Though no precise figures are available, other armies seem to have suffered in proportion.

In Germany the phenomenon was put under the rubric of *Nervenkrankheiten* (nervous diseases) as opposed to *Geisteskrankheiten* (mental diseases). The British, pragmatic as ever, called it "shell shock." As the difference in terminology indicates, doctors could not agree either on its origin or on the best way to treat it. Some suspected a background of hereditary "degeneration," a term made popular by the Jewish-French physician Max Nordau in his best-selling book of the same name. The French military authorities, and after them the Italian ones, were inclined to regard stricken soldiers as malingerers. They accused them of cowardice in front of the enemy and even shot a few so as to teach the rest a lesson. Early on the British tried doing the same. Later, though, they relented and prescribed various forms of treatment instead.

Those who, in view of their history during the Civil War, ought to have known about the problem were the Americans. In fact, they did not have a clue. Instead, having sent over medical personnel to take a look at their various allies' approaches, they ended up by adopting the British one. By the end of the war a consensus had emerged that the best thing to do—best in the sense that it enabled most soldiers to return to their units after a relatively short period of absence—was to treat them as near to the front as possible. Only very severe cases were evacuated to hospitals in the rear. Once they had arrived there, the treatment they received was sometimes so barbaric as to be akin to torture.[51]

As in so many other ways, in respect to psychiatric casualties the Second World War was largely a repetition of the First. The principal term the Allies used, combat fatigue, was not the same. But most of the symptoms were. As the name indicated, the most important one was extreme fatigue. Others were paralysis, loss of speech and hearing, blindness, uncontrollable trembling, anxiety, stomach contractions, nightmares, bedwetting, impotence and its opposite, priapism, confusion, hysteria, and obsessional-compulsive behavior. In short, almost every kind of disturbed behavior psychiatrists and psychologists know. At one point in 1943, so many American soldiers were affected that the number of those discharged for this reason exceeded that of recruits coming in, prompting General Marshall to demand an investigation.[52] What he probably did not know was that, in proportion to their number, his forces suffered *ten times* as many psychiatric casualties as their most important opponent, the German Wehrmacht, did.[53]

The best way to explain the difference is to consider the principles on which the two armies were organized and led. German soldiers have often been presented as soulless robots caught in a ruthless machine and blindly obeying orders. That they were much better disciplined than the Americans is true enough. During the second half of 1944, the latter raped so many women in France as to almost make parts of the population wish that the Germans would come back.[54] Yet the Wehrmacht was much more attuned to the social and psychological needs both of individual soldiers and of groups. That applied to fields as different as the way units and formations were put together and the way punishments were meted out and decorations awarded.[55] Throughout the war it displayed far greater cohesion and what the Germans called *Kampfkraft*, fighting power, than did its more bureaucratically run, less cohesive, opponent.

What figures are available also suggest that the American Army did worse in the Second World War than in the First. One possible explanation is the duration of the conflict. Another, the fact that, in 1917-18, public opinion had generally been unsympathetic to the men in question. It called them by various derogatory names, making it clear that to avoid having to fight in this way was not acceptable and forcing them to think twice before they threw in the towel. Not so in 1941-45, when the unofficial, but physician-approved, slogan was "every man has his breaking point." When General Patton slapped two soldiers in hospital in 1943, so great was the uproar that he almost lost his job.[56]

Clearly there had taken place, in the meantime, some kind of cultural change or drift. Presumably the problem itself remained much as it had been a quarter-century earlier. However, the way society related to it, and made its armed forces relate to it, was different indeed. Partly responsible for the change were a number of post-World War I, mostly female, novelists such as Rebecca West, Virginia

Woolf, and Dorothy Sayers. All three spent time visiting the hospitals where psychiatric casualties were held, often for years after the conflict had ended. Later they described what they had seen in lurid detail.[57]

An excellent method for illustrating the way all kinds of non-medical factors dictate the incidence of psychiatric casualties, as well the way society and doctors relate to them, is to compare the situation in the two Germanys as it developed after 1945.[58] After all, West and East German psychiatrists had studied at the same universities. They served in the same military and followed the same guidelines issued by the physician-general. They also, treated the same soldiers.

Americans took the existence of breaking points for granted. Not so the Nazis. Throughout the twelve years of their rule they never ceased to emphasize the innate mental strength of people and their ability to cope with the most extreme stress if necessary. To quote just one typical slogan spread by Hitler's minister of propaganda, Joseph Goebbels, in the face of the allied air bombardments which were destroying one city after another: "Our walls break, our hearts don't." *Haltung*, proper conduct, was expected not just of soldiers and men but of women and even children. When necessary it was enforced by police methods.

Nor did the end of the war bring immediate change. The early postwar years were a period when millions of Germans were facing the prospect of hunger, if not actually experiencing it. Millions more fled their homes or were driven from them, often by violence. The number of cripples and others who carried their war wounds around was astronomical.[59] Most people had more important things to worry about, and any complaints remained unattended to.

That explains why, in Germany and many other European countries, attention only shifted to PTSD during the mid-1950s, when things had returned more or less to normal. Particularly interesting is the fact that in West Germany, many psychological problems afflicting veterans were seen as due to the harsh conditions under which the Soviet Union had held their prisoners of war. Not so in East Germany, where saying as much was enough to land the speaker in prison. Nothing can better illustrate the extent to which PTSD was, and presumably is, influenced by politics.

In the Federal Republic persons showing the symptoms could obtain disability benefits. To do so they had to a.) Prove that their symptoms had emerged during the war rather than after it; and b.) Find a psychiatrist who supported their claim. In the Democratic Republic, owing to the emphasis the government put on equality and productive work, doing so was much more difficult. At least one East German psychiatrist argued that, in his country, "pension-neuroses, aggravation neuroses, [and] greed neuroses have become virtually unknown." The reason, he wrote, was because "the understandable wish to be a state pensioner is now pointless."[60] More, even: "An overhasty decision in favor of disablement and the right to a pension on account of a mental ailment without organic damage was even harmful from a therapeutic standpoint, as it would only lead to a chronification of the symptoms."[61] Instead of providing pensions, the East German authorities did their best to re-integrate cases into the workforce.

The West German system was governed, at least in part, by the need to reintegrate the country into the Western world of which the country now claimed to be part. The desire to blacken the Soviet Union as much as possible also played a role. Not so the East German one. The latter rested on ideological considerations and the country's alleged fraternal relations with the same Soviet Union, which was held up as a shining example. Indeed, it is possible to argue that, in this as well as some other ways, the Volksarmee remained closer to the old Wehrmacht than the Bundeswehr did.[62]

Overall, there can be no doubt that social factors—politics, culture, organization, leadership, what have you—do much to determine the way PTSD is treated. The same seems to apply to its frequency and, perhaps, even to its very existence. That much being understood, how did it turn into the massive problem it has become? On that, more in the following section.

4. The Great Epidemic

During the 1950s and most of the 1960s concern for PTSD seems to have been limited. Possibly that was because, initially at any rate, the problem was not nearly as widespread as it had been during World War II. Certainly not in absolute terms, given that armed forces were shrinking fast. In the case of European forces, the fact that the fighting no longer took place in or near home but in the colonies far, far away, must also have discouraged public interest in it. By one set of figures, in 1941-45 twenty-three percent of all American medical evacuees were psychiatric casualties. In Korea the figure declined to six percent. During the early, so-called "forward" phase of the Vietnam War it even went down to five percent; an indication, perhaps, that President's Kennedy undertaking, in his inaugural speech, to "bear any burden, meet any hardship" in defense of liberty enjoyed strong support.[63]

As things in Vietnam went sour, the figures shot upward and PTSD became nothing short of an epidemic. In 1972 the symptoms accounted for no less than sixty percent of the evacuees.[64] Strangely so, since this was the period of "Vietnamization," when US military involvement in the fighting as well as the number of casualties was going down very fast. The figure of sixty percent was never reached again. Assuming it reflected any kind of reality, which is anything but proven,[65] it must have been due to some special circumstances, such as unrest at home and the demoralization brought about by impending defeat, which cannot be examined here. Be that as it may, clearly the Vietnam War formed a turning point.

If "a poll conducted by the *Washington Post* and the [decidedly left-wing] Kaiser Family Foundation" may be believed, "more than half of the 2.6 million Americans dispatched to fight the wars in Iraq and Afghanistan struggle with physical or mental health problems stemming from their service [and] feel disconnected from civilian life." Others put the figure at a more modest, but still massive, thirteen to twenty percent.[66]

As the numbers rose, the terminology used to describe the phenomenon changed. In 1968 a physician writing for an American military-medical journal could still examine not only "combat fatigue" but its opposite, "pseudo-combat fatigue," as well.[67] Thirteen years later PTSD, like a debutante presenting herself at her first ball, made its entry into the pages of the Diagnostic and Statistical Manual of Mental Disorders (DSM). In 1987 another edition of the same publication dropped the requirement that stressors be outside the range of "normal" human experience. Meaning, one supposes, that any- and everything could now lead to PTSD just as well as war could.

By that time publications on the topic could be counted in the thousands, perhaps more. Reflecting the idea that PTSD is an inherent consequence of war, even some computer games now incorporate it and enable people to play with it. The more numerous the publications, the more divergent the opinions of those involved concerning the causes behind the phenomenon.[68] Some drew attention to the fact that many casualties in Iraq and Afghanistan were produced by so-called IEDs, improvised explosive devices. Following this logic, they went back to the idea, first raised in connection with "railway brain" and then adopted by military doctors in 1914-18, that the cause was concussion.[69] Others pointed to the sheer terror of modern war; or to the guilt feelings caused by the fact that, amidst so many comrades who had lost their lives, one was left alive; or else, to the contrary, to the guilt feelings that killing others can occasion, especially if it is done at such close quarters that one can watch the victim's sufferings.

As with the attempt to explain why the Civil War was the first to witness PTSD, none of these interpretations seems to hold much water. Concussion is ruled out by the fact that, as some World War I psychiatrists noted, by no means all who were exposed to it contracted PTSD. The reverse is, of course, equally true.[70] Recently even some drone operators sitting behind consoles thousands of miles away from the theater of war have been affected, or so it had been claimed.[71]

One only has to read some ancient authors to realize that war has always been terrible, often almost beyond belief. "The Field [of Bedriacum, near Cremona, Italy, where a two Roman armies fought one another in 69 AD]," says Tacitus, "presented a horrible and shocking sight... maimed bodies, lopped-of limbs, decaying shapes of men and horses, the ground tainted and foul, the trampled trees and crops presented a scene of dreadful desolation."[72] Archaeological excavations at places such as Visby in Demark, where the remains of thousands of dead medieval soldiers have been found, amply confirm Tacitus' observations.

Or take a look at Urs Graf's drawing of the Battle of Novara, in Piedmont, which was fought by Swiss, French, and German troops in 1521.[73] The foreground is crowded with bodies: decapitated bodies, limbless bodies, disemboweled bodies, and bodies that have been trampled into the ground by the pike-carrying phalanxes on both sides. All of these were promiscuously strewn about and intermingled with the carcasses of dead horses lying about in equally grotesque poses—not to mention two corpses prominently dangling from trees. Florange, a French captain who was in the thick of it, says that out of perhaps three or four hundred men who fought in the first ranks, only six survived the clash.[74] Further back, the losses were hardly less atrocious.

Of 230 men recruited for service in one Swedish village in 1621-39, 215 never returned.[75] The French artist Jacques Callot, who worked at the time of the Thirty Years War and produced a series of etchings known as "The Great Miseries of

War," also has a few interesting things to say about the subject.[76] So did a much greater artist, Francis Goya, who documented the Spanish people's uprising against the Napoleonic occupation early in the nineteenth century. Limbless bodies, decapitated bodies, bodies in the act of being sawn in half, impaled bodies in all kinds of grotesque postures, and the remains of bodies being eaten by dogs are everywhere. So are women in the act of being raped in front of their weeping children, or else while their dead babies lie nearby.

Indeed one may argue, as Harari does, that war in some ways has grown *less* terrible than it used to be. One reason for this is because we no longer have those huge "pitched battles" of which Bedriacum and Novara provide such excellent, if grisly, examples. Instead, so dispersed is modern warfare—Vietnam, Afghanistan, and Iraq specifically included—that many, perhaps most, soldiers will only meet relatively few casualties spread over a considerable amount of time.[77] Another is that, owing to improved medical treatment and prompt evacuation, the proportion of dead to injured personnel has gone down from about one to three or four during World War II to one in eight or nine today.

Enforced passivity in front of the enemy is very hard to endure. But its role in causing PTSD is put into question by the history of World War II at sea. Sailors crossing the world's various seas and oceans could never know when their ships would be sent to the bottom by some unseen submarine suddenly emerging and launching its torpedoes. Yet they hardly suffered from the problem at all. Guilt feelings occasioned by the death of comrades are a real problem, which is also familiar from the lives of concentration-camp survivors.[78] However, there is no reason to think that it is worse today than it has ever been. Given the anonymous nature of modern mass society, the opposite may well be the case.

Nothing is less likely than the idea that men have some kind of built-in reluctance to kill opponents whose faces they can see, and that doing so is major cause of PTSD. Had that been true, then almost the whole of military history, when weapons were edged and soldiers fought hand to hand, would have been impossible. But it is not. Little if anything of the kind is to be found in the *Iliad*; or in the Peloponnesian War, fought mostly with the aid of spears some two meters long; or in the Viking sagas, which tell us not only of dead warriors but of the wolves and birds that devour their cadavers; or in Renaissance military memoirs, written at a time when the most important weapon was the pike.

The vast majority of warriors did not have to undergo *asubhā* (foulness) training to get accustomed to the gruesome scenes war so often generates. To the contrary: Many of them prided themselves on what they did in such situations. They still do. In one of Rolf Hochhuth's plays a young Wehrmacht lieutenant is teased for using a woman's garter button to hold one of his medals in place. He responds by saying that both the medal and the button were won in close combat; adding that, on both occasions, he had been scared stiff. Neither mutilating dead enemies nor collecting body parts are entirely *passé*. Had not the regulations, often initiated by people who never in their entire lives had even been *near* a battlefield, prescribed severe penalties for such practices, no doubt they would have been much more prevalent than they are.

Nor do Daesh, Boko Haram, and any number of similar organizations in many Muslim countries seem to have realized that face-to-face killing is bad for you. Let alone did they call for mental health workers to diagnose and treat their members. In many cases the question has become largely academic. So long is the range of modern weapons that many, perhaps most, soldiers do not even see those whom they kill. Others are so dependent on electronic circuitry that they reduce them to oddly shaped blips on a screen. Thus there is no opportunity to talk to them beforehand or hear them scream in agony as their bodies are pierced, burnt, or crushed—or as their brains, guts, and blood are splattered all over one's own body. As, for example, happened to King Agamemnon while he was leading an attack at the head of his men.[79] None of this is to say that we are born to kill.

Only that, many modern psychologists to the contrary, we can do so without compunction when necessary and very often when it is not as well.

So what brought about the increase? Again, comparisons help. Gathering data from various Western Forces, we quickly discover that the Wehrmacht in World War II was not the only force to suffer proportionally far fewer psychiatric casualties than the Americans did. In comparison with Vietnam, the same also applied to the British during the 1982 Falkland Campaign.

To be sure, in terms of duration the Falkland Campaign cannot stand comparison with any of the others mentioned in the present study. Just forty-four days passed from the moment the first British forces arrived in the vicinity of the islands until the Argentinian commander and his troops surrendered. On the other hand, British recruits were not screened for their vulnerability to PTSD as had been standard American practice from 1943 on. Nor were units in this campaign accompanied by psychiatrists charged with dealing with the problem. The last two factors make the British achievement look even greater.[80]

Two to two-and-a-half decades later, the situation in Iraq and Afghanistan was somewhat different. Enough British soldiers developed PTSD as to make the Ministry of Defense admit that the problem was serious and would be given all due attention. Still, by most accounts they did not do so nearly as often as their American comrades in arms did.[81] The most important reason, it seems, is the regimental system of recruitment and organization. Going back for centuries, it deliberately keeps men and officers together for relatively long periods, enabling them to get to know each other, trust each other, and forge strong bonds with each other.

As was also the case with the Wehrmacht, the outcome is units far more tightly-knit and cohesive than most American ones. Not long after the end of the Vietnam War the US Army considered adopting a somewhat similar system known as COHORT.[82] However, little came of it. Soon enough bureaucratic convenience reasserted itself as, in that army, it almost always does.

And how about non-Western troops who fought, and usually defeated, Western ones? About North Vietnam, one American psychotherapy with experience in the field, Dr. Edward Tick, wrote that veterans there "suffer a far lower incidence of PTSD than do American veterans, with fewer instances of nightmares, depression, alienation and dysfunction."[83] According to the Serb Medical Military Academy in Belgrade only one percent of the 400,000 men who served in the Serb Army during the civil wars of 1992-95 and 1999 suffered from the syndrome. This is in tune with the Serb military attaché in Tel Aviv, Colonel Rasa Lazovic, who told me that, in his country, "PTSD is not a hot topic."[84]

Many of these armies, organizations, and people lived and fought under conditions incomparably harsher than anything most people in the West can even imagine. All also found themselves on the receiving end of Western, mainly American, firepower and suffered very heavy casualties as a result. Did these facts make America's military take the beam out of their eyes? By no means. Instead, the US Air Force and Army have been trying to force PTSD down the Serbs' throats![85] Clearly, in the kingdom of the West—the Western militaries specifically included—something is very, very rotten.

5. Damaged Goods?

To repeat, victory is the best cure for the soul. The fact that, before 1945, most of the armies in question, and the societies in which they were rooted, emerged victorious from the various struggles they waged must have helped their members cope with the problem of PTSD. However, the Germans in 1914-18, the Wehrmacht in 1939-1945, and the Serbs in 1992-95 and 1999, kept fighting almost to the very end. Clearly, then, the link between defeat and PTSD is anything but absolute. Earlier we saw how different countries related to the issue in different ways. Could it be that post-1960s Western societies, with American society at their head, are actively, sometimes even deliberately, pushing their troops to become psychiatric casualties?

It is social expectations which, to a large extent, govern the lives of people in general and soldiers in particular. Presumably a society that links war to excellence will get precisely that, at least up to a certain point. That is because, as the case of Aristotle instructing Alexander shows, people will be taught to admire it and emulate it. The same applies to honor, which, during the Middle Ages was transmitted by means of the *chansons de geste*, as well as the kind of knowledge vouchsafed by "the ultimate experience"—an expression, incidentally, that in January 2015 registered almost 600,000 hits on Google.com. So why not PTSD?

Is it really war that is generating PTSD? Or is it present-day society's *idée fixe* that war is bad both in itself and for the soul of those who participate in it, so that over enough time anybody who does so *must* break down? And does not this idea itself help explain why PTSD has become as much of a problem as it is? The suggestion that all returning soldiers be screened for the symptoms, not just once but on a recurrent annual basis, points to the second and third answers.[86] So does the fact that, starting in 2010, no American combat veteran can be discharged without being examined for PTSD first.[87]

In other words, the cure may be driving the disease. If not in all cases, then at any rate in many. As has been said, psychotherapy works by helping patients construct a story they can live with.[88] If so, then the idea that war can and will make anybody break down—and that, as a consequence, there is nothing disgraceful in doing so—becomes very useful indeed.

Moving from the individual to society, the most important factor behind the process is fear of liability. Whatever the precise statistics, there can be little doubt that the number of those who claim to have the syndrome is enormous. Many feel that the Government should do more for them.[89] Nor is there any shortage of lawyers who are waiting to sue on their behalf. Both are assisted by armies of mental health workers who have a vested interest in identifying and treating as many cases as they can and tracing their problems back as far as they can. Between them, the three groups threaten to drive the cost of the war from the stratosphere, where it is now, right into intergalactic space—and, what is more, keep it there for years and even decades to come.

Some of the costs are occasioned by screening and treatment. Requiring, as it does, the long-time employment of highly-paid medical specialists, the latter tends to be very expensive. Others are incurred by the need to pay compensation and pensions. No doubt the Romans would have been bemused. Whether, had they followed the modern Western system, they would have conquered the world and ruled it for as long as they did is doubtful.

Clearly the East German doctor who drew attention to the "chronification" of the problem was on to something. Is it conceivable that the compensations and pensions are providing at least some soldiers with an incentive to invent or exaggerate symptoms and retain them for as long as they can? And that, as a result, many of them will be falsely diagnosed as suffering from PTSD when, in fact, nothing serious is the matter with them? And that, which is worst of all, some of them will be made to suffer from syndromes they do not have? That may be exactly what is taking place both in the military world and the civilian one. By one estimate, as many as one half to two thirds of all diagnoses are false.[90] And no wonder, given how vague and elastic the relevant criteria have become or, if truth be said, have always been.

One man who, long after the Civil War but decades before the term PTSD came into use, thought along such lines was Theodore Roosevelt. Roosevelt read Stephen Crane's book *The Red Badge of Courage* shortly after it was published

147

in 1895. At first he admired it very much, as many of his contemporaries as well as subsequent generations did. However, having formed the Rough Riders and seen action in Cuba, he changed his mind. Here is what he had to say about it:[91]

> I did not see any sign among the fighting men, whether wounded or unwounded, of the very complicated emotions assigned to their kind by some of the realistic modern novelists who have written about battles. At the front everyone behaved quite simply and took things as they came.

Is history repeating itself? So powerful is the pro-PTSD lobby that cases are known when soldiers and units which did not suffer from the problem were practically compelled to declare that they had, in fact, done just that.[92] However, even that is not the worst of it. How about those who have answered the call, gone through the hell that is war without flinching, and returning home—instead of being praised, feasted, and rewarded for doing so—find themselves denounced as insensitive brutes by people who have never heard a shot fired in anger? Isn't *their* honor being dragged through the mire? Should we, perhaps, start rewarding those who do *not* get PTSD, instead of those who do?

Supposing things are allowed to continue as they do, what are the probable consequences for fighting power going to be? Listen to the previously mentioned General James Mattis. In and outside the US, few people have as much combat experience as he does. He went through battle not once, as Roosevelt and his Riders did, but on a hundred different occasions in several wars. Speaking to the Marine Memorial Club, he is reported to have said:[93]

> I would just say there is one misperception of our veterans and that is they are somehow damaged goods. I don't buy it.

If we tell our veterans enough that this is what is wrong with them they may actually start believing it.

While victimhood in America is exalted I don't think our veterans should join those ranks.

There is also something called post traumatic growth where you come out of a situation like that and you actually feel kinder toward your fellow man and fellow woman.

We are going to have to have young people in our country who are willing to go toe to toe with this because two irreconcilable wills exist.

There is no room for military people, including our veterans, to see themselves as victims even if so many of our countrymen are prone to relish that role.

As we saw, whether Achilles did indeed suffer from PTSD is doubtful, to say the least. Supposing he did, though, he would have agreed that such a thing as post traumatic growth where "you actually feel kinder toward your fellow man and fellow woman" does exist. It did, after all, melt his heart, moving him to grant old King Priam's request to ransom Hector's body. But who is paying attention? So heretical did the editors of *USA Today*, which published the speech, consider these thoughts that they took care to add the words "he said" at the end of each separate sentence. And so heretical did some others consider similar words, uttered on other occasions, that the general, who incidentally is well-known for his urbane manner and wide reading, became known as "'Mad Dog' Mattis"!

Finally, is it really true that war, in the words of Jonathan Shay, must "destroy the social contract binding soldiers to each other, to their commanders, and to the society that raised than as an army?"[94] Not necessarily, it turns out. Jean de Bueil (1406-77) was an immensely experienced French soldier. Early in his career he fought side by side with Jeanne d'Arc at the siege of Orleans. Here is what he had to say about the matter:[95]

> You love your comrade so much in war. When you see your quarrel is just and your blood is fighting well, tears rise to your eyes. A great sweet feeling of love and pity fills your heart on seeing your friend so valiantly exposing his body to execute and accomplish the command of our Creator. And then you prepare to go and live or die with him and for love not to abandon him. And out of that there arises such delectation, that he who has not tasted it is not fit to say what a delight is. Do you think that a man who does that fears death? Not at all. For he feels strengthened, he is so elated he does not know where he is. Truly he is afraid of nothing.

So strong are some of the ties war creates that they last into death and, not seldom, even beyond. There is nothing new about dead comrades-in-arms appearing in the dreams of soldiers (and commanders!) and talking to them. Both Odysseus and Virgil visited the underworld. There they met with, and talked to, their former fellow combatants without, apparently, suffering any particular psychological damage. What *is* new is the idea that such encounters are one of the symptoms of PTSD and should be treated accordingly.

Just how strong such ties can be is made clear by a famous German military mourning song, "I had a comrade." It was written in 1809, twelve years after Schiller's "Cavalry Song." This was a time when much of Germany was under French occupation, and long before anybody had heard either of PTSD or of political correctness. Sixteen years later it was put to music:

PUSSYCATS

I once had a comrade,
A better one you won't find.
The drum called to battle.
He marched at my side,
In the same step and tread.

A bullet came flying,
Is it my turn or yours?
It caught him,
He lies at my feet,
As if he were a part of me.

He still stretches his hand to me,
Just when I'm about to reload.
"I cannot give you my hand.
Rest you in eternal life,
My good comrade."

Chapter V. Delegitimizing War

1. Of Might and Right

To wage war two things are indispensable: armed force and legitimacy. Why the former is needed is not worth explaining. The reason why the second is required is because, without it, there would be no way to distinguish between war on one hand and every other kind of violence on the other. To put it another way: In any civilization, at any time and place, some people, groups, communities, and organizations have the right to resort to force in order to achieve their objectives, whether defensive or offensive. Provided they do successfully, they will be rewarded. Others do not have that right—with the result that they will be, or at least are supposed to be, punished both when they are not successful and when they are.

In general, the more sophisticated the polity the more restricted the right. Compared to the overall number of people, groups, communities, and organizations, it remains so today. For example, the US is said to have 22 million active corporations.[1] But of those just one, which in the US is called "the Government" and elsewhere "the State," is legally entitled to go to war. That is why so many of those who do have the right, and whom others recognize as having it, pride themselves on that fact. Ancient monuments from Egypt and Mesopotamia bristle with the military deeds of kings, performed either in person or by means of their armies. Greek cities counted the right to go to war as an essential part of *eleutheria*—liberty, the one thing they considered most precious of all. That was one reason why they so often put military symbols on public monuments, coins, etc., and why any number of festivals were held in honor of wars fought, and victories won, in the past.[2]

From the time of Augustus on, the first and most important title of all Roman emperors was Imperator, no translation needed. Medieval noblemen regularly identified themselves to each other as well as to non-nobles by means of their "coats of arms." Starting in the first half of the eighteenth century, heads of state regularly wore uniforms both in war and in peace. And with good reason, for it was primarily on the military that their power rested. In 1901, when they gathered in London for the funeral of Queen Victoria, the only ones who did *not* do so were the presidents of France and the US. As a result, they struck a somewhat poor figure among the rest with their abundance of plumes, crests, helmets, ribbons, medals, and high riding boots. During the interwar period Mussolini, Hitler, Pilsudski, Mannerheim (Polish and Finnish heads of state, respectively), Hirohito, Chiang Kai-Shek, and Stalin all went on making many of their public appearances while dressed in uniform. After 1945 many leaders of "developing" states also continued the tradition. Some do so still.

Developments in political theory both reflected the trend and bolstered it. Constructing his imaginary *polis*, Plato decreed that the members of one out of the three classes into which the population was divided would devote their lives to preparing for war and waging it if necessary.[3] Aristotle, in the *Politics*, says that civic duties are of two kinds, those of peace and of war.[4] It is as if modern countries, instead of having perhaps eleven to twenty ministries—the great majority of which are in charge of various aspects of civilian life, as is normally the case—had only two. No sooner had Jean Bodin coined the term "sovereignty" in *Six Books of the Commonwealth* (1576) than he made it very clear that waging war was one of the seven fundamental rights and duties of the sovereign ruler and his alone.[5] Seventy-five years later Hobbes, in *Leviathan*, increased the number of duties to nine.[6]

As Frederick the Great's dictum to the effect that "I am the first servant of the state"[7] indicates, around the middle of the eighteenth century the right to wage war began passing from the sovereign to the state that he, less often she, "carried" (to use Hobbes' term). That, in turn, initiated a process whereby the state itself came to be understood not just as a machine for defense and the imposition of order but as an ideal, in fact the highest ideal of all—one that both demanded blood sacrifice and was worthy of it. Nobody did more to establish this view than the great political scientist, philosopher, and historian Georg Friedrich Wilhelm Hegel (1770-1831). "What is the state?" he rhetorically asked, and then answered his own question: "The echo of God's footsteps on earth; *that* is the state."[8]

If only because many of them had gone through it in one way or another, none of these authors looked at war as if it were some lighthearted game. For example, Bodin's main reason for writing his book was to suggest a way in which the civil wars of 1562-98, which may have been the bloodiest in the whole of French history, might be brought to an end. The same applies to Hobbes, who had to flee for his life during the civil war of 1642-51. Frederick the Great once complained that he was doomed to wage war just as a dolphin was condemned to swim in the sea. A look at the map of Prussia as it was when he ascended the throne in 1740 will explain why this was so. In 1798 Hegel, while observing war at first hand, wrote that not a village was left that did not lie half in ruins.[9] Eight years later his own house in Jena was burnt down during Napoleon's campaign against Prussia. He and the rest, however, never wavered in their opinion that waging war was both a prerogative and a duty of the state.

As the idea of war as a necessary—necessary because there was, by definition, no other way to settle disputes between sovereign rulers and entities—function of the state asserted itself, the older Judeo-Christian tradition of "just war" was largely pushed aside.[10] The way the great jurists Hugo Grotius (1583-1645), Samuel Pufendorf (1632-94) and, above all, Emmerich de Vattel (1714-67) saw it, war, as long as it was waged by legitimate authority, was just on both sides. In *Candide*, Voltaire caricatured this attitude by describing how, following a battle, both the Bulgars and the Abares had their men sing the Te Deum, "each in his own camp."[11] One outcome was a shift of interest from *ius ad bellum* to *ius in bello.*[12] Starting around 1700, the latter probably did something to make war a little less bloody and a little less terrible than it would otherwise have been.

Looking at what we now know as the West, perhaps at no time were all these beliefs more strongly held than during the nineteenth century, precisely the classical period when Western power vis-à-vis the rest of the world was at its height. Possibly they were a reaction to the "horrors and uncertainties" of industrialization.[13] No doubt the fact that this was also the period when one state after another introduced conscription, turning the military into "the school of the nation," helped. After all, one could hardly draft millions of men and keep them under the colors for a considerable part of their lives (generally two to three years) without explaining to them, in terms they could understand, why doing so was good or, at any rate, indispensable. This was also true of the frequently made attempts to link war with the new Darwinist theories concerning the struggle for life, natural selection, the survival of the fittest, and the like.

Not just conservatives but many liberals subscribed to these views.[14] So did most socialists and, from the 1890s on, communists. The only difference was that the latter in particular hoped to do away with war on behalf of, and as waged by, states against each other—not in order to abolish it, but to replace it by armed struggles by the proletariat against the bourgeoisie. Paradoxically, in view of all this belligerence, the century was also the most peaceful one in the whole of European history. In fact, the belligerence—or jingoism, as it was known in England—may well have been a *reaction* to peace. Wasn't it the French philosopher Blaise Pascal (1623-62) who said that the one thing humans could not do was to sit quietly in a room alone? And suppose we could do so; would we be human or some kind of slugs?

These are important questions, but not such as form part of our subject. Suffice it to say that the list of those who considered war a necessary instrument in the hands of the state could be extended forever. Perhaps the most prominent among them was General Erich Ludendorff (1865-1937). Ludendorff was a militarist—none more so—and an anti-Semite. Early on he associated with Hitler and the nascent Nazi Party. For that he has been rightly condemned. For us, though, what matters is that, at his post as army quartermaster general from 1916 to 1918 Ludendorff acted as Germany's virtual dictator. He ran not only the military but large parts of the economy as well. He knew and understood war, especially modern total war, as few people before or after him have done. He also lost two sons to it. As he wrote, "the war has spared me nothing."[15]

All this caused him to formulate his views with a frankness and brutality seldom equaled before or since. In his 1936 book, *Der Totale Krieg*, he drew the conclusions from his experiences. "All the theories of Clausewitz [concerning the need to subordinate war to policy/politics]," he wrote, "should be thrown overboard. Both warfare and policy/politics are meant to serve the preservation of the people. But warfare is the highest expression of the national 'will to live.' And policy/politics must, therefore, be subservient to the conduct of war."[16] And not just in wartime either. Preparing for modern war was an enormously complex, enormously expensive, enterprise. It drew on a vast number of different fields, including not least that of propaganda intended to mobilize the people's spirit and prepare it for battle. All of this had to be carefully coordinated and took a long time to complete. Hence the only way to manage a nation was by means of a permanent military dictatorship, such as he himself had tried to exercise— but, as he saw it, had failed to bring to fruition because Germany's resources were insufficient and because too many others stood in his way.

PUSSYCATS

2. The Rise of Rights

Back in 1937 in the English-speaking world, a critically important, if almost totally unnoticed, development took place. For the first time two curves, one going up, the other down, crossed one another. Based on millions of scanned books, one of the curves traced the frequency with which printed books used the word "rights" (not right, which in English as in some other languages can also mean the opposite of "left" and "correct"; as in the right side, the right direction, and so on). The other did the same for the word "duty." From that time on the gap between the two has kept growing. As of the year 2000, readers were more than three times as likely to see the former term as the latter.[17]

On Google.com, as of early 2015, "rights" registered ten times as many hits as "duty." The way the curves moved in other countries was not the same. However, and again focusing on the turn of the century, the actual outcome was the same. Returning to Ngram, in Spanish books the ratio of *derechos* to *obligatorio* was about two to one. That of *Rechte* to *Pflicht* in German ones was more than two to one; that of *droits* to *devoir* in French ones almost three and a half to one. The most extreme case was Italian. In books printed in that language, *diritto* was used almost eight times as often as *dovere*. Quite obviously, Mussolini's attempt to re-educate them has failed. Italians do not seem to feel they owe anything to anybody.

As "certain inalienable rights" (the US' Declaration of Independence, 1776) and the "Declaration of the Rights of Man" (France, 1789) show, in a modern liberal-democratic society rights are the first concern of the citizen. As "Duty, Honor, Country" (the motto of West Point Military Academy, founded in 1802) and "England expects every man to do his duty" (Admiral Nelson before the Battle of Trafalgar, 1805) show, duty is the first thing any society and any army must and do demand of their soldiers. Or take the last words of Empress Eugénie,

157

wife of Emperor Louis Napoleon, addressed to her fourteen-year-old son as the latter departed for the war against Prussia in 1870 in his father's suite: *"Louis, fais ton devoir."*[18] That is why the balance—the changing balance—between the two concepts is of vital concern to the topic at hand.

To start with the former, the idea that all men—a term, incidentally, which was meant to cover women too—were born with certain rights "nature" had bestowed on them goes back to the first half of the eighteenth century. As the above quotes suggest, its role in helping shape first the American Revolution and then the French one can hardly be overestimated. However, not everybody accepted the idea. Throughout the nineteenth century many did not. Later, during the twentieth century, both Fascism and National Socialism denied that such a thing as human rights did in fact exist.

The need to fight Italy and Germany, and the Allied victory over them, gave the idea of "rights" a tremendous boost. That explains why, as soon as World War II ended, attempts got under way to take it out of the somewhat vague realm of "nature" and codify it into positive international law. The outcome was the 1946 Charter of the United Nations, destined to become the most subscribed-to document in the whole of history. The Charter's very first article proclaimed its purpose: "to promot[e] and encourag[e] respect for human rights and for fundamental freedoms for all."[19]

Just two years later the Universal Declaration of Human Rights was signed.[20] Together, these two documents gave the signal. Slowly but inexorably over the next few decades, a vast body of legislation was stamped out of the ground. The most important documents were a Convention on the Prevention and Punishment of the Crime of Genocide, and a Convention against Torture. As of the early twenty-first century the total was about two dozen.

As the fact that Stalin was one of the original signatories shows all too clearly, not all the countries in question had as clean a human-rights record as purists might desire. Quite a few spiked their letters of acceptance with so many reservations as to make their signatures meaningless. Others only signed by way of paying lip service to the concept.[21] Probably even more signed with no intention of changing their behavior, and proceeded as they always had. By 1994 even Iraq, which at that time was governed by the unspeakable dictator Saddam Hussein, had joined five treaties protecting human rights. In 2003 Libya, then under the scarcely less unspeakable dictator Muammar Gadhafi, was actually elected chair of the United Nations Human Rights Commission! One hardly knows whether to laugh or to cry.

Human rights were taken much more seriously in the West, the part of the world in which they had been invented and from which they spread, to the extent that they did spread, over the rest of the world. But things did not develop in the same way in Europe as in the United States. The former resembled the United Nations in that the main driving force was the need to ensure that nothing like Fascism and National Socialism, with all their injustices and atrocities, would ever resurge. The outcome, the Convention on Human Rights, was adopted by the Council of Europe, an organization established in 1949 for the purpose of facilitating cooperation among member states. Originally there were ten: Belgium, Denmark, France, Ireland, Italy, Luxembourg, the Netherlands, Norway, Sweden, and the United Kingdom (which, at that time, still liked to call itself "Great Britain").

The European Convention on Human Rights was signed in 1950 and went into force in 1953.[22] Article by article, it listed the rights in question. To wit: the right to life, liberty, security (against arbitrary arrest), fair trial, privacy ("the right to respect for privacy and family life"), conscience and religion, expression, association, marriage, and effective remedy. Torture, servitude, and discrimination were prohibited. To guarantee the rights and uphold the prohibitions, a European Court of Human Rights was established. Its judges,

159

equal in number to that of the contracting states, were authorized to rule over cases submitted both by states and by individuals.

The Court of Human Rights has always had its hands full. Currently the number of applications runs into the tens of thousands and the backlog is in proportion. To be sure, the impact of law and courts on reality is always much more limited than many people imagine. There always exists a gap between the spoken or written word on one hand and practice on the other. Still, to the extent that they do influence reality and shape it, law and courts have helped turn the European Union, all of whose members are also Council members, into what is one of the freest, most liberal regions in history. Although given the rise of political correctness on one hand and of extreme Islam on the other, how long it will remain so is unclear.

The most important difference between Europe and the United States is that, in the former, the "rights revolution" first instituted in 1950-53 started the top of the political hierarchy. From there it worked its way downward. Any country that wanted to join the Council had to sign the Convention first. By the end of the first decade of the twenty-first century forty-seven of them had done so. That even includes Russia, where whatever rights and liberties existed have never been more than short-lived guests. The Court responsible for enforcing it was considered superior to any single state and also, as long as the Convention remained in force, to all of them together.

Across the Atlantic things were quite dissimilar. In the US, the idea that citizens possessed "certain inalienable rights" *against* the Government had existed from the beginning and was rooted in the country's very foundations. Consequently there was no need to dig them up, institute them, or impose them on anybody. Another difference was that the Supreme Court, which ruled over such cases as it did over all others, did not stand above the Government but was very much part of it. The outcome was a more or less permanent, three-cornered, struggle between the Court—or rather the court system of which it formed the apex—the executive, and all sorts of plaintiffs. The last-named were always trying to use the first against the second in an attempt to defend or extend their "rights." They do so still.

How successful, or at least prominent, has the struggle been? One way to answer the question is to look at the growth of ACLU, the American Civil Liberties Union. Throughout its century-long history it has seen its task as defending people's "rights" and "liberties" against the big bad government in Washington, DC, which is always intent on limiting them and taking them away. A glance at Ngram, which throughout his study has enabled us to form an idea of the frequency with which this or that word appears in printed books, yields a fascinating insight. In just two years, from 1958 to 1960, that frequency went up 2,500 percent!

Since then the curve has had its ups and down. However, it still remains much higher than it used to be before 1958. The ACLU itself has waxed big and fat. In the two decades between 1978 and 1999 alone its annual income grew more than tenfold, and its endowment fund fifty-two fold.[23] In 2011 it was able to spend more than $100 million.[24] It has also served as a model for similar organizations in other Western and would-be Western countries.

The time of the increases, as well as their size, is easily explained. The 1960s were the years of the civil rights movement, which shook the US to its very foundations. It acted as a model for, and was followed by, many similar ones: women's rights, gay rights, minority rights, the rights of the handicapped.... Each movement or group claimed that its members were being discriminated against and victimized by the government, all kinds of organizations, and the public in general. Each asked the courts to redress their grievances. Very often, their requests were granted. The legislature too got involved, enacting many laws that prohibited "discrimination" and enforced "diversity." This also occurred not least of all in the military, which was compelled to grant female soldiers in particular their "rights," very often against its will.

No wonder Ronald Dworkin (1931-2013), "widely respected as the most original and powerful philosopher of law in the English-speaking world,"[25] believed that "the language of rights now dominates political debate in the United States."[26] This has been carried to the point where not just people but even animals and plants are supposed to have—and soon may have—"rights," and should be treated accordingly.[27]

In both the US and in Europe, the rise of rights led to the creation of what is, in some ways, the freest, fairest, and most liberal society of all time. Gone, hopefully for good, is arbitrary government of the kind still often found in other parts of the world. Gone too are many kinds of discrimination, if not always in practice then at least in law. That includes several kinds of government-exercised discrimination which used to make the lives of those who suffered from them hard if not, in some cases, all but intolerable. As, for example, the regulations that affected gay people of both sexes.

If certain psychologists may be believed, it is not just society but personalities that have changed. Since society is made up of individual people, and since individuals influence society as well as the other way around, that is not surprising. Returning to Ngram, we find that, in the forty years after 1960, use of the term "narcissism," defined by the DSM as "self-centeredness; firmly holding to the belief that one is better than others; condescending toward others," went up two had a half times. Another study suggests that, between 1999 and 2009 alone, its incidence among the population has gone up tenfold![28]

The two figures are neither consistent nor strictly comparable. Nevertheless, for the average adult, the words *mon droit*, with the emphasis on *mon*, seem to have taken on a new lease on life.

3. The Demise of Duty

Broadly speaking, duties may be divided into two principal categories. The first, which may be referred to as negative, is of the kind that obliges one *not* to do certain things such as kill one's fellows, rob them, rape them, etc. The second, which may be referred to as positive, is of the kind that obliges them to do a whole series of other things. The first does not concern us here. In what follows, we shall focus on the second.

While rights have been going up, their mirror-image, duty—especially but not exclusively the kind of duty individuals owe not to other individuals but to the society in which they live—has been going down.[29] In the four-hundred-odd pages of Dworkin's book *Taking Rights Seriously*, duty only takes up a few lines.[30] In no part of the world is this truer than in the "advanced" West where, since 1970 or so, the public sector and its demands has been in full retreat before the private one and its offers. So much so that, as applied to almost anything from water to schools, "public" now means "cheap and bad," whereas "private" means "good but expensive."[31] To be sure, the 2008 economic crisis has increased the former's supervision of, and interference with, the latter. Far from increasing the prestige of the public sector, though, in the eyes of most people the outcome has been to make it into an ever greater nuisance than it was before.

Wits claim that "I am from the government; I am here to help you," is one of the three greatest lies in the English language (the other two are "the check is in the mail" and "I'll divorce my wife and marry you, honey"). Things have not always been that way. So enamored of duty was Immanuel Kant (1724-1804), one of the greatest philosophers of all time, that he addressed it in almost lyric terms:[32]

Duty! Thou sublime and mighty name that dost embrace nothing charming or insinuating, but requirest submission, and yet seekest not to move the will by threatening aught that would arouse natural aversion or terror, but merely holdest forth a law which of itself finds entrance into the mind, and yet gains reluctant reverence (though not always obedience), a law before which all inclinations are dumb, even though they secretly counter-work it; what origin is there worthy of thee, and where is to be found the root of thy noble descent which proudly rejects all kindred with the inclinations; a root to be derived from which is the indispensable condition of the only worth which men can give themselves?

For both Kant and his younger fellow German, Hegel, duty was far more than the indispensable lynchpin without which no society can exist. It was that, of course, but it also provided the only possible basis in which real freedom could be anchored. Freedom, they argued, does not mean the individual's right to do whatever he (or she) pleases. Such freedom would be possible only if he lived alone in a desert and is very likely to lead to madness. What it does or should mean is his complete, voluntary, submersion in society.[33] Take duty away, and what are probably the most famous words former British Prime Minister Margaret Thatcher ever said would become horribly true: "There is no such thing as society."[34] Let alone an organized state with a government, if indeed it is worthy of being called that, based on anything other than the bluntest, crassest, forms of punishment and reward.

Starting in ancient Egypt, home to the pyramids, countless rulers made large parts of the male population perform forced labor, or *corvées* as they were known in French, either as the authorities ordered them to or on a seasonal basis. In simple agricultural economies where most people did not have access to money for day-to-day use, is it easy to see how there would be no other way that large-scale public works such as building roads, canals, and fortifications could have been carried out. Adam Smith in *The Wealth of Nations* (1776) called such labor "cruel and oppressive... one of the principal instruments of tyranny by which [officers of the state] chastise any parish or *communeauté* which has had the misfortune to fall under their displeasure."[35] Yet at that time even Britain, as the most advanced and most liberal country of all, still had it in the form of the notorious press gangs that roamed coastal cities in search of fit men whom they could kidnap for service in the Navy.[36] In France it took the Revolution to bring forced labor to an end. In Eastern Europe such labor, which had to be performed either for the state or for the land-owning nobility, persisted until the middle of the nineteenth century.

The abolition of *corvées* left only two really important civic duties: to wit, paying taxes and military service. Here we are concerned with the latter. During the Ancien Régime, at any rate in principle, most countries relied on volunteers to fill the ranks. This state of affairs changed in 1793, when the French National Assembly famously "requisitioned" all unmarried able-bodied men between eighteen and twenty-five with immediate effect.[37] Though there were many ups and downs, a century later Germany, France, Russia, Austria-Hungary, Italy, and Japan had all adopted the system in one form or another. So had smaller countries, many of which hoped that, by granting as few exceptions as possible, they would go a little way to compensate for their demographic and economic weakness. During World Wars I and II even the island nations, Britain and the US, took that road. Having done so, they continued to draft their young men even after World War II had ended.

The first important country to do away with the draft was Britain in 1960. One Western nation after another followed. In 1996 even France, the original home of the *levée en masse*, decided to do without it; five years later, the decision was implemented. Though circumstances varied from one country to another, generally the reasons behind the decision were as follows: First, the introduction and proliferation of nuclear weapons, including so-called tactical weapons suitable for use on the battlefield, made mass armies both impossible and useless. Second, so expensive were many modern conventional weapons that states could only afford very few of them to arm their troops with.

The following is one, admittedly extreme, example of the process. America's P-51 Mustang is widely believed to have been the best fighter-bomber of World War II. So much so that it was sometimes referred to as "the Cadillac of the sky." Yet it could be had for only $50,000 or so. Seven decades later an F-22 Raptor came at about $150,000,000. Taking inflation into account, the difference meant an increase of approximately 1,500 percent. No wonder that, whereas 15,000 of the former were built, Secretary of Defense Robert Gates in 2009 decided to cap the number of the latter at 187. Which meant that, factoring in the cost of research and development, each aircraft actually cost upward of $350,000,000.[38]

Other factors were also involved. In some ways, it was the Vietnam War which provided the decisive turning point. So divisive was the conflict that it threatened to tear American society apart, paralyzing the government's ability to use the armed forces for almost any political purpose it might have in mind. President Nixon's decision to abolish the draft solved the problem, if not completely—the so-called Colin Powell Doctrine still stated, among other things, that enjoying the support of the American people was an essential prerequisite for going to war—then at any rate to a considerable extent.[39] A military made up of volunteers was expected to give, and in fact did give, rise to far fewer objections on the part of the pulblic. In addition, the troops themselves could be relied upon to do their duty. Or so it was thought.

Throughout the Cold War, Western European armed forces, backed up by American ones, were supposed to prepare to defend their borders against a possible, if always rather unlikely, Soviet invasion of what was known as "the Central Theater." As the Soviet Union imploded, though, the emphasis shifted to other kinds of operations such as expeditionary warfare and peacekeeping. To draft young men, train them, and oblige them to defend the homeland was one thing; to do the same in order to send them to fight, and perhaps die, for some obscure cause hundreds if not thousands of kilometers away, quite a different one.

Something has already been said about the role feminism has played in all this. In the age of equality between the sexes, logically conscription should have been applied to women as well as men. Except in Israel, though, doing so was simply inconceivable. And even in Israel women always served for a shorter period, and found it much easier to obtain a discharge, than men did.[40] Understood in this way, the switch from conscription to an all-volunteer force was a direct response to the rise of the women's-liberation movement. As its name implies that movement, claiming as it does to represent half the population, has always put far greater emphasis on rights than on duties. Surely it is no accident that, on Google.com, the combination of "women's liberation" with "rights" yielded five times as many hits as "women's liberation" with "duties." Ngram shows that, between 1960 and 2000, the use of the term "women's rights" went up almost twice as fast as "women's duties" did.

Two renowned World War I British suffragettes, Emmeline and Christabel Pankhurst, strongly supported conscription so as to prove that they were patriotic and supported the war—conscription for men, needless to say, not for themselves and their sisters.[41] To this day, when feminists speak and write about conscription they practically always refer to the historical fact that men used to be drafted, not to the possibility that the same methods will one day be applied to women.[42]

All this was part outcome, part cause, of the abovementioned powerful anti-militarist feelings that have come to pervade Western societies, European ones in particular. Looking back, governments and nations tend to look at the replacement of conscripts by professional volunteers as a great blessing, as do the commanders of the forces themselves. And so, in many ways, it is. But it has not been without cost. Like many other government agencies, the military cannot compete with private business when it comes to paying competitive wages and salaries. Especially in modern Western societies, which unlike more traditional ones provide individuals with plenty of other ways by which, if they have what it takes, they can raise to the top, the more qualified the people, both women and men, the military needs the greater the difficulty it has in attracting them and keeping them.

Nor is the difficulty of recruiting such people the only problem. War is the most terrible of all human activities by far. It brings out not just every human strength but every human weakness as well. That is why even an army consisting entirely of enthusiastic volunteers, such as the one Britain raised and fielded in 1914-16, cannot avoid operating an extensive system of courts-martial to make sure orders are obeyed even when death is looking the troops in the face.

In such a situation there is only so much the courts, and the punishments they mete out, can do. That even applies in the most strictly administered, best-disciplined forces of all. Where rights reign supreme and duty has become an object of neglect, suspicion, and even derision—as it has in most Western societies—whether, if, and when the test comes, they will be sufficient is anybody's guess.

4. Learning to Say No

In the past, not everybody agreed to be drafted for military service, let alone volunteered for it. Principled resistance to such service can be traced back as far as early Christianity under the Roman Empire. Whether, at that time, it was rooted in any moral objections to war as such or in religion—after all, the army was pagan and its commander-in-chief, the Emperor, was himself a god—has long been moot.[43] The fact is that, no sooner did the empire turn Christian in the fourth century AD than Christians started joining the army in large numbers, suggests that the latter interpretation is closer to the truth. Once God had told Emperor Constantine that *in hoc signo vinces* ("in this sign you will win)," most "moral" objections disappeared. From the time of Charlemagne's campaigns in Spain and Saxony to that of Oliver Cromwell during the English Civil War, countless Christians went into battle under the sign of the cross. As the Serb forces, fighting Kosovarian and Albanian terrorists in 1999, showed, on occasion they do so still.

Starting with the Reformation, some Protestant sects took the opposite tack. Luther himself had said that the essence of Protestantism—a term, of course, he did not use—consisted of each person's right to interpret the Bible as his or her conscience dictated. Citing Jesus' command to "love your enemies"[44] the members of some sects refused to fight. Instead they asked to be exempted from military service on religious grounds. Among them were the Anabaptists, the Hutterites, the Mennonites, and, in Poland, the Nontrinitarians. Some of the sects' members had to leave their countries of origin and settle elsewhere. However, in the Netherlands, in Switzerland, and in parts of Germany they were often able to get their way. Usually they did so in return for agreeing to pay a special tax or "contribution."[45]

England, too, had some sects whose members refused to take part in the Civil War of 1642-51. However, neither there nor in other Protestant countries did they have a very significant impact on the military. First, the numbers involved were never large. Second, starting around 1660 one country after another started creating professional armed forces made up, in principle at any rate, entirely of volunteers. The various medieval militias that still existed were broken up. In

Prussia, even the term itself was prohibited. The change made dealing with objectors much easier than it had been.

In late seventeenth- and eighteenth-century America, where there was no "standing army" but where each colony had its own militia, the situation was different. As in England, the most important and best organized sect was the Quakers. Like the rest, they were sometimes willing to contribute money for building fortifications and maintaining the various state militias. They also provided shelter to (white) refugees from war. Still, they adamantly refused to take up arms and fight.[46] On the eve of the War of the American Revolution, so strong were the sects that every one of the Thirteen Colonies recognized conscientious objection as a valid ground for exemption from service. This did not prevent a few objectors from being imprisoned for periods of up to two years.[47] Both in America and in Europe, exemption was a question not of right but of privilege. It was always understood that the powers that granted that privilege also had the right to withdraw it if they wanted to.[48]

Nevertheless, the two continents were separated by an important difference. At the time the US was a remote country with fewer than two and a half million (white) inhabitants. It did not really have an army but only a host of separate state militias. By contrast France, with twenty-seven million, was the greatest power of the age. It also maintained the largest, most powerful army in the Western world. The 1793 switch to general conscription formed a critical turning point. In France itself the near-complete absence of radical Protestant sects meant that the impact of conscientious objection, as opposed to draft-dodging and the like, was limited-to-nonexistent. The mere handful who did object were often assigned to depots, lines of communication, hospitals, and the like, a solution subsequent armed forces also adopted on occasion. However, when Napoleon tried to extend conscription to the Netherlands and the parts of Germany under his rule, he quickly found himself opposed by the American groups' parent sects. Typically for the times, his response was to allow the people in question to hire substitutes to serve in their place. Since few of them had the means to do so, this concession did not carry very far. Several attempts by the sects' leaders to plead with the emperor did not lead to results.

As conscription spread from France to other countries, objections to military service were bound to increase in number. As before, some were religiously based. During the American Civil War both sides followed the old practice of permitting objectors to hire substitutes. Those who could or would not do so were sent to jail. Lincoln personally, at one point, pardoned some Quakers and Mennonites who were serving time for this reason. It was, after all, hard to fight for freedom while at the same time keeping those who demanded it in their own way in prison.

Seeing themselves as the underdogs, the Confederate authorities, though they did recognize conscientious objection in principle, were not as tolerant in practice. Many Southern objectors were mobbed, arrested, abused, starved, and whipped. It has even been claimed that a few of them had muskets strapped to their bodies and were forcibly transported to the battlefield, to no avail.[49]

That is not to say that, in the US and in other countries, all of those who refused to fight did so because they objected to war as such. Presumably many did so for other, less praiseworthy, reasons. There were also those who did not agree with the specific cause their governments claimed to represent while waging this war or that, as the American writer Henry Thoreau did when his county went to war with Mexico. Others were socialists of a certain kind. They justified their refusal to fight by their opposition to states which, following Karl Marx, they saw as instruments of class oppression.[50]

What made the period different from all its predecessors was the rise of secular pacifism. Its adherents condemned war and violence not on religious grounds but on purely moral ones. No longer as isolated as they had normally

171

been in the past, pacifists could be found in many walks of life, from the highest to the lowest. They set up countless organizations, systematically used the most modern communication techniques to conduct propaganda, and held national and international congresses.[51] The most prominent pacifist of all was the Russian writer Leo Tolstoy (1828-1910). Having seen action during the Crimean War, during the 1880s he converted to nonviolence. From then on he issued a whole series of treatises, denouncing war as "the absolute evil." His supporters set up organizations in Britain, the US, the Netherlands, and Austria-Hungary, but he had sympathizers in many other countries as well.

Tolstoy himself described how those who refused military service were sent first to priests, then to doctors, then to various penal battalions, and finally to the lunatic asylums.[52] Another well-known pre-1914 pacifist was an Austrian noblewoman, the agitator, lecturer, and troublemaker Bertha von Suttner (1843-1914). Her 1889 novel *Die Waffen Nieder* went through thirty-seven German editions and was translated into sixteen languages. Her efforts earned her a Nobel Peace Prize. Much later, her portrait was chosen to grace Austria's two Euro coins.

These efforts bore fruit, if that is the right word, during World War I. It was the first time that so-called "conscientious objectors" appeared in significant numbers outside well-established sects such as the Quakers and the Mennonites. As one historian was later to note, "just as the individual psyche of the shell-shock victims was beginning to be deemed by the progressive minded more important than their... obligations, so the individual conscience of the objectors and war protestors was coming to be thought deserving of protection."[53] To that extent, PTSD and conscientious objection rose at the same time and formed two sides of the same coin.

Neither Tolstoy's followers nor those of von Suttner (many of them women, and many of them members of various suffragist movements),[54] had a noticeable impact on the outbreak and course of World War I. For example, in 1917-18 the US drafted some three million men, but only about two thousand objectors of all kinds were arrested and convicted.[55] What they did accomplish was to act as harbingers of what the future would bring. Even while the conflict lasted the British government decided to mitigate the effects of conscription and improve its own image by recognizing conscientious objectors and granting them the right to perform alternative civil service. In part, its actions were directed by the need to assuage those veteran anti-war activists, the Quakers. Later, taking their cue from Britain, several other countries, mostly Protestant ones in Western and Northern Europe, passed similar legislation. Denmark did so in 1917, Sweden in 1920, the Netherlands in 1922, and Finland in 1931.

In 1921 the War Resisters' International was founded with headquarters, appropriately called Broederschapshuis (Fraternity House) in the village of Bilthoven, the Netherlands. It adopted, as its slogan, "War is a crime against humanity. I am therefore determined not to support any kind of war and to strive for the removal of all causes of war." Its symbol was a broken rifle. Along with its branches in various countries, it kept the issue alive.

In 1933 two Belgian citizens, Léo Campion and Hem Day (pseudonym for Marcel Dieu) were put on trial for refusing to be conscripted. The stir they caused was enormous. As one British author wrote three years later, "one pacifist create[s] another."[56] During World War II totalitarian countries persecuted conscientious objectors might and main. In Germany some Jehovah's Witnesses were executed, but most were put into concentration camps where they were treated as viciously as any other group.[57] In the Soviet Union they were more likely to be shot out of hand.

Democratic countries generally took a line similar to the British one a generation earlier. Special commissions staffed by officers, psychologists, and priests were set up to decide who was a genuine objector and who was not.

American men who came before the commissions were likely to be asked whether they would refuse to fight to prevent their sister (if they had one) from being raped. Those who said yes to this and similar questions were sent to work in hospitals and the like. As a character in Joanne Greenberg's 1964 novel, *I Never Promised You a Rose Garden*, explains, the government in its wisdom had decided to rub objectors' noses in "it." And it was the patients in a mental asylum who formed the "it."[58]

Compared with those who were drafted, the number of those who refused to be inducted on grounds of conscience and obtain a release remained rather small. Still in many cases they were able to get what they wanted, or at least obtain some public sympathy for their views. This in turn signified the various states' tacit admission, previously all but inconceivable, that they themselves no longer necessarily held the moral high ground. As the saying goes, if you cannot lick them, join them, or at least try to ignore them as best you can. Increasingly, states gave up their own absolute right to rule over conscience. If not in every respect, then at any rate in relation to the most important question of all: namely, that of citizens' right, and duty, to kill and die for their countries.

A landmark of sorts was reached in January 1967 when the Council of Europe adopted Resolution No. 337. The resolution declared that "persons liable to conscription for military service who, for reasons of conscience or profound conviction, arising from religious, ethical, moral, humanitarian, philosophical or similar motives, refuse to perform armed service shall enjoy a personal right to be released from the obligation to perform such service. This right shall be regarded as deriving logically from the fundamental rights of the individual in democratic Rule of Law states."[59] It was based on Article 9 of the European Convention on Human Rights, which binds member states to respect the individual's freedom of conscience and religion. By issuing the declaration, the states in question to a large extent pulled the objectors' sting. Previously a

174

principled refusal to serve had often had something heroic about it. Now it became just one of the numerous, if rather tepid and uninteresting, rights citizens in liberal democracies enjoy or are told they enjoy.

Concurrently, on the other side of the Atlantic, the Vietnam War led to a sharp rise in the number of US citizens who made similar claims.[60] Almost ten thousand were put on trial and convicted. The number of those who refused to serve and found various ways to do so was much larger still. For the first time the objectors, merging as they did into a much broader protest movement that opposed US policies in Southeast Asia, seriously interfered with a national war effort. Doing so, they were helped by several Supreme Court rulings that expanded the right to gain an exemption in such a way as to include not only those who based their objections on religious belief but on "deeply held moral and ethical" ones as well.

Logically the end of conscription should have caused conscientious objectors to war to become an extinct species. But this did not happen. The more rights they were granted, the greater—some would say the more impudent—their demands. Not that, among those who claim to be acting in the name of "rights," doing so is at all unusual. Three factors, more or less common to all Western societies, led to those demands being granted. The first was the fact that, as we saw, "militarism" had become one of the worst terms of abuse of all. Niagaras of ink were spilled in an effort to expose it and denounce its evils.

The second factor, also mentioned before, was the decline of mass armies. The third was the "rights revolution" and the demise of duty. Nowadays in the US even uniformed military personnel, i.e., people who joined out of their own free will and were paid for doing so, are entitled to cite conscientious objection to war and ask for an exemption from deployment.[61] The same is true in Germany, where quite some soldiers became objectors as soon as they discovered that, rather than spending their service sitting in a comfortable room behind a computer as they had hoped, they might actually have to be deployed.[62] The

Bundeswehr has great difficulty attracting manpower. Consequently, it fears the bad publicity any refusals to meet soldiers' demands, however preposterous, may generate. That is why, of more than one thousand Bundeswehr soldiers who sought this way out in 2014, no fewer than three quarters got their way.[63]

With this *reductio ad absurdum*, the Western states' surrender to "rights" was complete.

5. The Absolute Evil

Great or small, right- or left-wing, most thinking Europeans who lived between 1750 and 1914 would probably have subscribed to the idea that war was a legitimate, sometimes necessary and unavoidable, business. Especially during the nineteenth century, quite a few went further still. They argued that war, though horrible and destructive—in fact, *because* it was horrible and destructive—was indispensable for the health both of states and individuals. Absent war, both would degenerate into a morass of cowardice, selfishness, materialism, and, last not least, feminism.[64] In the words of German Chief of Staff Helmuth von Moltke, an otherwise exceptionally urbane, well-educated man with sufficient perspective to joke about his own profession: "Eternal peace is a dream, and not even a beautiful one."[65]

But "most" is not everybody. Already during the Enlightenment, a minority view had emerged. It saw war not as an essential instrument in the hands of the state but as a murderous game—one that spoiled aristocrats, with the king at their head, played at the expense of their hapless troops as well as society in general. The most important eighteenth-century representatives of this approach were the so-called physiocrats.[66] Their basic idea, going back to John Locke, was that all wealth originated in productive work—primarily, but not necessarily, agricultural work. War interrupted productive work, killed those who did it, and destroyed its fruits. The culprits were those who, while not engaging in such work, filled the most important positions at the head of the state.

The obvious solution was to overthrow existing institutions so as to institute representative forms of government. Pointing to Switzerland and the Netherlands as his examples, Immanuel Kant suggested that, as a condition for "eternal peace," all countries turn themselves, or let themselves be turned, into republics. Albeit he remained sufficiently realistic to say, at the opening of his book, that the kind of peace he was looking for only existed in graveyards.[67]

Starting in the seventeenth century, which until 1900 was the bloodiest in the whole of European history, occasional proposals were raised to render war "absurd and impossible from its own monstrosity," as the American philosopher William James put it in 1896.[68] Most involved the establishment of some kind of international organization. Made up of sovereigns and states, it would adjudicate disputes between those sovereigns and those states. A few visionaries even suggested, with obvious relish, that the organization in question raise armies and use armed force against anybody held guilty of disturbing the peace. More or less seriously meant schemes of this kind are associated with the names of such luminaries as William Penn, Jean-Jacques Rousseau, Immanuel Kant, John Stuart Mill, and, during the second half of the nineteenth century, the Swiss jurist Johann Bluntschli.[69]

In 1899 the idea that there were, or any rate ought to be, better ways to settle international disputes than by engaging in mutual slaughter led to the creation of the Permanent Court of Arbitration in The Hague. The declared purpose was to help resolve conflicts involving states, state entities, intergovernmental organizations and private parties. As of 2014 the relevant conventions had been signed by 116 out of some 190 countries on earth. Over a century and a quarter, the total number of cases submitted to the Court for arbitration runs into several dozen. Unfortunately, though, that number only includes very few involving sovereign organizations entitled to wage war, i.e., states, on both sides.[70] How the Justices spend the rest of their time is not very clear. But it does not look as if they are at all short of leisure.

As World War I ended, the concept of war-guilt was introduced. Not only Vattel, but "blood and iron" Bismarck would have been appalled. To be sure, there was nothing new about rulers and polities blaming each other for engaging in armed aggression. As that great cynic, Vattel's contemporary Frederick the Great, is supposed to have said: "The world is in order; my armies are marching, my professors are researching the causes of the war." Never before, however, had any country been compelled to sign a formal document in which it admitted its guilt. The Treaty of Versailles provided the legal basis for disarming Germany as well as the payment of reparations. Perhaps even more important, it did as much to foster bitterness and hatred as any other written instrument has ever done. By doing so, it helped create the basis for the outbreak of World War II twenty years later.

World War I also provided the impetus for the establishment of the League of Nations.[71] However, the League's inability to prevent war quickly became both obvious and notorious. Ere World War II broke out in 1939, the only other advance towards the abolition of armed conflict was the Kellogg-Briand Pact of 1928. Named after the foreign ministers of the US and France, respectively, ultimately it was signed by sixty-one other states as well. The signatories undertook "to renounce war as an instrument of national policy."[72] Though the pact failed to prevent the outbreak of war, it did provide a legal basis for the 1946 war criminals' trials in Nuremberg and Tokyo. Technically it remains in force to the present day.

Less than thirteen months after the end of World War II, and still very much influenced by the immense death and destruction it had occasioned, the United Nations came into being. In time, every state on the planet joined the organization. "All members," read Article 2.4 of the Charter, "shall refrain in their international relations from the threat or use of force against the territorial integrity or political independence of any state, or in any other manner inconsistent with the Purposes of the United Nations." In 1970, Resolution No. 2734 repeated the prohibition.[73] With the right to use armed force for any purpose except strict self-defense gone, age-old concepts such as "the right of conquest" and "subjugation," which earlier during the twentieth century had been very much part of legal discourse, also went into oblivion.

To be sure, enforcing the prohibition proved harder than proclaiming it. As, for example, the universal replacement of the term "war department" by "department of defense" shows, in many places the only thing that changed was the terminology. That even applies to the Stockholm International Peace Research Institute (SIPRI). In reality it is a strategic-studies think-tank much like all the rest. Yet these changes, superficial and not seldom hypocritical as they are, hint at a brave new world which was being born. Especially in the West, and especially among what Americans call liberals and Europeans, left-wingers or socialists, a new idea not only took hold but was institutionalized: namely, that going to war is an absolute evil and that those who do so are either criminals or some kind of madmen (and, increasingly madwomen) in need of psychotherapy.

Spoken or written, the words of some peace researchers or conflict resolvers—or bleeding hearts or peaceniks as, less respectfully, they are sometimes known—can only be described as hallucinatory. We have already commented on the way Sweden's foreign minister hopes to counter Putin's "macho aggression" by means of a "feminist foreign policy" based on representation, resources, and respect. But she is just the harbinger of an avalanche that threatens to bury much of the West under its weight. To a considerable extent, it has done so already.

Take Noam Chomsky, the American "linguist, philosopher, cognitive scientist, logician, political commentator and anarcho-syndicalist activist" (Wikipedia). Starting as far back as the late 1960s, he has been denouncing US capitalism, imperialism, war-mongering, and other assorted evil deeds. There is hardly a terrorist organization around the world whose actions he has not justified to one extent or another. There is hardly an attempt by his own country, as well as other Western ones, to cope with terrorism by using armed force if necessary that he has not condemned. To him, America's worldwide use of its intelligence services, special forces, and drones is not simply an attempt, however heavy-handed it may sometimes be, to prevent another 9/11 either in New York or anywhere else. No, it is "the world's greatest terrorist campaign," waged by "the world champion in generating terror" bent on enforcing its hegemony by means fair or foul.[74]

Early in 2015 Chomsky repeated the claim—which, ever since Hiroshima, has been wrongly made so many times that it has almost turned into a joke—that the world "is ominously close to nuclear war."[75] Never mind that in reality nuclear weapons, in other words the balance of terror, have probably been the one thing which has maintained the so-called "long peace" between the most powerful countries and does so still.[76] For these and similar pearls of wisdom the prestigious Britannica Educational Publishing House has listed Chomsky as "one of the 100 most influential philosophers of all time."[77] This may be an exaggeration, but not a very great one. As of February 2015 on Google.com, Chomsky got almost nine million hits.

Chomsky's European counterpart is the Norwegian Johan Galtung, widely known as the doyen of peace research, peace studies, and similar worthy disciplines. Disregarding an estimated 45 million people who died during the "Great Leap Forward" and the Cultural Revolution of 1958-76, at one point he called Mao Zedong a "liberator." For him and his followers all disputes are due to misunderstandings, which a little imagination and a little goodwill may solve. The way to deal with belligerents, protect civilians in war-torn countries, and bring armed conflicts to an end is as follows:[78] "Send teams with military and police training, nonviolence and mediation training, to protect with hand weapons, and as eye witnesses and escorts, but above all as mediators organizing dialogues, focused on understanding what it is all about and finding viable solutions beyond diplomats far away from reality—50 percent women—so numerous that they constitute a carpet of blue caps, and you will get results. Give them heavier arms, and so will the other side; arms are cheap these days. Train them well, also in empathy."

Thus both intellectuals and politicians keep promising their audiences security without sacrifice, privilege without responsibility. But what if, as has been known to happen, terrorists/guerrillas/insurgents/freedom fighters refuse to answer empathy with empathy? What if, as the "dialogues" proceed, instead of moderating their demands, they increase them? What if, since arms *are* cheap these days, they take the initiative and bring in heavier ones so as to outgun the "teams," defeat them and chase them away? What if they confront blue caps, with military-style helmets and the fifty percent women, with tough, no-nonsense fighters who know how to kill and, if necessary, be killed? And what if, having done so, they take the "team" members hostage and, unless their governments pay a huge ransom, sell, rape, and kill the women—not necessarily in that order—and decapitate, crucify, or burn the men? And what if, as the adherents of Daesh in particular keep saying, their ultimate objective is to take over the world, killing or subduing anyone who stands in the way?[79] Surely in that case we are back to square one?

Peace is the greatest blessing of all. What is more, where it does not prevail all other good things are almost certain to be absent as well. But isn't it also true that, among so many who are not good, a man who wishes to make a profession of goodness in everything must necessarily come to grief?[80] Did not Clausewitz, when he said that it is always the attacker who wants peace, have right on his side? All he wants is, first, to occupy our country; and second, take away our freedom and our property. Normally it is only when we try to resist that he will kill us. However, there may also be occasions when he does so *pour encourager les autres*. Or else, hard as Galtung and others may find it to believe, simply for fun. Hitler wanted peace, except that he wanted Danzig and Poland and Scandinavia and the Low Countries and France and the Balkans and Russia and perhaps a few other countries first. Many others before and after him also came "in peace." Almost by definition, it is the defender who must take up arms and is the first to do so.

"When they poured across the border/I was cautioned to surrender/This I could not do," sang Leonard Cohen (1934-). Is defending home and hearth such a bad thing? Should we always turn the other cheek? Some Christian, Hindu, and Buddhist sects considered being killed a lesser sin than killing. So did Jesus, Saint Francis, and Mahatma Gandhi. The reason why these and other sects could do so was because they felt protected by the larger societies that surrounded them. As to the three leaders, they were lucky to be preachers and leaders with a following small or large. Had they been in charge of a polity under siege and responsible for its existence their behavior would hardly have been seen as heroic. Instead it could have, almost certainly would have, been considered criminal if not treasonous.

The day when wolves lie down with sheep is still far off. Even then, being a wolf will not be without its advantages. Nobody doubts that war is a very great evil and should be avoided and/or prevented if at all possible. What *must* be doubted is the idea that it is always and necessarily the greatest evil of all. Aren't some things even worse? How about being forced to give up one's identity, to become what one is not? How about injustice? How about persecution? How about genocide? To avoid war, should Abraham Lincoln have permitted slavery to continue? Should Britain in 1940 have accepted Hitler's offer, made peace, and left Norway as well as many other countries to the Nazis' tender mercies? Have freedom and dignity ceased to matter? Have survival and comfort become the only goals of life? Doesn't war engage our enterprise, our courage, our desire to test ourselves to the utmost? And how about our love, out of which wells our willingness to suffer, sacrifice, and, should there be no other way, die for something or somebody else?

What to do with these, the very best qualities we have? Put them in the icebox, perhaps? If so, will they be there when we need them? Failing to cultivate them, shan't we turn into pussycats and be easily defeated?

Conclusion: Hannibal *intra Portas*

Seventy years have now passed since any Western country has waged a major war anywhere near its frontiers—let alone sent a major part of its population to fight, and perhaps die, in it. During this period much has changed. In part, that was precisely because there has been no major war.

Still remaining in the West, the decline in fertility has led to a drastic reduction in the number of children. Ongoing profound demographic changes have caused their parents to grow old, cautious, and controlling. The schools to which they entrust their offspring, as well as society as a whole, have moved in the same direction. All seem to be engaged on a conspiracy whose aim is to prevent the young from growing up and entering the workforce for as long as possible. The outcome has been to make a great many of them incapable of looking after themselves. At times it looks as if their arteries are filled with bouillon, not blood. The hypocritical nature of the enterprise is made clear by the fact that adults are not made to give up these activities. In the words of my late father-in-law: The congregation does as the priest does, not as he preaches.

No human organization, not even the professional military, is an island into itself. Hence it is not surprising that similar problems have affected them, too. Though the precise situation varies from one country to another, over the last few decades most of them have been defanged, robbed of their pride, infantilized, and humiliated. They have, so to speak, been domesticated in much the same way as many animals are. Like other domesticated animals, in many ways the process has caused them to become weaker than their cousins in nature. "Wildcats into pussycats" might be the motto.

The time is in sight, if it has not arrived already, when the only men with any guts will be the members of the motorcycle gangs. The culprits are political correctness on one hand and the nanny state on the other. But it is by no means all society's fault. As General Dempsey's statement concerning the need to reduce sexual assault by integrating women into combat units illustrates, part of the problem was brought about by the forces' own astonishing obsequiousness and readiness to bend with the wind. To this must be added their selfishness and wastefulness. They have been much sinned against; but they have also sinned.

When the women came marching in from about 1970 on, they compounded these problems. Whatever the proponents of "gender" may say, physically speaking men and women are not the same. So great is the gap that, if those who are always pushing for the rights of servicewomen may be believed, the latter are in constant need of protection against their own male comrades in arms. That, incidentally, was already the case with the female "battalion of death" raised by the Russians in World War I.[1] In all coed courses and posts where physical strength and endurance are required, the outcome was gender-norming. It led to a very large number of injured female service personnel on one hand and a general lowering of standards on the other. In this way, the military actually got the worst of both worlds.

Much more serious still, the quest for "gender equality" in the forces has run at cross-currents with the fact that, in reality, women are privileged. To start with, in both the US and Britain servicewomen seem to enjoy easier access to commissioned rank.[2] The last-named difference may seem puzzling until we realize that, whatever feminists may say, not only have women been banned from ground combat but very few of them want to join the combat arms in the first place. Conversely, proportionally more of them are found in various rear-services, especially such as require an academic education, special training, or special skills.

The exact situation varies from one Western country to another. Generally, though, the privileges include, or have included until recently, freedom from registration for military service; freedom from alternative forms of civil service;

not being required to meet the same physical standards as men; and all sorts of policies pertaining to pregnancy and childbirth. Judging by the situation in the civilian world, there is also good reason to believe that the military disciplinary and justice systems treat women much more leniently than it does men. Information on that topic is unavailable, quite possibly because it is deliberately withheld.

The final outcome is that combat troops, aka "grunts," do not form a privileged group as they deserve to be and as, in any military worth its salt, they have always been. To the contrary: They are discriminated against in favor of better-educated personnel, especially women. I have visited enough military bases, and talked to enough soldiers in various countries, to realize that everybody knows it and the vast majority resent it. However, as with the king's new clothes, nobody dares say it aloud. That even includes some retired personnel. For example, one former student of mine, a retired US Army captain with experience in Afghanistan, told me in private that while he had nothing against military women he was glad that, in his unit, there had been none. But when I asked him to explain his reasons in class he declined, and for very good reason. Censorship is strong, and walls have ears. To that extent, the entire modern feminized military is based on a sordid, impudent lie. Men's fear that their female colleagues will falsely accuse them of sexual harassment or worse, which is often quite justified, does not make things any easier.

Another very serious problem is PTSD and, perhaps even more so, the way it is being handled both by society and by the military themselves. Among other things it makes nonsense of the claim that today's American soldiers are better trained to kill than ever before.[3] The phenomenon itself is real and cannot be simply swept under the carpet. However, the experience of all generations until the middle of the nineteenth century seems to imply that it need not be nearly as common, or have as many bad consequences for the military as a whole, as is the case today. Comparing various armed forces at various times and places, we find that organization and leadership play a major role in preventing PTSD. Whereas fear of liability, the hope for pensions, and the idea that war is necessarily bad for the souls of those who fight it work in the opposite direction.

Starting around 1960 "the rights revolution" got under way. As it did so duty, the one thing without which no armed force can exist, let alone fight successfully, went by the board. The first conscientious objectors, to use the modern term, made their appearance shortly after the Reformation. Increasingly during the second half of the nineteenth century they shifted from religious arguments to secular ones. At first they formed a small minority that did not have a perceptible effect on society. Later, however, things changed, causing their rights to be recognized and extended—to the point that, in the end, they were applied not just to civilians but to professional soldiers who, acting out of their own free will, had joined and taken the oath to defend their country even unto death.

Nietzsche believed that nothing is better for the soul than victory. Contemporary Western society seems to hold the opposite view: namely, that war is bad for the soul even when it is victorious. Not that, in all the decades since World War II ended in 1945, Westerners have had many opportunities to celebrate victorious wars. That is one reason why war has been progressively delegitimized, with all that implies for fighting power.

I shall not repeat the arguments showing this is not necessarily so. Jesus was the most peaceful of men. Yet he famously said, "Think not that I am come to send peace on earth: I came not to send peace but a sword," a sentence which has since been subjected to countless different interpretations.[4] No less a pacifist than Mahatma Gandhi wrote: "better to be violent... than to put on the cloak of nonviolence to cover impotence."[5] He also made it clear, however discreetly, that, should *satyagraha* not work and his demands not be granted, other options were always available.

187

So numerous are the restrictions surrounding modern Western forces, and so intense the criticism to which they have often been subjected by their own public, especially the educated public, as to make one wonder how they manage to survive at all. To those of them which have somehow succeeded in maintaining their fighting spirit as well, hats off! Unfortunately, they are a drop in the ocean. Even a few good men have become hard to find.

*

For good or ill, a nonviolent world without war is as likely to come about as a chaste one without sex. How ready to fight is the West? Back in 1976 the late John Keegan—a great military historian and, in his last years, a friend—had the following to say about this question:[6]

> Today... wireless keeps one *au courant* from minute to minute whether in the bath or in a slit trench... the quality, though not the volume, of battlefield noise is made familiar by the showing of war films... men and women employed in continuous process industries are made indirectly familiar with many... battlefield phenomena: they are to a considerable degree inured to very high constant noise levels and to emissions of intense light, they work in proximity to dangerous machinery and chemicals, including poison gases.... Modern industry, moreover, teaches its work people—though the same lessons are learnt by almost all citizens, first in school and later as the *administrés* of the state's bureaucracy—habits of order, obedience and uniform behavior which the embryo armies of the sixteenth century could not expect to find in any of their doltish recruits.... If to this pre-conditioning of battle we add the undoubted

power which nationalist and ideological feeling exerts in opposition to the human instincts for self-preservation, we ought to conclude that twentieth-century man is potentially a better soldier than those of any other age.

Unfortunately, Keegan got it completely wrong. Proceeding in reverse order, many sixteenth-century soldiers were anything but doltish.[7] More important, they did not get PTSD every time they took a blow, killed an enemy, or watched a comrade die, and certainly not in such numbers as to enable historians to identify the phenomenon. The state's bureaucracy and schools, coed schools in particular, have not so much habituated people—young people in particular—to discipline as they have rendered a great many of them cautious, helpless, and tearful. Deindustrialization, which in 1976 was already starting to happen, has created a situation where fewer and fewer people work in factories. Thankfully, too, what factories still remain have improved out of all recognition. The West still has plenty of workers who perform heavy, dirty, sometimes dangerous physical labor. By now, however, a great many of them have an immigrant background.

The media have in fact brought many people much closer to the battlefield. However, the effect has often been the opposite from what Keegan says it is. That is true in spite of the fact that, whether because of censorship or for commercial reasons, they rarely show war's real horrors. If only because the West has won no victories, movies depicting them have grown very rare. Essentially they only portray two kinds of heroes. The first consists of muscular but socially inept supermen. Driven by some kind of personal grievance, they go on wild killing sprees without the support of society and, in some cases, even against its wishes.

The second consists of wonder-women. Why such freaks have become as popular as they are, is something a Freudian psychologist might explain. Clearly it has to do as much with sex, shamelessly put on show, as with any martial prowess.[8] However that may be, for good or ill they do not have any link with reality at all. Other movies display the kind of "heroes" who resist their own officers ("the enemy is within") or are the victims of both war and society. At best, all of them reflect only part of the reality of war. None can provide a faithful picture of it, let alone a substitute for it.

*

Pussycats or no pussycats, currently there can be no question but that no Third World country is even remotely capable of invading and taking over any Western one. Should they try to mount a serious challenge, superior Western firepower will easily take care of them—as happened, for example, when Saddam Hussein had to be quashed back in 1991.

When it comes to tackling non-state opponents, the situation is very different. Currently there are plenty of terrorist movements around the world. They make life in large regions a misery and threaten to do the same in others. Among those regions are some, particularly the Middle East and North Africa, in which the West has very considerable, perhaps vital, interests. Others have served in the past, and may very well serve in the future, as bases from which terrorist strikes may be launched against it. After all, Bin Laden—the leader whose organization, Al Qaeda, has the dubious honor of having killed more people in a single act of terrorism than any other in history—was based in Afghanistan. When the Taliban, who at that time were in control of the country, were called upon to surrender or expel him, they refused to do so.

If the record of failure is any guide, then not even the United States, which currently spends almost as much on its military as do all other countries combined, has what it needs to take care of the movements in question. At best it is able to contain them, more or less. The remaining Western countries are essentially helpless. Had it not been for US leadership they would not even have been able to put an end to the war in the former Yugoslavia, right on their own doorstep.

Much worse still, almost all of them already have the enemy within their gates, some more so, some less. In most European countries that harbor considerable numbers of immigrants, encounters between them and the local population did not lead to better mutual understanding. Too often, the result was just the opposite. The list of grievances the latter harbor against the former, especially but not exclusively Muslim ones, would take up volumes.[9] Supposedly what drove the people in question to leave their homelands was not extreme danger to life and limb but "merely" economic need. Having made their way and crossed the border, often illegally, they were accused of being violent and criminal, as well as of being unwilling to integrate into the surrounding societies and intolerant of the rights of women and gays. Some even had the effrontery to distribute free Korans in the street!

The men in particular are seen as uneducated, good-for-nothing bums. Supposedly they cannot be entrusted with any proper job, preferring to live on welfare at the taxpayer's expense. They routinely abuse women and children, both their own and others. There is no shortage of statistics—some real, others bogus—to back up these claims. To cite just one, on the average foreigners make up one quarter of the entire prison population in the forty-seven member states of the European Council. In some countries, notably Cyprus, Greece, Luxembourg, and Austria, they actually form more than half.[10]

Famously, the members of the minorities in question tend to concentrate in the main cities, especially such as have ports or are located on important communication knots. Their birthrates are much higher than those of the surrounding communities. So much so that in the four largest Dutch cities, for example, "Mohammed" has become the single most common boys' first name.[11]

As a result, their populations contain relatively much larger numbers of young men—precisely the group that, in all societies since the beginning of the world, have been most prepared to use violence and to do so with, without, or even against the will of their elders.

Whether out of their own free will or because they cannot afford anything better, most of them live in ghettoes which, for lack of proper maintenance, tend to turn into slums. Many cannot speak the language of their host countries. The leaders whom they respect and to whom they listen are not democratically elected politicians but imams. Based in the mosques, which have sprouted up like acne on the face of teenagers, many of them have made a career by preaching hatred for anyone who is not a Muslim. They do not believe in state law but in the Koran or Sharia, which they try to impose on the neighborhoods where they live. Not seldom with some success, as the municipal authorities close an eye.

Not all Muslim immigrants are extremists—far from it. Let alone prepared to use violence in defense of what the late Professor Samuel Huntington in *The Clash of Civilizations* called "identity." Meaning, "views on the relations between God and man, the individual and the group, the citizen and the state, parents and children, husband and wife, as well as differing views of the relative importance of rights and responsibilities, liberty and authority, equality and hierarchy."[12] Not to mention relations between the sexes and the rights, or lack of them, of homosexuals. However, as the fact that hundreds attended the funeral of a terrorist who attacked a synagogue in Copenhagen in February 2015 shows, many, perhaps most, share the extremists' ideas as to what a proper society should like.[13] Violence has a built-in tendency to escalate. Should it do so, no doubt they too will become extremists. As Winston Churchill wrote over a century ago, "Mohammedanism is a militant and proselytizing faith… [capable of] raising fearless warriors at every step."[14] Having fought them along India's

Northwestern frontier in 1897 and at Omdurman in 1898, he ought to have known.

On the other hand, there is no shortage of hooligans—some of whom actually call themselves that, and some of whom wear police uniforms—prepared to physically assault immigrants.[15] Attacks on buildings where immigrants live have become commonplace. According to the European Union Agency for Human Rights (FRA) survey of December 2013, eighteen percent of Roma (Gypsies) had experienced hate crimes during the previous twelve months, or so they claimed. Eighteen percent of sub-Saharan Africans, nine percent of North Africans, and eight percent of Turks living in the EU said the same.[16] Things have certainly not improved since then. Nor is the US entirely without anti-Muslim hate-crimes of its own.

It may very well be true, as the great Galtung wrote, that peace is a situation where "concern and togetherness" dominate over violence.[17] If so, then many districts in many Western cities, including some in his native Scandinavia, are either already at war or very, very close to it. Slowly, surely, and at times spectacularly, things seem to be moving from ordinary crime toward the kind of politically and/or ideologically motivated version commonly known as terrorism. From there it is an easy step toward other even more violent forms of armed conflict.

Should immigration continue and "integration" fail, as may very well happen, what will such conflict look like? The rest of the world provides plenty of models to follow. They start with very low-intensity hostilities of the kind that used to take place in Northern Ireland between 1969 and 1997. They end with large-scale, absolutely murderous, struggles, such as are currently taking place in quite some Asian and African countries, not to mention events in the Ukraine. War, like a smorgasbord, comes in all sizes, colors, and tastes. Let the reader in each country select his or her choice.

Suppose this scenario comes true, how will Western countries, especially in Europe, respond? Here Keegan seems to have hit the nail on its head. "The young," he wrote, "have already made their decision. They are increasingly unwilling to serve as conscripts"—or even as volunteers—"in armies they see as ornamental. The militant young have taken that decision a stage further. They will fight for the causes they profess not through the mechanism of the state and its armed power, but where necessary against them, by clandestine and guerrilla methods."[18] With the exception that Keegan did not mention immigrants, who at the time he wrote were few in number, forty years later his prediction seems to be coming all too true.

*

Given these problems, can the West hold on to its dominant position and with it, its culture, its traditions, and its values? Or will it go down a slippery slope? For an answer, look to history. Today most people, used to the kind of time sometimes known as "Newtonian," look at history as linear. It proceeds from past through present to future and is non-repetitive. That is not how many of our ancestors saw it. From Lycurgus, Solon, Heraclitus, Herodotus, and Plato on, many ancient statesmen, philosophers, and historians believed history was cyclical. Rise and fall, rise and fall, repeated over and over again.[19] Medieval sages such as Honoré Bonet, and in the Islamic world Ibn Khaldun, agreed. So did some notable twentieth-century scholars such as Oswald Spengler, the abovementioned Arnold Toynbee, and, much more recently, Paul Kennedy in his famous book, *The Rise and Decline of the Great Powers* (1987).

As one would expect, the details vary from one thinker to the next. Still, the gist of the argument is always more or less the same. The first to wage war were the men of poor, nomadic tribal societies of which, long ago, all of us used to be a part. They started by fighting each other over such things as access to water, hunting and grazing ground, domestic animals, and, not least, women. The last-named were valued not only for the sexual possibilities they offered but also, which was as important, for their fertility and their labor.[20]

At some stage one tribe, often headed by a particularly able leader, defeated all the rest and united them into some kind of league, confederation, or federation. As, for example, the ancient Assyrians, Babylonians, Persians, Huns, Magyars, and Mongols (first under Genghis Khan, then under Timur) all did. Next, the victors took on their richer, settled, neighbors. They fought, triumphed, conquered, and subjugated. Having done so, the former tribesmen discarded their nomadic traditions and took up life in the cities under their rule. Exploiting the labor of others, they grew rich and soft. They also indulged in every kind of luxury, allowed themselves to be governed by women, and witnessed a sharp decline in fertility.

Having abandoned the military virtues, at some point they started looking down on them. Hiring foreigners to fight in their stead, they ended by losing the qualities that had made for their greatness. Attempts to substitute technology for fighting power, such as were made both in fourth-century AD Rome and, repeatedly, in China, did not work.[21] Nor is there any reason why they should, given that the barbarians could often capture or imitate the technologies and find renegades ready to operate them as, for example, the horse-riding Mongols did.[22] Each empire in turn was overrun by its poorer but more virile and aggressive neighbors. More often than not subjected peoples, long oppressed, rose and joined the invaders. The end was always the same: ignominious collapse.

The cycle formed the stuff of which history was made. Polybius, the sober, businesslike second-century BC Hellenistic historian, says that, in his time, "men turned to arrogance, avarice and indolence [and] did not wish to marry. And when they did marry, they did not wish to rear the children born to them except for one or two at the most." And he goes on: "When a state has escaped many serious dangers and achieved an unquestioned supremacy and dominion, it is clear that, with prosperity growing within, life becomes more luxurious and men more tense in rivalry about their public ambitions and enterprises."[23] The historian Livy, a contemporary of Augustus who saw the empire's power as it was approaching its zenith, says that Rome was "struggling with its own greatness."[24] As the Roman poet Juvenal, who lived around 100 AD, put it:[25] "We are now suffering the calamities of a long peace. Luxury, more deadly than any foe, has laid her hand upon us, and avenges a conquered world."

Some of these thinkers and doers also came up with solutions, or at any rate tried to do so. Lycurgus prohibited his Spartans from using gold and silver, and made them lead lives so austere that they have become proverbial. Plato wanted his imaginary state to avoid external trade, as far as possible, so as to prevent it from growing luxurious. Interestingly, both of these also emancipated women. The former gave them much greater freedom than they had in other Greek city-states, with the result, Aristotle says, that they became licentious and utterly useless.[26] The latter liberated them from the need to look after their children, thus putting them on an equal footing with men in everything but physical strength.

Isocrates, the fourth-century BC Athenian statesman, argued that, if Athens wanted to avoid repeating the cycle that had led to the ruin of its first empire, moderation and benevolence were the right tools to use. Three centuries later Cicero, the Roman orator and statesman, did the same.[27] Polybius, on his part, claimed that Rome made war on the Dalmatians in 150 BC because "they did not at all wish the Italians to become effeminate owing to the long peace... [and] to recreate, as it were, the spirit and zeal of their own troops."[28]

In 101 BC Metellus Numidicus, censor and therefore in charge of Roman public morality, gave a famous speech. The Republic, he said, was short of military manpower. But the solution was not to open the legions to propertyless men as his rival Marius had suggested. Instead, he demanded that upper- and middle-class men should share the burden, marry, and have children. The title of the speech? *De ducendis uxoribus*, "about leading (marrying) women." A hundred years later the problem still persisted, causing the Emperor Augustus to pass legislation with an eye toward raising the birth rate among Roman citizens.[29]

Both austerity and raising the birthrate continued to be proposed throughout the Middle Ages and the Renaissance. Machiavelli argued that whereas gold could not obtain soldiers, soldiers could and would obtain gold.[30] True, scientifically and technologically the civilizations in questions were light years behind ours. Yet the similarities, including (in the case of Rome) a growing aversion to casualties,[31] are, perhaps, even more astonishing. What *that* may harbor for the future, I leave it for the reader to contemplate.

*

Some Westerners, Europeans in particular, have already more or less given up. Looking into the future, they paint it in the darkest imaginable colors. Take Henryk Broder's *Hurra, Wir Kapitulieren* (Hurray, We Surrender, 2004), whose title speaks for itself. Or Thilo Sarrazin's *Deutschland schafft sich ab* (Germany is abolishing itself, 2010). Or Michel Houellebecq's *Soumission* (2014). The first uses black humor to describe the process of decline and what is more, the way *Gutmenschen*, bleeding hearts, are cheering it along. The second and third paint a dark picture of its possible outcome. All three were bestsellers, as were quite a number of others that focused on the same problem.

Can the West still be saved? Perhaps. But doing so will require much more than increasing military spending from one to two percent as some European countries, in a "non-binding" resolution, pledged to do when they met in

September 2014.[32] Terrorism is nasty and brutish; the struggle against it will be just the same. It will also be prolonged.

First, parents, school, the law, and society in general have gone much too far in "protecting" the young against all sorts of dangers, real and imaginary. Combining this with the drive towards the kind of "self-esteem" that is unlinked to any kind of real achievement, in too many cases they have turned them into "excellent sheep." Demolishing their ability to help themselves and cope both with life in general and with the kind of challenges just described. Like H. G. Wells' Eloi in *The Time Machine* (1896), they, and the societies of which they form a part, have become easy prey for tougher types emerging from the great, unwashed, submerged, dark, "non-integrated" immigrant communities in particular. This will have to change.

Second, in the words of George Orwell, "we sleep safe in our beds because rough men stand ready in the night to visit violence on those who would do us harm."[33] But only as long as we do not treat them as babies, defang them, humiliate them, and denounce much of what they hold dearest as "militarism." Doing so makes most young people, and the most highly qualified among them in particular, reluctant to serve. It also drives away some of the toughest and best fighters, the "pack of bastards" (an Australian soldiers' marching song) without whom no war can be fought. Sick and tired of being underappreciated and humiliated at every step, they prefer to become mercenaries instead. The pay is better and the risks often smaller. This will have to change.

Third, there are any number of capable women whom the military could use in a great variety of important capacities. However, as the fact that the deployment of German armored personnel carriers will have to be delayed to make them protect the amniotic fluid of pregnant women illustrated only too well, the way they have integrated them since 1970 or so is an absolute disaster.[34]

Disastrous for the military; for servicewomen; and, judging by the skyrocketing divorce rates, for the women's families as well. This will have to change.

Fourth, the belief that PTSD is a necessary outcome of war, and that it should be treated accordingly, is itself one of the reasons why it has become as great a problem as it is. The outcome is a lethal combination of vast suffering, tremendous financial cost, and military ineffectiveness that is almost literally turning the services into putty. This will have to change.

Fifth, both European and American societies, each in its own way, have come to give rights near-absolute priority over duty. That has been carried to the point where serving soldiers, who are volunteers, are entitled to raise conscientious objections to war so as to avoid participating in it. Large parts of those societies have also come to see war not simply as an evil that is sometimes made absolutely necessary by circumstances but as the ultimate one that almost nothing can justify. This will have to change.

Or else.

Thanks

To Jeff Clement, Samuel Finlay, and Emile Simpson, whose books, written from the bottom up, taught me as much about war as Clausewitz did.

To Colonel (ret.) Dr. Moshe Ben David, who over the course of thirty years has been a true friend in need.

To Colonel (ret.) Raz Sagi, in the hope that he will continue to teach me about the IDF.

To Jason Pack, my one-time student and currently an expert on Arab affairs, who has kindly read the manuscript and commented on it.

To Brigadier (ret.) Dr. Erich Vad, to whom I can say anything and everything, and his family.

To Shmulik Alkelai and Amihai Borosh, who taught me that "different" need not be different and who, to me, are quite as good as the best family there is.

To Adi Raz, my delightful stepdaughter, and her family. My family.

To my stepson Jonathan Lewy, whose integrity and readiness to give his honest opinion sometimes leaves me awestruck.

To my son Eldad van Creveld, who has returned to me, and his family. My family.

To my daughter, Abigail, who has finally come back to me, and her family. My family.

To my son Uri van Creveld, computer expert *cum* psychotherapist of whom I am so proud, and his family. My family.

To Dvora, who to me is the best, most beautiful woman God has ever given a man.

Bless you all. Thanks to you, my cup runneth over.

Endnotes

Preface

[1] Quoted in J. Wallach, *Kriegstheorien*, Frankfurt/Main, Bernard & Graefe, 1972, p. 94.
[2] See, for a short history, M. van Creveld, *The Training of Officers*, New York, NY, Free Press, 1990.

Introduction

[1] A German translation of the ultimatum is available at http://www.tuerkenbeute.de/res/pdf/forschung/nachweise/quellen/TuerkenkriegHabsburg.pdf.
[2] See, for the causes of Europe's ascent, E. Jones, *The European Miracle*, Cambridge, Cambridge University Press, 2003 [1985].
[3] S. M. Stanley, *How I Found Livingstone*, Knoxville, TN, Wordsworth, 2010 [1871], p. 95.
[4] See, on the war in question, W. B. Harris, *France, Spain and the Riff War*, Uckfield, Naval and Military Press, 2010.
[5] See, on contemporary estimates as to what defeating Saddam would take, S. Biddle, *Military Power: Explaining Victory and Defeat in Modern Battle*, Princeton, NJ, Princeton University Press, 2004, pp. 1-2; also M. O'Hanlon, "Estimating Casualties in a War to Overthrow Saddam Hussein," pp. 1-2, at http://slantchev.ucsd.edu/courses/pdf/ohanlon-estimating-casualties-iraq.pdf.
[6] See for a recent statement of this view, R. Kagan, *Of Paradise and Power: The US and Europe in the New World Order*, New York, NY, Vintage, 2007.
[7] See, on this mood, M. Dayan, *Vietnam Diary* [Hebrew], Tel Aviv, Dvir, 1977, p. 27, 40; also D. Halberstam, *The Best and the Brightest*, New York, NY, Random, 1969, pp. 123-24.
[8] Figure from *The Pentagon Papers*, Gravel edition, Boston, MA, Beacon, 1971, vol. 4, p. 11, reference to CIA memorandum of 25.6.1967.
[9] S. Shah, "US War in Afghanistan, Iraq, to Cost $6 Trillion," Global Research, 20.9.2013, at http://www.globalresearch.ca/us-wars-in-afghanistan-iraq-to-cost-6-trillion/5350789.
[10] N. Ferguson, *Colossus: The Rise and Fall of the American Empire*, New York, NY, Penguin, 2005.
[11] A. J. Bacevich, *The New American Militarism*, New York, NY, Oxford University Press, 2005.
[12] In 2013, military spending varied between 0.9 percent (Spain) and 2.6 percent (Greece) of GDP. France, Britain and Germany spent 2.5, 2.3 and 1.3 percent

respectively. SIPRI figures at
http://data.worldbank.org/indicator/MS.MIL.XPND.GD.ZS.

[13] See, e.g., M. Gebauer, "Neuer Maengelbericht der Bundeswehr," Spiegelonline, 24.9.2014, at http://www.spiegel.de/politik/deutschland/bundeswehr-schwere-maengel-bei-ausruestung-a-993530.html.

[14] Russian Federal Security Bureau, valid for mid-2015, Heavy News, 11.11.2015, at http://heavy.com/news/2015/11/how-many-fighters-militants-jihadist-soldiers-are-in-isis-islamic-state-nationalities-where-do-they-come-from-numbers/.

[15] See, on the nature of this world, W. S. Lind, *The Four Generations of Warfare*, Kouvola, Finland, Castalia, Kindle ed., 2014.

[16] See, for instance, W. C. Westmoreland, *A Soldier Reports*, New York, NY, Dell, 1976, pp. 81-3, 89, 553-58.

[17] Mao's speech to the Sixth Plenary Session of the Central Committee of the Chinese Communist Party, 6.11.1938. Part of the text is available at http://en.wikipedia.org/wiki/List_of_Maoist_China_rhetoric_and_political_slogans.

[18] M. Bowden, *"Black Hawk Down,"* Atlantic Monthly, 1999, p. 37.

[19] S. Finlay, *Breakfast with the Dirt Club*, CreateSpace, 2012, Kindle 3rd ed., loc. 1495.

[20] F. Nietzsche, *Daybreak*, Cambridge, Cambridge University Press, 1982 [1881], fifth book, aphorism No. 571.

[21] R. D. Sawyer, *The Seven Military Classics of Ancient China*, New York, NY, Basic Books, 2007, p. 202.

[22] For what is happening in Europe see G. Chailand, *Pourquoi Perd-on la Guerre?* Paris, O. Jacob, 2016.

[23] J. Davidson, "How NATO's Military Spending Has Evolved Since 1949," Council on Foreign Relations, 4.9.2014, at http://blogs.cfr.org/davidson/2014/09/04/explainer-this-graph-shows-how-natos-military-capability-has-evolved-since-1949/.

[24] J. S. Nye, *Soft Power: The Way to Success in World Politics*, New York, NY, Public Affairs, 2009.

Chapter I. Subduing the Young

[1] See H. Assa and Y. Yaarv, *Fighting Differently* [Hebrew], Tel Aviv, Hemed, 2015.

[2] A. Schlegel and H. Barry, *Adolescence: An Anthropological Inquiry*, New York, NY, Free Press, 1991, especially p. 2.

[3] See H. Cunningham, *The Invention of Childhood*, London, BBC Books, 2006.

[4] The next few paragraphs are based on R. Epstein, *Teen 2.0: Saving Our Teens and Children from the Torments of Adolescence*, Sanger, CA, Quill Driver Books, Kindle ed., 2010.

[5] See on this H. Cunningham, *Combating Child Labor: The British Experience*, in H. Cunningham and P. P. Viazzo, eds., *Child Labor in Historical Perspective, 1800-1985*, Florence, UNICEF, 1996, pp. 42-52.

[6] See H. A. Giroux, *America's Education Deficit and the War on Youth*, New York, NY, Monthly Review, 2013; and M. A. Males, *The Scapegoat Generation: America's War on Adolescents*, Monroe, ME, Common Courage, 1996.

[7] See, e.g., UNICEF Report, November 2014, at http://data.unicef.org/child-protection/child-labour; L. McKenna, "Child Labor Is Making a Disturbing Resurgence around the World," *Business Insider*, 6.1.2012.

[8] A. S. Wald, "Gingrich Calls Child Labor Laws 'Stupid,'" ThinkProgress, 20.11.2011, at http://thinkprogress.org/politics/2011/11/20/372918/gingrich-calls-child-labor-laws-stupid-wants-to-replace-janitors-with-poor-kids; B. Mathis-Lilley, "Rand Paul Suggests Disturbingly That He Enjoyed Having Summer Jobs as a Teen," Slatest, 7.4.2015, at http://www.slate.com/blogs/the_slatest/2015/04/07/rand_paul_summer_jobs_fun.html.

[9] B. Bettelheim, *The Children of the Dream*, London, MacMillan, 1969, p. 164.

[10] T. Simmons and P. Ingram, "The Kibbutz for Organizational Behavior," in B. M. Staw and R. I. Sutton, eds., *Research in Organizational Behavior*, vol. 22, Amsterdam, Elsevier, 2000, pp. 21-31.

[11] B. Igou, "The Traditional Family and the Amish," Amish Country News, 1994, at http://www.amishnews.com/amisharticles/traditionalfamily.htm.

[12] J. Laucius, "Many Benefits for Teenagers Who Work During the School Year, Study Finds," *Ottawa Citizen*, 23.8.2014.

[13] See, e.g., "How to Get into Harvard," n.d., Wikihow, at http://www.wikihow.com/Get-Into-Harvard-University.

[14] S. Freud, *Civilization and Its Discontents*, London, Hogarth, 1968, standard edition, vol. 21, p. 80, note 1.

[15] B. Friedan, *The Feminine Mystique*, New York, NY, Norton, 1962, pp. 343-78; S. de Beauvoir, *The Second Sex*, New York, NY, Knopf, 1971 [1959], p. 760.

[16] See T. J. Matthews and B. E. Hamilton, "Delayed Childbirth: More Women Are Having Their First Child Later in Life," Europe Pubmed, 21, 2009, pp. 1-8, at http://europepmc.org/abstract/MED/19674536; also M. J. Bailey, "More Power to the Pill," *The Quarterly Journal of Economics*, 121, 1, February 2006, especially pp. 288-92.

[17] "Europeese Unie Gaat Social Media Verbieden," Geenstijl, 25.4.2016, at http://www.geenstijl.nl/.

[18] C. Mercer, "Europe's Soft Drink Firms Ban Adverts to Children," Beveragedaily.com, 26.1.2006, at http://www.beveragedaily.com/Markets/Europe-s-soft-drinks-firms-ban-adverts-to-children.

[19] Schlegel and Barry, *Adolescence*, pp. 40, 105, and 107-32.

[20] P. E. H. Hair, "Bridal Pregnancies in Rural England in Earlier Centuries," *Population Studies*, 20, 2, November 1966, pp. 233-43; and J. Knodel, "Law, Marriage and Illegitimacy in Nineteenth-Century Germany," *Population Studies*, 20, 3, 1967, pp. 279-94.

[21] See W. A. Deresiewicz, *Excellent Sheep*, New York, NY, Free Press, Kindle ed., 2014, locs. 551-83.

[22] A. Gomstyn, "When 'Super Mom' Is Super Sad: Pressures Haunt New Parents," Today's Parents, 19.8.2014, at http://www.today.com/parents/when-super-mom-super-sad-pressures-haunt-new-parents-1D80081732.

[23] See, for a breezy, but very good, account of the way parents are being pressed into overprotecting their offspring against all kinds of (almost entirely) imaginary fears, see L. Skenazy, *Free Range Kids*, San Francisco, CA, John Wiley & Sons, Kindle ed., 2009, locs. 492-80, 592-738, 764-858.

[24] See A. Parks, *An American Gulag: Secret POW Camps for Teens*, Eldorado Springs, CO, The Education Exchange, 2000.

[25] A. Pierce, "California Lawmakers to Raise the Legal Smoking Age to 21," *Utah People's Post*, 31.1.2015.

[26] City of Hilliard Curfew Law, at http://hilliardohio.gov/police/don't-be-a-victim/curfew-laws.

[27] "Dallas City Council Enacts Daytime Juvenile Curfew in 12-2 Vote," *Dallas Morning News*, 13.5.2009.

[28] Center for Problem-Oriented Policing, "Responses to the Problem of Cruising," n.d., at http://www.popcenter.org/problems/cruising/3.

[29] J. Fowels, *The Case for Television Violence*, Berkeley, CA, Sage, 1999, especially pp. 1-3, 3-6, 25, 30.

[30] Epstein, *Teen 2.0*, loc. 873.

[31] J. Huggler, "German Beaches in Schleswig-Holstein Ban Sandcastles," *Telegraph*, 12.8.2014; "You Can't Do That on Our Beaches, Says Italy," World News, 26.7.2001, at http://www.theguardian.com/world/2011/jul/26/no-sandcastles-on-italian-beaches..

[32] L. Stanford, "Bizarre School Rules," ParentDish, at http://www.parentdish.co.uk/news-and-views/bizarre-school-rules-strict-uniforms/#!slide=aol_1005005.

[33] Skenazy, *Free Range Kids*, locs. 999 and 1007.

[34] J. Goodwin, "Less Play Time = More Troubled Kids," USNews, 22.9.2011, at http://health.usnews.com/health-news/family-health/brain-and-behavior/articles/2011/09/22/less-play-time--more-troubled-kids-experts-say.

[35] SRTS Guide, "The Decline of Walking and Bicycling," n.d., at http://guide.saferoutesinfo.org/introduction/the_decline_of_walking_and_bicycling.cfm; "The Decline of Children's Right to Roam," *The Telegraph*, 13.1.2013.

[36] M. De Lacey, "Mum's Taxi Service," MailOnline, 29.8.2013, at http://www.dailymail.co.uk/femail/article-2405436/Mums-taxi-service-Average-mother-drives-children-1-248-miles-EACH-YEAR--London-Zurich-round-trip.html; "Children Still Hail Mum's Taxi at 30," *Daily Mail*, 3.9.2014.

[37] See, e.g., "Eltern werden zur Verkehrsgefahr auf Schulwegen," *Die Welt*, 25.8.2014.

[38] "Student Criticizes Studies on Twitter" [German], Koelner Stadt-Anzeiger, 13.1.2015, at http://www.kstADe/koeln/lehrplan-schuelerin-kritisiert-lehre-auf-twitter,15187530,29557736.html.

[39] M. Mecija, "Parents: Local School Policy Is Making Kids Sick," ABC10 News, 14.7.1014, at http://www.10news.com/news/investigations/parents-local-schools-bathroom-policy-is-making-kids-sick-061214; American Booksellers Association, "Banned Books That Shaped America," September 2014, at http://www.bannedbooksweek.org/censorship/bannedbooksthatshapedamerica; Ma. Zandian and others, "Children Eat Their School Lunch Too Quickly," Public Health, 14.5.2012, at http://www.biomedcentral.com/1471-2458/12/351.

[40] See, e.g., South Bay's Neighbor, "Schools in Place to Protect Promgoers," n.d., at http://www.theneighbornewspapers.com/promandgraduation/article0014.html.

[41] See, for one list of banned foods, School at Killarney, Cork; see http://www.monkillarney.net/our-school/history/.

[42] "Banned Books That Shaped America."

[43] K. Roberts, *Finding Your Element: How to Discover Your Talents and Passions and Transform Your Life*, London, Penguin, 2013.

[44] C. O'Keefe, "Dad Zones," GreenBuilder, 24.6.2014, at http://www.greenbuildermedia.com/blog/dead-zones-cell-phones-can-kill; Epstein, *Teen 2.0*, loc. 1470.

[45] W. Dersiewicz, *Excellent Sheep, passim.*

[46] J. M. Twenge and others, "It's Beyond My Control: A Cross-Temporal Meta-Analysis of Increasing Externality in Locus of Control, 1960-2002," *Personality and Social Psychology Review*, 8, 3, 2004, pp. 308-19.

[47] Aspen Education Group, *Your Child and ADHD*, n.p., n.d., p. 14, at http://www.4-adhd.com/youchildandadhd.pdf/

[48] See J. Hechinger and D. Golden, "When Special Education Schools Go Easy on Students," *Wall Street Journal*, 25.6.2006.

[49] US Department of Labor, "Bureau of Labor Statistics-Social Workers," 2003, available at www.bls.gov/oco/ocos060/htm; and Psychiatric News, 36, 5, 2.3.2001, available at http://pn.psychiartyonline/prg/cji/content/full/36/5/3.

[50] Figure from G. E. Zuriff, "Extra Examination Time for Students with Learning Disabilities," *Applied Measurement in Education*, 13, 1, 2000, p. 99.

[51] L. E. Booren and B. K. Hood, "Learning Disabilities in Graduate School," Observer, March 2007, at http://www.psychologicalscience.org/observer/getArticle.cfm?id=2146.

[52] See, out of the vast literature, J. Lorin and J. Smialek, "College Graduates Struggle to Find Employment Worth a Degree," Bloomberg News, 5.6.2014, at http://www.bloomberg.com/news/2014-06-05/college-graduates-struggle-to-find-employment-worth-a-degree.html; and R. Able and others, "Are Recent College Graduates Finding Good Jobs?" *Current Issues in Economics and Finance*, 20, 1, 2014, pp. 1-8, at http://www.newyorkfed.org/research/current_issues/ci20-1.pdf.

[53] See, for some figures on this, S. Pinker, *The Better Angels of Our Nature: Why Violence Has Declined*, New York, NY, Viking, 2011, pp. 221, 227, 230, tables 5-11, 6-16, 6-18.

[54] R. L. Mayers, "Semantic Connotations of the Words 'Adolescent,' 'Teenager,' and 'Youth,'" *The Journal of Genetic Psychology*, 129, 1, 1976, p. 1.

[55] Online Etymology Dictionary; Dictionary.com.

[56] J. Haltung and T. Hoivik, "Structural and Direct Violence," *Journal of Peace Research*, 8, 1, 1971, p. 73.

[57] Wikipedia, "Structural Violence."

[58] Merriam-Webster, "Oppression."

[59] *Ibid.*

[60] P. Evans, *Verbal Abuse Survivors Speak Out*, Avon, MA, Adams, 1993.

[61] J. Donovan, *The Way of Men, Milwaukie, OR,* Dissonant Hum, *Kindle* edition, 2013, loc. 574.

[62] J. Leicester, "A Cricketer's Courageous Battle with Stress," The Big Story, 25.11.2013, at http://bigstory.ap.org/article/cricketers-courageous-battle-stress.

[63] D. J. Siegel, *Brainstorm: The Power and Purpose of the Teenage Brain*, New York, NY, Tarcher/Penguin, 2015, p. 7.

[64] SSCB Event Checklist—Safety Advisory Group, unsigned at http://sheffieldscb.proceduresonline.com/pdfs/events_check.pdf.

[65] See J. Gruber and D. A. Weiss, eds., *Social Security Programs and Retirement Around the World: The Effect on Youth Unemployment*, Chicago, IL, University of Chicago Press, 2005.

[66] Ph. Aries, *Centuries of Childhood*, New York, NY, Vintage, 1962, p. 30.

[67] L. S. Stepp, "Adolescence: Not Just for Kids," *Washington Post*, 2.1.2002.

[68] V. Woolastone, "Adult at 18? Not Any More," MailOnline, 24.9.2013, at http://www.dailymail.co.uk/health/article-2430573/An-adult-18-Not-Adolescence-ends-25-prevent-young-people-getting-inferiority-complex.html.

[69] Ph. Wilan, "Italian Court Tells Father to Support Stay-at-Home Son, 30," *The Guardian*, 6.4.2002.

[70] D. Albrecht, "A: Now the Most Common Grade in College," 17.7.2011, at http://profalbrecht.wordpress.com/2011/07/17/a-now-the-most-common-grade-in-college/.

[71] National Research Council, *Juvenile Crime, Juvenile Justice*, Washington DC, National Academy Press, 2001, pp. 5-6.

[72] Substance Abuse and Mental Health Services Administration, "Results from the 2007 National Survey on Drug Use and Health: National Findings," at http://www.samhsa.gov/data/nsduh/2k7nsduh/2k7Results.htm.

[73] G. Kant, "Radical Increase in Kids Prescribed Ritalin," WND, 24.7.2014, at http://www.wnd.com/2013.04.radical-increase-in-kids-prescribed-ritalin/.

[74] Associated Press, "Psychiatric Drugs Used by Youths Surges," *LA Times*, 13.1.2003.

[75] Mehr Kinder rutschen in eine Depression ab," *Naturheilkunde und Naturverfahren*, 28.12.2014, at http://www.heilpraxisnet.de/naturheilpraxis/mehr-kinder-rutschen-in-eine-depression-ab-901853447201.php.

[76] "Ritalin Side Effects and Warnings," DrugEnquirer, 5.8.2014, at http://ritalinsideeffects.net/.

[77] Donovan, *The Way of Men*, locs. 1643-49. See also, in much greater detail, C. Hoff Sommers, *The War Against Boys*, New York, NY, Simon & Schuster, 2013 [2001].

[78] M. Kaldor, *New and Old Wars: Organized Violence in a Global Era*, Oxford, Polity, 2nd ed., 2006.

[79] The exact figures were 4,944 men and 143 women. Figures from "America's Wars; US Casualties and Veterans," Infoplease, at http://www.infoplease.com/ipa/A0004615.html; and Center for Military Readiness, "Grim Toll of Military Women Killed in War," 1.1.2013, at http://www.cmrlink.org/content/home/35891/grim_toll_of_military_women_killed_i n_war.

[80] *Heeres Dienstvorschrift* 300, *Truppenfuehrung,* Berlin, Mittler, 1936, article 15. The translation is mine.

[81] See, for Palmach, the relevant article at http://en.wikipedia.org/wiki/Palmach.

Chapter II. Defanging the Troops

[1] See B. D. Rostker, *"I Want You!" The Evolution of the All-Volunteer Force*, Berkeley, CA, RAND, 2006.

[2] Figures from A. Searle, *Wehrmacht Generals*, Westport, CT, Praeger, p. 18, as well as "Von der Leyen plant Frauenquote bei der Bundeswehr," *Focus*, 10.1.2015.

[3] Figures from J. Shay, *Achilles in Vietnam*, New York, NY, Simon & Schuster, Kindle edition, 2010, loc. 603.

[4] D. MacGregor, "Five Rules for Defense Spending," BreakingDefense.com 26.1.2015, at http://fortunascorner.com/2015/01/27/five-rules-for-defense-spending/.

[5] R. Sisk, "Gates and Panetta Blast Obama for Micromanaging Military," Militarycom, 17.1.2014, at http://www.military.com/daily-news/2014/11/17/gates-and-panetta-blast-obama-for-micromanaging-military.html.

[6] The figures are 9,087,000 and 2,709,918 respectively; "Vietnam War: Facts, Stats and Myths," US Wings, at http://www.uswings.com/about-us-wings/vietnam-war-facts/.

[7] Athenaeus, *Deipnosophistae*, 561e; the translation of *aphrodisiazein* comes from Liddell and Scott's *Greek-English Lexicon*. For the exact meaning of the term in the context under consideration see also B. Bertosa, "Sacrifice and Homosexuality in the Spartan Army," *War and Society*, 28, 2, October 2009, especially p. 10.

[8] Plato, *The Republic*, 460b.

[9] Suetonius, *Caesar*, 67, 51.

[10] I. Sherer, "Warriors for a Living: The Experience of the Spanish Infantry Soldiers in the Italian Wars, 1521-1546," dissertation submitted to the Hebrew University, Jerusalem, 2014, pp. 8, 46.

[11] B. R. Haydon, *Autobiography*, London, Longman, 1853, vol. 1, p. 117.

[12] LZ Center, "Myths and Facts of the Vietnam War," at http://www.lzcenter.com/Myths%20and%20Facts.html; Statistic Brain, "Demographics of Active US Military," at

http://www.statisticbrain.com/demographics-of-active-duty-u-s-military/.

[13] E. Slavin, "Restrictions on US Servicemembers in Japan Could Create More Issues," *Stars and Stripes*, 6.12.2012.

[14] E. Slavin, "Curfew Eased for Servicemembers in Japan," *Stars and Stripes*, 12.2.2013.

[15] "Military Curfew in South Korea to Continue," *Stars and Stripes*, 17.1.2013; "G. I. Korea, "Is Infantilization the New Leadership Philosophy of the US Military," ROK Drop, 12.12.2012, at http://rokdrop.com/2012/12/12/is-infantilization-the-new-leadership-philosophy-of-the-us-military/.

[16] J. Vandiver, "US Troops in Europe Banned from Wearing Uniform off Base," *Stars and Stripes*, 23.3.2011.

[17] Josephus Flavius, *The Jewish War*, 2:254-57; *The Antiquities of the Jews*, 20:186

[18] See P. Fussell, *Uniforms*, Boston, MA, Houghton Mifflin, 2002, pp. 8-10.

[19] B. Fleming, "The Few, the Proud, the Infantilized," *The Chronicle of Higher Education*, 8.10.2012, at http://chronicle.com/article/The-Few-the-Proud-the/134830/.

[20] A. Brenneman, "Why the Viet Cong Were Called 'Charlie,'" TodayIFoundOut, at http://www.todayifoundout.com/index.php/2013/04/why-the-viet-cong-were-called-charlie-during-the-vietnam-war/

[21] See M. van Creveld, *The Culture of War*, New York, NY, Ballantine, 2008, pp. 243-44.

[22] See, e.g., D. Bar Tal, "Delegitimization: The Extreme Case of Stereotyping and Prejudice," *Springer Series in Social Psychology*, 1989, pp. 169-82.

[23] See, e.g., D. Grossman, *On Killing*, New York, NY, Back Bay Books, Kindle ed., 1996, locs. 2656, 3051, 3076, 3203, 3399, 3401, 5040, 4914.

[24] USAREC Regulation 600-25, Prohibited and Regulated Activities," 2009, at http://www.usarec.army.mil/im/formpub/rec_pubs/r600_25.pdf.

[25] "Cucolo: No. 1 Priority is Training to Serve," *The Frontline*, 44, 4, 29.1.2009, at http://www.fortstewartfrontline.com/archivedFrontline/Frontline01-29-09News.pdf.

[26] C. Carroll, "Air Force Finds Thousands of Inappropriate Items, Including Pornography," *Stars and Stripes*, 18.1.2013.

[27] J. Dunnigan, "The US Navy Breaks the Wrong Record," Strategy Page, 11.1.2012, at http://www.strategypage.com/dls/articles/US.-Navy-Breaks-The-Wrong-Record-1-20-2012.asp.

[28] R. Scarborough, "Navy Too Politically Correct for 'Old Salts,'" *Washington Times*, 28.5.2011.

[29] B. Mathis-Lilley, "Blue Angels Scandal Involves Genitalia Painting So Large That It Could Be Seen on Google Maps," *Slatest*, 23.7.2014.

[30] R. Powers, "Adultery in the Military," About.com, at http://usmilitary.about.com/od/justicelawlegislation/a/adultery.htm.

[31] *Psychopathia Sexualis*, (English), 12th ed., New York, NY, Pioneer, 1939, p. 79.

[32] 1999 figures. GAO Report, "Military Personnel: Actions Needed to Better Define Pilot Requirements and Increase Retention," Washington DC, 1999, p. 18.

[33] P. J. Boyer, "Admiral Boorda's War," *The New Yorker*, 6.9.1996.

[34] See "A Tale of Two Paulas," Military Corruption.com, 2003, at http://www.militarycorruption.com/paulas.htm.

[35] CMR: "Military Sexual Assault Numbers Inflated for Political Purposes," 8.4.2014, at http://www.onenewsnow.com/national-security/2014/04/08/cmr-military-sexual-assault-numbers-inflated-for-political-purposes#.VKFpOsDm7U.

[36] L. C. Baldor, "Sex Is a Major Reason Military Commanders Are Fired," Associated Press, 21.1.2013, http://news.yahoo.com/sex-major-reason-military; M. Thompson, "Military Misbehavin'," *Time*, 1.10.2012.

[37] T. Zakaria and S. Cornwell, "US Military Faces Scrutiny over Its Prostitution Policies," Reuters, 29.4.2012, at http://www.reuters.com/article/2012/04/29/us-usa-agents-military-idUSBRE83S09620120429.

[38] Suetonius, *Caesar,* 50-2, 67-8.

[39] D. Chandler, *The Campaigns of Napoleon*, New York, NY, MacMillan, 1966, p. 369.

[40] D. Showalter, *Patton and Rommel: Men of War in the Twentieth Century*, New York, NY, Berkeley, 2005, pp. 126, 411-12.

[41] D. Frum, "Top Ten Military Sex Scandals," The Daily Beast, 15.11.2012, at http://www.thedailybeast.com/articles/2012/11/15/top-ten-military-sex-scandals.html.

[42] *Othello*, Act I scene 3.

[43] S. de Beauvoir, *The Prime of Life*, Harmondsworth, Middlesex, Penguin, 1962, pp. 452, 454.

[44] See M. L. Roberts, *What Soldiers Do: Sex and the American GI in World War II France*, Chicago, IL, University of Chicago Press, Kindle ed., 2013, loc. 1263; and P. Goedde, "From Villains to Victims: Fraternization and the Feminization of Germany, 1945-47," *Diplomatic History*, 23, 1, 2002, pp. 1-20.

[45] "Down by the Bahnhof, American Soldat/Ich habe Zigaretten, und beaucoup Chocolat. Dass ist prima dass ist gut, A zwanzig Mark/fuer fuemp Minute. Wieviel, Lili Marlene."

[46] C. Hedges, *War Is a Force That Gives Us Meaning*, Kindle ed., locs. 1532-86.

[47] R. Scarborough, "Doubts on military's sex assault stats as numbers far exceed those for the US," *Washington Times*, 26.4.2014; M. Conzachi, "The Sexual Assault on US Military Members," A Voice for Men, 30.11.2013, at http://www.avoiceformen.com/feminism/feminist-governance-feminism/the-sexual-assault-on-us-military-members/; and "The Rape Differential," The Ledger, 24.11.1996, at http://news.google.com/newspapers?nid=1346&dat=19961124&id=IwQwAAAAIBAJ&sjid=6fwDAAAAIBAJ&pg=6674,2194602.

[48] Thompson, "Military Misbehavin'."

[49] R. J. Maginnis, *Deadly Consequences: How Cowards Are Pushing Women into Combat*, New York, NY, Back Bay, 2009, Kindle ed., loc. 1109.

[50] J. Huang, "ClassicWHO: Why Petraeus Takedown May Have Been an Inside Job," WhoWhatWhy, 25.6.2014, at http://whowhatwhy.com/2014/06/25/classicwho-why-petraeus-takedown-may-have-been-an-inside-job/.

[51] L. M. Schenck, "Sex Offenses under Military Law: Will the Recent Changes in the Uniform Code of Military Justice Re-traumatize Sexual Assault Survivors in the Courtroom?" *Ohio State Journal of Criminal Law*, 11, 2, 2014, pp. 438-85.

[52] A. Jones, "Some Marines Fear Innocent Men Are Being Convicted of Rape," The Wire, 18.2.2014, at http://www.thewire.com/politics/2014/02/some-marines-fear-innocent-men-are-being-convicted-rape/358220/; D. Lee, "Women in Combat; Marines Fear Spike in Sexual Harassment Allegations," USAttorneys.com, 5.2.2013, at http://sexual-harassment-lawyers.usattorneys.com/women-combat-marines-fear-spike-sexual-harassment-allegations/.

[53] See, for a short but excellent discussion of the meaning of the term, B. Lind, *On War*, Kouvola, Finland, Castalia, 2014, column for 19.11.2009.

[54] See on her, "Protect Our Defenders," at http://www.protectourdefenders.com/leadership/.

[55] The text is available at http://protectourdefenders.com/downloads/Smith_ExhibitSelects_20121101.pdf.

[56] Amazon does in fact have a publication titled *The Fighter Pilot's Handbook*, but it has nothing to do with the one I am discussing here.

[57] The original is: "Whom does woman hate most? Thus spoke the iron to the magnet: "I hate you most, because you attract me, but are too weak to draw me to you." *Thus Spake Zarathustra*, R. J. Hollingdale, trans., London, Penguin, 1969, p. 91.

[58] The original is available at http://www.westernfrontassociation.com/great-war-people/48-brothers-arms/372-songs-war.html.

[59] F. Fukuyama, *Trust: Human Nature and the Reconstitution of Social Order*, New York, NY, Free Press, 2008.

[60] See, for some comparative figures on urban population density, www.demographia.com/db-intluadens-rank.htm.

[61] See, for the British and German figures, L. Long, *Migration and Residential Mobility in the United States*, New York, NY, Russell Sage, 1988, table 2.6; for the Chinese one, C. Cindy Fan, "Interprovincial Migration, Population Redistribution, and Regional Development in China," *The Professional Geographer*, 57(2) 2005, p. 295.

[62] According to D. Brooks, *Paradise Drive*, New York, NY, Simon & Schuster, 2004, p. 76.

[63] According to M. A. Glendon, *Legally Speaking: Contemporary American Culture and the Law*, Boston, MA, University of Massachusetts Press, 1999, pp. 76-89.

[64] See, for some comparative figures, F. K. Upham, *Law and Social Change in Postwar Japan*, Cambridge, MA, Harvard University Press, 1987, pp. 166-227.

[65] J. R. Glater, "In a Complex World, Even Lawyers Need Lawyers," *The New York Times*, 3.2.2 004.

[66] See, for a short account of the way the profession is organized, L. M. Friedman, *American Law in the Twentieth Century*, New Haven, CT, Yale University Press, 2002, pp. 457-504.

[67] See A. K. Bailey, "Military Employment and Spatial Mobility across the Life Course," in J. M. Wilmoth and A. S. London, eds., *Life Course Perspectives on Military Mobility*, New York, NY, Routledge, 2013.

[68] Annual Report to Congress Pursuant to the Uniform Code of Military Justice, 1.10.1997-1.10.1998, section III, p. 8.

[69] "Active Duty Military Personnel, 1940-2011," at http://www/infoplease.com/ipa/A5498html.

[70] B. Gertz and R. Scarborough, "JAG Proliferation," *Washington Times*, 15.9.2006.

[71] B. Farmer, "MoD Lawyers Soar as Armed Forces' Budgets Cut," *Telegraph*, 1.11.2011.

[72] Lt. Jeffrey Clement, personal communication.

[73] S. Rayment, "£340 Million Bill as Compensation Culture Infects Our Armed Forces," MailOnline, 20.4.2013, at http://www.dailymail.co.uk/news/article-2312242/340million-compensation-culture-infects-Armed-Forces-36-000-claims-payouts-past-seven-years.html.

[74] C. Dickens, *Bleak House*, London, Penguin, 1991 [1853], pp. 6, 11, 13, and 83.

[75] See, on these men, van Creveld, *The Culture of War*, pp. 203-8.

[76] T. O'Brien, *The Things They Carried*, Boston, MA, Houghton Mifflin, Kindle ed., 2009, locs. 871-89.

[77] CNN.com, 2.4.2005, at http://edition.cnn.com/2005/US/02/03/general.shoot/.

[78] "Chaos: General James Mattis Announced as Next Commandant of the Marine Corps," 17.8.2012, at http://www.abovetopsecret.com/forum/thread872700/pg1.

[79] See http://www.bartleby.com/266/63.html/.

[80] A. Chaniotis, *War in the Hellenistic World*, Oxford, Blackwell, 2005, pp. 36, 210, 229.

[81] See van Creveld, *The Culture of War*, p. 93.

[82] See M. Polner, *No Victory Parades: The Return of the Vietnam Veteran*, New York, NY, Holt, Rinehart and Winston, 1971.

[83] At http://www.goodreads.com/quotes/300507-militarism-has-been-by-far-the-commonest-cause-of-the breakdown of civilizations: and http://oxforddictionaries.com/definition/english/militarism.

[84] W. Eckhardt and G. A. Newcome, "Militarism, Personality and Other Social Attitudes," *Journal of Conflict Resolution*, 13, 2, June 1969, p. 212, table 1.

[85] Chaniotis, *War in the Hellenistic World*, p. 192.

[86] See on all this van Creveld, *The Culture of War*, pp. 209-28.

[87] A. Vagts, *A History of Militarism*, New York, NY, Free Press, 1959 [1937], pp 13-4.

[88] See on this van Creveld, *The Culture of War*, pp. 412-13.

[89] Thucydides, *The Peloponnesian War*, I, 3.

[90] See M. Domarus, *The Complete Hitler, 1932-1945*, Wauconda, IL, Bolchazy-Carducci, Kindle edition, 2013, p. 407.

[91] C. von Clausewitz, *On War*, Princeton, NJ, Princeton University Press, 1976, p. 605.

[92] Alex Ashbourne-Walmsley, quoted in "How Europe's Five Female Defense Ministers Could Impact the Ukraine Conflict," The Daily Beast, 5.3.2014, at http://www.thedailybeast.com/witw/articles/2014/03/05/how-europe-s-five-female-defense-ministers-could-impact-the-ukraine-conflict.html.

[93] N. Rothschild, "Swedish Women vs. Vladimir Putin," Foreignpolicy.com, 5.12.2014, at http://foreignpolicy.com/2014/12/05/can-vladimir-putin-be-intimidated-by-feminism-sweden/.

[94] L. Wurster and T. Nollau, "Ursula von der Leyen: Deutschland muss fuehren—zumindst ein bisschen," Focus-Online, 6.2.2015, at http://www.focus.de/politik/ausland/ukraine-krise/ratlosigkeit-und-zurueckrudern-ursula-von-der-leyen-deutschland-muss-fuehren-zumindest-ein-bisschen_id_4459645.html.

[95] C. Dale and C. Gilroy, "The Effects of the Business Cycle on the Size and Composition of the US Army," *Atlantic Economic Journal*, 11, 1, March 1983, pp. 42-53.

[96] J. G. Bachman and Others, "Who Chooses Military Service? Correlates of Propensity and Enlistment in the US Armed Forces," *Military Psychology*, 12, 1, 2000, pp. 1-30

[97] "The US Military Helps Naturalize Non-Citizens," Military.com, at http://www.military.com/join-armed-forces/eligibility-requirements/the-us-military-helps-naturlize-non-citizens.html.

[98] J. Dunnigan, 'Why Foreigners Make Better Soldiers," *Strategy Page*, 7.8.2012, at http://www.strategypage.com/dls/articles/Why-Foreigners-Make-Better-Soldiers-8-7-2012.asp.

[99] Ministry of Foreign Affairs of Denmark, "Danish Military Service for Foreign Nationals," at http://usa.um.dk/en/travel-and-residence/defense-and-security/danish-military-service-for-foreign-nationals/.

[100] Personal communication by Prof. Col. Alexandre Vautravers, Geneva.

[101] "List of Militaries that Recruit Foreigners," February 2010, at http://en.wikipedia.org/wiki/List_of_militaries_that_recruit_foreigners.

[102] See, for an overview of the subject, P. W. Singer, *Corporate Warriors: The Rise of the Privatized Military Industry,* Ithaca, NY, Cornell University Press, 2011.

[103] See, for the US, S. Lendman, "The World of Mercenary Companies and Private Military Contractors," Global Research, 11.1.2012, at http://www.globalresearch.ca/the-world-of-mercenary-companies-and-private-military-contractors/28603; for Britain, I. Traynor, "The Privatization of War," *The Guardian*, 10.12.2003.

[104] A. Bones, "How Much Do Private Military Contractors Get Paid?" The Nest, n.d., at http://woman.thenest.com/much-money-private-military-contractors-paid-23196.html.

Chapter III. Feminizing the Forces

[1] E. Flock, "Gadhafi's Female Bodyguards Say They Were Raped, Abused by the Libyan Leader," *Washington Post*, 28.11.2011.

[2] C. Bigg, "Army Puts on a Pretty Face," Radio Free Europe, 18.1.2015, at http://www.rferl.org/content/article/1059432.html.

[3] See, for a short summary of the roles women have played in various militaries, M. van Creveld, *Men, Women and War*, London, Cassell, 2001, pp. 41-169.

[4] J. Holm, *Women in the Military: An Unfinished Revolution*, Novato, CA, Presidio, 1992, chapter 10; J. Ebbert and M-B. Hall, *Crossed Currents: Navy Women from WWI to Tailhook*, Washington DC, Brassey's, 1993, p. 97 ff.

[5] Holm, *Women in the Military*, p. 184.

[6] Holm, *Women in the Military*, p. 181; Ebbert and Hall, *Crossed Currents*, p. 122; Breuer, *War and the American Woman*, pp. 70-1.

[7] See Holm, *Women in the Military*, chapter 15; W. B. Breuer, *War and American Women: Heroism, Deeds, and Controversy*, Westport, CT, Praeger, 1997, p. 79; H. Rogan, *Mixed Company: Women in the Modern Army*, Boston, MA, Beacon Press, 1981, p. 16; Ebbert and Hall, *Crossed Currents*, pp. 160-61, 168, 222-23.

[8] M. Binkin and J. S. Bach, *Women in the Military*, Washington DC, Brookings, 1977, pp. 2, 12-3.

[9] Quoted in J. Stiehm, *Arms and the Enlisted Woman*, Philadelphia, PA, Temple University Press, 1989, p. 55.

[10] J. J. Mansbridge, *Why We Lost the Era*, Chicago, IL, University of Chicago Press, 1986, p. 72; B. Mitchell, *Women in the Military: Flirting with Disaster*, Washington DC, Regnery, 1998, pp. 24-5.

[11] See the testimonies quoted in Binkin and Bach, *Women in the Military*, p. 49 ff.

[12] Binkin and Bach, *Women in the Military*.

[13] Ebert and Hall, *Crossed Currents*, pp. 163-4.

[14] See Holm, *Women in the Military*, chapter 18.

[15] See Breuer, *War and the American Woman*, p. 116 ff.

[16] Holm, *Women in the Military*, p. 205.

[17] N. Montgomery, "Army Uniform Designed for Women Now for All," *Stars and Stripes*, 28.9.2012.

[18] Stiehm, *Arms and the Enlisted Woman*, p. 55.

[19] See on these cases Stiehm, *Arms and the Enlisted Women*, p. 113 ff.

[20] Presidential Commission on the Assignment of Women in the Armed Forces, *Report to the President*, Washington DC, 1992, GPO, *passim*.

[21] E. Bumiller and Th. Shanker, "Pentagon Is Set to Lift Combat Ban for Women," *The New York Times*, 23.1.2013.

[22] "Dempsey: Combat Ban Contributed to Sexual Assault Problem," *Washington Free Beacon*, 24.1.2013.

[23] For details see E. Klick, "Utilization of Women by the NATO Alliance," *Armed Forces*

and Society, 4, 4, August 1978, pp. 673-94.

[24] E. MacAskill, "US Hands Command of Libya Air Strategy to Senior Female Officer," Guardian, 23.5.2011.

[25] "Von der Leyen plant Frauenquote bei der Bundeswehr," FocusOnline, 10.1.2015, at http://www.focus.de/politik/deutschland/von-10-5-auf-15-prozent-von-der-leyen-plant-frauenquote-bei-der-bundeswehr_id_4394796.html.

[26] Iliad, III, 184. For the meaning of antianeirai see J. H. Blok, The Early Amazons: Modern and Ancient Perspectives on a Persistent Myth, Leiden, Brill, 1995, pp. 155 ff., 167, 173, 223 ff.

[27] Data summarized in Mitchell, Women in the Military, pp. 141-42.

[28] According to J. Diamond, Guns, Germs and Steel, New York, NY, Norton, 1997, p. 375.

[29] D. Morris, Manwatching: A Field Guide to Human Behavior, New York, NY, Abrams, 1977, pp. 239-40.

[30] Presidential Commission on the Assignment of Women in the Armed Forces, Report to the President, p. c-74.

[31] G. Zorpette, "The Mystery of Muscle," Scientific American, 10, 2, summer 1999, p. 48.

[32] J. F. Tuten, "The Argument against Female Combatants," in Loring Goldman, ed., Female Soldiers, Beverly Hills, CA, SAGE, 1976, pp. 247-48.

[33] Morris, Manwatching, pp. 230-32.

[34] D. Kimura, "Sex Differences in the Brain," Scientific American, 10, 2, summer 1999, p. 27.

[35] Presidential Commission on the Assignment of Women in the Armed Forces, Report to the President, p. C-64.

[36] J. Caba, "Women's Breast Size Could Be Hindering Their Participation in Physical Activity," Medical Daily, 24.6.2014, at http://www.medicaldaily.com/womens-breast-size-could-be-hindering-their-participation-physical-activity-289626.

[37] Sallust, Jugurthine War, Harmondsworth, Middlesex, Penguin, 1963, p. 120. In fact, for fear of them being attacked, even in the most "progressive" modern military very few women stand guard.

[38] Rogan, Mixed Company, p. 62; see also Stephanie Gutman, The Kinder, Gentler Military, pp. 31-43, 72-3.

[39] Rogan, Mixed Company, p. 65.

[40] US Army Research Institute for Environmental Medicine, Incidence of Risk Factors for Injury and Illness among Male and Female Army Basic Trainees, 1988.

[41] Figures from L. B. de Fleur, D. Gilman, and W. Marshal, "Sex Integration at the US Air Force Academy: Changing Roles for Women," Armed Forces and Society, August 1978, p. 615.

[42] "First Woman to Lead Troops in Battle Praised," Kansas City Star, 4.1.1990.

[43] Gutman, The Kinder, Gentler Military, p. 266; A. McDonald, "Canada Offers Lessons

on Women in Combat," *Wall Street Journal*, 24.1.2013.

[44] K. Wong, "Few Female Marines Step Forward for Infantry," *Washington Times*, 25.11.2012.

[45] R. Sagi, *Women Fighting the IDF* [Hebrew], Tel Aviv, Semrik, 2014, pp. 149-62.

[46] See K. J. Colson and others, *The Harvard Guide to Women's Health*, Cambridge, MA, Harvard University Press, 1996. pp. 238, 241, 322, 379, 388.

[47] M. J. Festle, *Playing Nice: Politics and Apologies in Women's Sports*, New York, NY, Columbia University Press, 1996, p. 270 ff.

[48] Gutman, *The Kinder, Gentler Military*, p. 248; *Wall Street Journal*, 3.12.1999.

[49] Ministry of Defense, "Women in Ground Close Combat," review paper, 1.12.2014, at https://www.gov.uk/government/publications/women-in-ground-close-combat-gcc-review-paper.

[50] On these problems see also GAO, *Improved Guidance and Oversight Are Needed to Ensure Validity and Equity of Fitness Standards*, Washington DC, Government Printing Office, 1998, pp. 3, 4, 5, 9, 12, 16, 26, and 28.

[51] M. Nichol, "Female RAF Recruits Get 100,000 Pounds Compensation Each... Because They Were Made to March Like Men," MailOnline, 23.11.2013, at http://www.dailymail.co.uk/news/article-2512412/Female-RAF-recruits-100-000-compensation--march-like-men.html.

[52] See, for some examples of the way foreign armies do these things, Maginnis, *Deadly Consequences*, locs. 1343-47.

[53] At https://www.google.co.il/webhp?sourceid=chrome-instant&rlz=1C1OPRB_enIL528IL528&ion=1&espv=2&ie=UTF-8#q=gender+norming+definition.

[54] Gutman, *The Kinder, Gentler Military*, pp. 44-79; Force System Directorate, "Valuation of the Military Entrance Physical Strength Capacity Test," Bethesda, MD, US Army Concepts Analysis Agency, October 1985.

[55] L. M. Bacon, "In Marines' New Fitness Plan, Pullups for Women Won't Be Mandatory," Marine Times, 18.4.2016, at http://www.marinecorpstimes.com/story/military/2016/04/18/marines-new-fitness-plan-pullups-women-wont-mandatory/82793128/.

[56] For a plethora of such complaints see Mitchell, *Women in the Military, passim*; L. H. Francke, *Ground Zero: The Gender Wars in the Military*, New York, NY, Simon & Schuster, 1997, p. 200; Gutman, *The Kinder, Gentler Military*, pp. 260-61.

[57] Thucydides, *The Peloponnesian War*, 5.66.3-4.

[58] Polybius, *The Histories*, 6, 38, 2.

[59] See, for the way it is created, M. van Creveld, *Fighting Power*, Westport, CT, Greenwood, 1983.

[60] M. Beal, "41-Year-Old Grandmother Joins the Army," 10News, 15.6.2010, at http://archive.wtsp.com/news/article/134225/8/41-year-old-grandmother-joins-the-Army.

[61] Presidential Commission, p. 40.

[62] "Zivildienst in Oesterreich," WienKonkret, n.d., at http://www.wien-konkret.at/leute/bundesheer/zivildienst/.

[63] Norway's Military Conscription Becomes Gender-Neutral," Deutsche Welle, 14.6.2013.

[64] J. Benenetto, "Childless Servicewomen May Sue MoD," *The Independent*, 7.9.1994.

[65] I. Drury, "200 Women Troops Sent Home for Being Pregnant," MailOnline, 16.2.2014, at http://www.dailymail.co.uk/news/article-2560898/200-women-troops-sent-home-pregnant-MoD-wont-impose-war-zone-pregnancy-tests-privacy-fears.html.

[66] Navy Personnel Command, Pregnancy FAQs, n.d., at http://www.public.navy.mil/bupers-npc/organization/bupers/WomensPolicy/Pages/FAQs-Women%27sPolicy.aspx.

[67] Mitchell, *Women in the Military*, p. 210.

[68] J. Wilson, "Unplanned Pregnancies May Be on Rise in the Military," CNN News, 23.1.2013, at http://edition.cnn.com/2013/01/23/health/unplanned-pregnancies-military/.

[69] J. Leopold, "Top Army Commander Rescinds Order Criminalizing Pregnancy," Truthout, 9.12.2009, at http://truth-out.org/archive/component/k2/item/87368:top-army-commander-rescinds-controversial-order-criminalizing-pregnancy.

[70] Brown and Safilios-Rothschild, "Greece: Reluctant Presence," in Goldman Loring, ed., *Female Combatants*, p. 173.

[71] Klick, "Utilization of Women in the NATO Military," *Armed Forces & Society*, p. 675; *Moniteur belge*, 7.5.1977, p. 236.

[72] Seidler, *Frauen zu der Waffen?* p. 381.

[73] Stiehm, *Arms and the Enlisted Woman*, p. 145.

[74] "Demographics of Active Duty US Military," 23.11.2013, at http://www.statisticbrain.com/demographics-of-active-duty-u-s-military/.

[75] See R. Bragg, *I Am a Soldier, Too: The Jessica Lynch Story*, New York, NY, Vintage, 2003.

[76] Center for Military Readiness, "Grim Toll of Military Women Killed in War," 1.4.2013, at http://www.cmrlink.org/content/home/35891/grim_toll_of_military_women_killed_in_war.

[77] Quoted in E. Donnelly, "Seven Reasons Why Women-in-Combat Diversity Will Degrade Tough Training Standards," Center for Military Readiness, 29.1.2013, at http://www.cmrlink.org/content/home/36488/seven_reasons_why_women_in_combat_diversity_will_degrade_tough_training_standards.

[78] Gutman, *The Kinder, Gentler Military*, pp. 15, 258.

[79] "Casualties of the Iraq War," at http://en.wikipedia.org/wiki/Casualties_of_the_Iraq_War; Maginnis, *Deadly Consequences*, locs. 1276, 1332 1484 and 1486.

[80] See on this G. Anderson, *The White Blouse Revolution: Female Office Workers Since 1870*, Manchester, Manchester University Press, 1989.

[81] Quoted in Ebbert and Hall, *Crossed Currents*, p. 14.

[82] *Ibid.*, p. 78.

[83] See M. van Creveld, *The Privileged Sex*, Amazon Digital Services, 2013.

[84] A. Platell, "What Did Single Mother Tilern Debique Expect?" MailOnline, 19.4.2010, at http://www.dailymail.co.uk/debate/article-1266654/What-did-single-mother-Tilern-Debique-expect-creche-Afghanistan.html; "Female Soldier Awarded 17,000 GBU by Employment Tribunal," *The Guardian*, 16.4.2012.

[85] R. H. Bork, *Slouching towards Gomorrah: Modern Liberalism and America's Decline*, New York, NY, Regan Books/Harper Collins, 1996, Kindle ed., 2010, locs. 3818-83.

[86] See W. B. Tyrell, *Amazons: A Study in Athenian Mythmaking*, Baltimore, MD, Johns Hopkins U.P, 1984, pp. 44-5.

[87] See M. van Creveld, *Wargames: From Gladiators to Gigabytes*, Cambridge, Cambridge University Press, 2013, pp. 294-97.

[88] G. Orwell, *1984*, Harmondsworth, Penguin, 1977 [1949], p. 31.

[89] See E. Donnelly, "Constructing the Co-Ed Military," *Duke Journal of Gender Law and Policy*, 14, 2, 2007, pp. 854-55.

[90] See on this Maginnis, *Deadly Consequences*, locs. 1637-64.

[91] Statement for the Record of M. E. Gebicke, Director, Military Operations and Capabilities Issues, GAO, "Gender Integration in Basic Training," at http://www.worldcat.org/title/gender-integration-in-basic-training-the-services-are-using-a-variety-of-approaches-statement-for-the-record-of-mark-e-gebicke-director-military-operations-and-capabilities-issues-national-security-and-international-affairs.

[92] "Military Leadership Diversity Commission, Decision Paper No. 3: Retention," February 2011, p. 8; A. McAvoy, "Commander: Navy Must Improve Female Retention Rate," Navy Times, 24.5.2014, at http://archive.navytimes.com/article/20140524/NEWS/305240032/Commander-Navy-must-improve-female-retention-rate.

[93] J. McGregor, "Women in Combat: Why Making It Official Matters," *Washington Post*, 25.5.2012.

[94] M. Thompson, "Women in Combat: *Vive la Différence*," *Time*, 25.1.2013.

[95] See Van Creveld, *The Privileged Sex*, pp. 207-26.

[96] See, out of the huge literature, C. Hedderman and M. Hough, *Does the Criminal System Treat Men and Women Differently?*, London, HMSO, 1994, pp. 3-4 (for Britain); as well as N. Levit, *The Gender Line: Men, Women and the Law*, New York, NY, New York University Press, 1998, p. 107, and R. J. Simon, "Women in Prison," in C. C. Culliver, ed., *Female Criminality: The State of the Art*, New York, NY, Garland, 1993, p. 375, (for the US).

[97] "Joseline," "Single Mothers in the Military Service," Feministing, 13.5.2013, at http://feministing.com/2013/05/13/single-mothers-in-the-military-service-the-silent-battle-for-their-children/.

[98] "Single Parent Families—Demographic Trends," at http://family.jrank.org/pages/1574/Single-Parent-Families-Demographic-Trends.html.

[99] "Females in Military Struggle with Higher Divorce Rate," *USA Today*, 8.3.2011.

[100] Thompson, "Women in Combat."

[101] R. Scarborough, "False Reports Outpace Sex Assaults in the Military," *Washington Times*, 12.5.2013.

[102] See, e.g., B. Redford, The Anatomy of False Accusations: A Skeptical Case Study," *Center for Inquiry*, 26.2.2014, at http://www.centerforinquiry.net/blogs/entry/the_anatomy_of_false_accusations_a_s keptical_case_study/.

[103] S. Tokar, "Almost One Third of Iraq/Afghanistan Women Veterans with PTSD Report Military Sexual Trauma," University of California News Service, 14.9.2011, at http://www.coe.ucsf.edu/coe/research/ptsd-sexualtrauma.html.

[104] E. O'Keefe, "Senate Easily Passes McCaskill's Military Sexual Assault Bill," *Washington Post*, 10.3.2014.

[105] See, e.g., M. O'Toole, "Military Sexual Assault Epidemic Continues to Claim Victims," The World Post, 6.10.2012, at http://www.huffingtonpost.com/2012/10/06/military-sexual-assault-defense-department_n_1834196.html.

[106] Hyginus, *Fabulae*, 191.

[107] *Beyond Good and Evil*, Harmondsworth, Penguin, 1987 ed., p. 83.

[108] K. Zivi, "Contesting Motherhood in the Age of AIDS," *Feminist Studies*, 31, 2, summer 2005, pp. 347-74.

[109] The literature on this subject is enormous. See E. Young-Bruehl, *Freud on Women*, New York, NY, Norton, 1990, pp. 346-62, 272-82; K. Horney, "The Flight from Womanhood," *International Journal for Psycho-Analysis*, 7, 1926, p. 330; *idem*, "The Dread of Women," *ibid.*, 13, 1932, p. 359; H. L. and R. R. Ansbacher, eds., *The Individual Psychology of Alfred Adler*, New York, NY, Harper & Row, 1956, pp. 50, 452; P. R. Sanday, *Female Power and Male Dominance: On the Origins of Sexual Inequality*, Cambridge, Cambridge University Press, 1987, p. 78; J. K. Conway and others, eds., *Learning about Women*, Ann Arbor, MI, University of Michigan Press, 1989, p. xxvi; J. Rutherford, *Men's Silences*, London, Routledge, 1990, pp. 180-81; and so many others that one cannot even list them.

[110] D. Siaz, "Trump Knocks Bush for Turning to 'Mommy,'" 23.1.2016, at http://edition.cnn.com/2016/01/23/politics/jeb-bush-donald-trump-barbara-bush-twitter/,

[111] See E. Badinter, *XY: on Masculine Identity*, New York, NY, Columbia University Press, 1997, chapter 3.

[112] See D. G. Gilmore, *Manhood in the Making: Cultural Concepts of Masculinity*, New Haven, CT, Yale University Press, 1990.

[113] F. J. Porter Pole, "The Ritual Forging of Identity," in Herdt, ed., *Rituals of Manhood*, p. 123.

[114] G. H. Herdt, "Fetish and Fantasy in Sambia Initiation," in Herdt, ed., *Rituals of Manhood*, p. 79.

[115] D. B. Gewertz, "The Father Who Bore Me: The Role of *Tsambunwuro* during Chambri Initiation Ceremonies," in Herdt, ed., *Rituals of Manhood*, p. 298.

[116] Plato, *Republic*, 455D.

[117] Exodus 12.36-7.

[118] Tacitus, *Germania*, 18.

[119] T. Spears, *Kenya's Past*, London, Longman, 1981, pp. 63-7; Ifi Amadiume, *Male Daughters, Female Husbands: Gender and Sex in an African Society*, London, Zed, 1987, pp. 94-6; Harry H. Turney-High, *Primitive War, Its Practice and Concepts*, Chapel Hill, SC, University of South Carolina Press, 1971 [1937], pp. 162-63.

[120] M. B. Davie, *The Evolution of War: A Study of Its Role in Early Societies*, New Haven, CT, Yale University Press, 1929, p. 33; Gilmore, *Manhood in the Making*, p. 67.

[121] For a discussion of the Greek terminology see E. Vermeule, *Aspects of Death in Early Greek Art and Poetry*, Berkeley, CA, University of California Press, 1979, p. 101; of the Hebrew one, Sion, *Images of Manhood*, pp. 90-2. For a general discussion of the terminology that war and sex have in common see D. de Rougemont, *Passion and Society*, London, Faber & Faber, n.d., pp. 248-50.

[122] See D. H. J. Morgan, "Theater of War: Combat, the Military and Masculinities", in H. Brod and M. Kaufman, eds., *Theorizing Masculinities*, Los Angeles, CA, Sage Publications, 1994.

[123] See the relevant source, "Aethiopis," at http://www.livius.org/source-content/epic-cycle/aethiopis/.

[124] Aristophanes, *Lysistrata*, lines 672-83.

[125] S. Siegel, "Story Claiming Obama Changes Marines' Hat Is Ridiculous," The Daily Beast, 24.10.2013, at http://www.thedailybeast.com/the-hero-project/articles/2013/10/24/story-claiming-obama-changed-marines-hat-is-flat-wrong.html.

[126] M. Mead, *Male and Female*, London, Gollancz, 1949, pp. 159-60; and, in much greater detail, B. F. Reskin and P. A. Roos, *Job Queues, Gender Queues: Explaining Women's Inroads into Male Occupations*, Philadelphia, PA, Temple University Press, 1997. For women's tendency to look down on women see L. Segal, *Is the Future Female?* New York, NY, Bedrick, 1988, p. 14; E. Reardon, *Sexism and the War System*, New York, NY, Teachers' College, 1985, p. 47; and V. Klein, *The Feminine Character*, London, Kegan Paul, 1946, p. 72.

Chapter IV. Constructing PTSD

[1] Arrian, *Anabasis*, 5.26.

[2] See Chaniotis, *War in the Hellenistic World*, p. 204.

[3] Vergil, *Aeneid*, 9.59.

[4] See, for the history of the idea, J. Bowman, *Honor: A History*, New York, NY,

Encounter, 2006, Kindle ed., locs. 759-906.

[5] See, on these aspects of the games, van Creveld, *Wargames*, pp. 62-3, 77-8.

[6] Froissart, *Chronicles*, Harmondsworth, Penguin, 1979 [1400], p. 179.

[7] Louis XIV, *Mémoires pour les années 1661 et 1666*, Paris, Bossard, 1923, pp. 124-25.

[8] Y. Harari, *The Ultimate Experience*, London, Palgrave, 2008, especially pp. 197-298.

[9] L. Tolstoy, *War and Peace*, Harmondsworth, Penguin, 1957 [1869], I, p. 162.

[10] See, for this Sassoon quote, J. M. Wilson, *Siegfried Sassoon: The Making of a War Poet*, London, Duckworth, 1998, pp. 179-80.

[11] R. Hoess, *Death Dealer: The Memoirs of the SS Kommandant at Auschwitz*, Boston, MA, Da Capo, 1996, p. 58.

[12] E. Juenger, *Storm of Steel*, London, Penguin, 1993 [1922], especially pp. 315-16

[13] G. Sajer, *The Forgotten Soldier*, New York, NY, Harper, 1971, p. 286.

[14] Clausewitz, *On War*, p. 75.

[15] "Hugh Selwyn Mauberley," 1920, at https://www.google.co.il/webhp?sourceid=chrome-instant&rlz=1C1OPRB_enIL528IL528&ion=1&espv=2&ie=UTF-8#q=hugh%20selwyn%20mauberley%20pdf.

[16] Chaniotis, *War in the Hellenistic World*, p. 1.

[17] J. K. Abdul Hamid and J. H. Huge, "Nothing New Under the Sun: Post-Traumatic Stress Disorders in the Ancient World," *Early Science and Medicine*, 19, June 2014, pp. 549-57.

[18] I Samuel 16.14.

[19] Shay, *Achilles in Vietnam*, loc. 250.

[20] *Ibid.*

[21] *Iliad*, 22.445-515, 24.

[22] C. Coker, *Men at War*, London, Hurst, 2014, 244-45.

[23] *Encomicum*, B. R. Donovan, trans., 16-7, at http://www.classicpersuasion.org/pw/gorgias/helendonovan.htm.

[24] Y. Ustinova and E. Cardeoa, "Combat Stress Disorders and Their Treatment in Ancient Greece," *Psychological Trauma*, 6, June 2014, pp. 739-48.

[25] Polybius, *The Histories*, 6.117.

[26] *Ibid.*, 7.152.

[27] See, above all, K. Yellin, *Battle Exhortation: The Rhetoric of Combat Leadership*, Columbia, NC, University of North Carolina Press, 2008.

[28] E.g., Ovid, *Heroides*, 1.31-5.

[29] See, on Marius' reforms, L, Keppie, *The Making of the Roman Army: From Republic to Empire*, London, Routledge, 1984.

[30] See, for what follows, K. van Lommel, "The Recognition of Roman Soldiers' Mental Impairment," *Acta Classica*, 56, 2013, pp. 155-84.

[31] A. N. Cabeza de Vaca, *Naufragias y Commentarios*, Madrid, Taurus, 1922, p. 32.

[32] O. de la Marche, *Mémoirs d'Olivier de la Marche*, Paris, Renouard, 1883, vol. II, pp. 45-6.

[33] Email of 25.5.2014.

[34] See S. Boym, "Nostalgia and Its Discontents," *The Hedgehog Review*, 9, 2, s summer 2007, pp. 7-8.

[35] J. C. Beaglhole, ed., *The Endeavour Journal of Joseph Banks 1768-1771*, Sydney, Public Library of New South Wales, 1962, 2, p. 145.

[36] See, e.g., the imaginative recommendations made by C. Reil, *Rhaphsodien ueber die Anwendung der psychischen Curmethode auf Geisteszerruetungen*, Berlin, Ebing, 1936 [1803], p. 209.

[37] S. Boym, *The Future of Nostalgia*, New York, NY, Basic Books, 2001, p. 5.

[38] S. J. Matt, *Homesickness: An American History*, New York, Oxford University Press, 2011, p. 7.

[39] C. OK, "The Upside of Nostalgia," *The Yale Herald*, 21.11.2013.

[40] See, for the symptoms in question, "Da Costa's Syndrome," at http://en.wikipedia.org/wiki/Da_Costa%27s_syndrome.

[41] S. A. M. Ford, "Suffering in Silence: Post-Traumatic Stress Psychological Disorders and Soldiers in the American Civil War," *Armstrong Undergraduate Journal of History* 3, no. 2 (April 2013).

[42] E. Hagerman, *The American Civil War and the Origins of Modern Warfare*, Bloomington, IN, Indiana University Press, 1988, p. xv.

[43] Thucydides, *The Peloponnesian War*, 7.87.

[44] G. Taylor, *Martyrs to the Revolution in the British Prison-Ships in The Wallabout Bay*, Ultimo, NSW, Keesing, 2007 [1855].

[45] Plato, *The Laws*, 1.629D.

[46] G.P's Notebook, "Da Costa's Syndrome," United Kingdom, n.d., at http://www.gpnotebook.co.uk/simplepage.cfm?ID=1818951721; R. I. Murray, *Mitral Valve Prolapse*, Edison, NJ, Medical Research Book Publishing Company, 1977, p. 154.

[47] See, for what follows, S. A. Ashley, "Railway Brain: The Body's Revenge against Progress," *Proceedings of the Western Society for French History*, 31, 2003, pp. 177-96.

[48] J. M. Charcot, *Leçons du mardi a la Salpêtriere*, Paris, Babé, 1893, 1, pp. 52-4.

[49] See, for a contemporary account, G. H. Savage and E. Goodall, *Insanity and Allied Neuroses*, London, Cassell, 1907, pp. 96-7.

[50] Unsigned, undated note, Bundesarchiv/Militaerarchiv, H20/480.

[51] See, for a short account of all this, van Creveld, *Fighting Power*, pp. 91-7.

[52] E. D. Cooke, *All But Me and Thee: Psychiatry at the Foxhole Level*, Washington DC, 1946, p. 11.

[53] W. C. Menninger, *Psychiatry in a Troubled World*, New York, NY, MacMillan, 1948, p. 345.

[54] Roberts, *What Soldiers Do*, loc. 501.

[55] See van Creveld, *Fighting Power, passim*.

[56] Eisenhower's letter to Patton after the incident may be found at http://boards.straightdope.com/sdmb/archive/index.php/t-259232.html.

[57] R. West, *The Return of the Soldier*, New York, NY, Century, 1918; V. Woolf, *The Return of Mrs. Dalloway*, London, Hogarth Press, 1925; D. Sayers, *The Unpleasantness*

at the Bellona Club, New York, NY, Payson & Clarke, 1928.

[58] See, for what follows, S. Goltermann, "Negotiating Victimhood in East and West Germany 1945-2005," in A. Mooij and J. Withuis, eds., *The Politics of War Trauma*, Amsterdam, Askant, 2010, pp. 107-40.

[59] See, on the way people lived and coped, K. Lowe, *Savage Continent: Europe in the Aftermath of World War II*, London, Penguin, 2012.

[60] W. Lindenberg, "Grundsatzliches zur Frage der Anerkennung von Hirnverletzungen," *Psychiatrie, Neurologie und medizinische Psychologie* 1, 1949, pp. 145-156.

[61] "Protokoll der Tagung der Medizinisch-wissenschaftlichen Gesellschaft fuer Psychiatrie und Neurologie an der Karl-Marx-Universitaet Leipzig, 1955," in *Psychiatrie, Neurologie u. med. Psychologie*, 8, 1956, p. 154.

[62] See O. Bluth, *Uniforme und Tradition*, Berlin (East), Ministerium fuer nationale Verteitigung, 1956, p. 73; also van Creveld, *The Culture of War*, pp. 364-65.

[63] See, for the text, http://www.presidency.ucsb.edu/ws/?pid=8032.

[64] Figures from H. H. Price, "The Falklands: Rate of British Psychiatric Combat Casualties Compared to Recent American Wars," *Journal of the Royal Army Medical Corps*, 130, 1984, p. 109.

[65] See D. W. Smith and D. C. Frueh, "Compensation Seeking, Comorbidity, and Apparent Exaggeration of PTSD Symptoms among Vietnam Combat Veterans," *Psychological Assessment*, 8, 1, March 1996, pp. 3-6.

[66] *Washington Post*, 29.3.2014; "Institute of Medicine: Returning Soldiers Should Be Screened for PTSD Each Year," CBS News, 13.7.2012, at http://www.cbsnews.com/news/institute-of-medicine-returning-soldiers-should-be-screened-for-ptsd-each-year/.

[67] R. E. Strange, "Combat Fatigue versus Pseudo-Combat Fatigue in Vietnam," *Military Medicine*, 133, 10, 1968, pp. 823-26.

[68] Two of the best known works about the subject are Shay, *Achilles in Vietnam*, and D. Grossman, *On Killing,* both mentioned above.

[69] E.g., A. Sahndera-Ochsner, "Outcome following concussion and psychological trauma: An investigation of long-term cognitive and emotional functioning in veterans with PTSD and deployment-related mild TBI," dissertation submitted to the University of Kentucky, 2013.

[70] See V. Pupavac, "Therapeutic Governance," *Disasters*, 25, 4, 2001, p. 364.

[71] A. Blaszczak-Boxe, "Drone Operators Suffer PTSD Just Like Those in Combat," Lifescience, 20.8.2014, at http://www.livescience.com/47475-drone-operators-develop-ptsd.html.

[72] *Histories*, 2.70.

[73] See, for Graf's etching, Google image at https://www.google.co.il/search?hl=en&site=imghp&tbm=isch&source=hp&biw=1097&bih=559&q=battle+novarra&oq=battle+novarra&gs_l=img.12...930.4384.0.5629.14.10.0.3.3.0.153.951.0j7.7.0.msedr...0...1ac.1.61.img..7.7.951.2BaUxgOq.

[74] Florange, R. de la Marck, *Mémoirs du Maréchal de Florange*, Paris, R. Goubaux and

P. A. Lemoisne pubs., Paris, 1923-24, 1, pp. 126-128..

[75] *The Life of Adam Martindale, Written by Himself*, R. Parkinson, ed., in The Cheltenham Society, ed., *Remains... Connected with the... Counties of Lancaster and Chester*, 1845, 4, 1, pp. 72-4.

[76] See "Les Grandes Misères de la Guerre," at http://en.wikipedia.org/wiki/Les_Grandes_Mis%C3%A8res_de_la_guerre.

[77] See Y. Harari, *Renaissance Military Memoirs*, Woodbridge, Boydell, 2004, pp. 71-7, and the sources there cited.

[78] See, e.g., A. Garwood, "The Holocaust and the Power of Powerlessness: Survivor Guilt an Unhealed Wound," *British Journal of Psychotherapy*, 13, 2, December 1996, pp. 243-58.

[79] *Iliad*, 11.143-78.

[80] Figures from H. H. Price, "The Falklands: Rate of British Psychiatric Combat Casualties Compared to Recent American Wars," *Journal of the Royal Army Medical Corps*, 130, 1984, p. 109.

[81] S. Slost, "The UK Understands How to Treat PTSD. Why Does the US Lag Behind?" *New Republic*, 28.2.2014.

[82] See J. G. Pulley, "The Cohort System," Carlisle Barracks, PA, Army War College, 1988, at file:///C:/Users/owner/Downloads/ADA195030.pdf.

[83] F. Tick, *War and the Soul*, Wheaton, IL, Quest, 2012, Kindle ed., locs. 3449-67.

[84] S. Milosevic, "Kosovo, Gypsy or PTSD," WorldPost, 22.4.2013, at http://www.huffingtonpost.com/sasa-milosevic/kosovo-gypsy-curse-or-pts_b_3124830.html; Lazovic, email of 15.2.2015.

[85] H. Haux, "AF, Army Train Serbians on PTSD Program," Ramstein Air Base, 29.2.2013, at http://www.ramstein.af.mil/news/story.asp?id=123342187.

[86] Institute of Medicine, "Returning Soldiers Should Be Screened for PTSD Each Year," chapter IV, fn. 66.

[87] L. Daniel, "Services Improve Diagnosis of Brain Injuries, PTSD," DoD News, 21.4,2010, at http://www.defense.gov/news/newsarticle.aspx?id=58849.

[88] See on this approach to psychotherapy M. White and. D. Epston, *Narrative Means to Therapeutic Ends*, New York, NY, Norton, 1990.

[89] *Washington Post*, 29.3.2014.

[90] E.g., D. Dobbs, "The PTSD Trap," Wired, 22.3.2012, at http://www.wired.com/2012/03/the-ptsd-trap/; S. Joseph, "Has PTSD Taken over America?" *Psychology Today*, 18.11.2011; and many others.

[91] L. Braudy, *From Chivalry to Terrorism: War and the Changing Nature of Masculinity*, New York, NY, Vintage, 2003, Kindle ed., loc. 11943.

[92] See on this fascinating story G. Chamayou, *A Theory of the Drone*, New York, NY, New Press, 2015, pp. 108-10; also, in a different context, Pupavac, "Therapeutic Governance," pp. 363-64.

[93] J. Michaels, "Mattis: Veterans Are Not Victims," *USA Today*, 25.5.2014.

[94] Shay, *Achilles in Vietnam*, loc. 689.

[95] Translation in J. R. Hale, *War and Society in Renaissance Europe 1450-1620*, London, Fontana, 1985, p. 177.

Chapter V. Delegitimizing War

[1] USA Business List, DMDatabases.com, at http://dmdatabases.com/databases/business-mailing-lists/how-many-businesses.

[2] Chaniotis, *War in the Hellenistic World*, pp. 18-9, 220-23, 227-40.

[3] Plato, *The Republic,* 374A-76E; 414D-15D.

[4] Aristotle, *Politics*, 1.6.

[5] J. Bodin, *Six Books of the Commonwealth*, Oxford, Blackwell, 1957 [1576], pp. 25-35. See also M. van Creveld, *The Rise and Decline of the State*, Cambridge, Cambridge University Press, 1998, pp. 176-84, 199-205.

[6] Th. Hobbes, *Leviathan*, London, Fontana, 1962 [1652], pp. 179-83.

[7] *Réfutation de Machiavell*, in *Oeuvres*, Berlin, Decker, 1857, 8, pp. 169 and 298.

[8] *Hegel's Philosophy of Right*, T. M. Knox, trans., Oxford, Clarendon, 1952, p. 279.

[9] Hegel to Nanette Endel, 25.5.1798, in G. W. F. Hegel, *The Letters*, Bloomington, IN, University of Indiana Press, 1984, p. 62.

[10] See, on just war, F. H. Russell, *The Just War Tradition in the Middle Ages*, Cambridge, Cambridge University Press, 1973, especially pp. 292-309.

[11] F. M. A. Voltaire, *Candide*, London, Jackson, 1789 [1759], p. 10.

[12] See G. Best, *Humanity in Warfare*, New York, NY, Columbia University Press, 1980.

[13] Vagts, *A History of Militarism*, p. 26.

[14] M. Howard, *War and the Liberal Conscience*, New Brunswick, NJ, Rutgers University Press, 1978, pp. 52-69.

[15] E. Ludendorff, *Ludendorff's Own Story*, New York, NY, Harper, 1919. The relevant passage may be found at http://www.allworldwars.com/Ludendorff%20Own%20Story%20by%20Erich%20von%20Ludendorff.html.

[16] E. Ludendorff, *The Nation at War*, London, Hutchinson, 1936, p. 24.

[17] This and all similar information from Google Ngram.

[18] L. Hegermann-Lindencrone, *In the Courts of Memory*, New York, NY, Harper, 1912, p. 100, entry for 28.7.1870.

[19] The Charter is available at http://www.un.org/en/documents/charter/.

[20] The text is available at http://www.un.org/en/documents/udhr/.

[21] See on this E. M. Hafner-Burton and others, "Human Rights in a Globalizing World: The Paradox of Empty Promises," *American Journal of Sociology*, 10, 5, March 2005, pp. 1373-411.

[22] See, for the text, http://www.echr.coe.int/Documents/Convention_ENG.pdf.

[23] *St. Petersburg Times*, 3.8.2000.

[24] http://en.wikipedia.org/wiki/American_Civil_Liberties_Union#Funding.

[25] G. Hodgson, "Ronald Dworkin Obituary," *Guardian*, 14.2.2013.

[26] R. Dworkin, *Taking Rights Seriously*, Cambridge, MA, Harvard University Press, 1977, p. 184.

[27] "Auch Pflanzen muessen wurdig behandelt werden," *Neue Zuericher Zeiting*, 14.4.2008.

[28] J. Twenge and others, *The Narcissism Epidemic: Living in the Age of Entitlement*, New York, NY, Atria Books, 2010.

[29] See on this J. D. Arras, "Taking Duties Seriously," in C. S. Campbell and B. A. Lustig, eds., *Duties to Others*, Dordrecht, Kluwer, 2010, pp. 3-16.

[30] *Taking Rights Seriously*, p. 171.

[31] See on this D. Marquand, *Decline of the Public: The Hollowing-out of Citizenship*, Oxford, Polity, 2004.

[32] I. Kant, *Ueber der Gemeinspruch: Das mag in der Theorie richtig sein, taught aber nicht fur die Praxis*, Berlin, Heimann, 1870 [1793], 7, p. 286. The emphasis is mine.

[33] See on this P. Singer, *Hegel: A Very Short Introduction*, Oxford, Oxford University Press, 2001, Kindle edition, locs. 858-86.

[34] Comments to *Women's Own Magazine*, 31.10.1987.

[35] A. Smith, *The Wealth of Nations*, Chicago, IL, Chicago University Press, 1976 [1776], p. 253.

[36] See N. Rogers, *The Press Gang: Naval Impressment and Its Opponents in Georgian Britain*, London, Bloomsbury, 2004.

[37] The original decree, in French, is available at http://ahrf.revues.org/1385#bodyftn15.

[38] See, for the figures, Lockheed-Martin F-22 Raptor," at http://en.wikipedia.org/wiki/Lockheed_Martin_F-22_Raptor#Production_and_procurement.

[39] See, for the text of the doctrine, http://en.wikipedia.org/wiki/Powell_Doctrine.

[40] See, for some statistics, "Exemption from Military Service in Israel," at http://en.wikipedia.org/wiki/Exemption_from_military_service_in_Israel.

[41] "Women and WWI," firstworldwar.com, http://www.firstworldwar.com/features/womenww1_three.htm.

[42] See, e.g., S. Zeiger, "She Didn't Raise Her Son to be a Slacker: Motherhood, Conscription and the Culture of World War I," *Feminist Studies*, 22, 1, spring 1996, pp. 6-39.

[43] See, for the debate, J. Hegeland, "Christians and the Roman Army AD 173-337," *Church History*, 43, 2, (June 1974), pp. 149-163.

[44] Matthew 5.44.

[45] See, for the history of these sects, P. Brock, *Pacifism in Europe to 1914*, Princeton, NJ, Princeton University Press, 1972.

[46] M. B. Weddle, *Walking in the Way of Peace: Quaker Pacifism in the Seventeenth Century*, Oxford, Oxford University Press, 2001, pp. 180, 228-29.

[47] S. M. Kohn, *Jailed for Peace: The History of American Draft Law Violators*, 1658-1985, Westport, CT, Greenwood, 1986, pp. 9-11.

[48] See, on the way these things worked before and during the War of the American Revolution, E. M. West, "The Right to Religion-Based Exemptions in Early America: The Case of Conscientious Objectors to Conscription," *Journal of Law and Religion*, 10, 2, 1993-1994, pp. 367-401.

[49] Kohn, *Jailed for Peace*, pp. 20-1.

[50] For Marx's own view on this see *The Communist Manifesto*, 1848, p. 2. The text is available at https://www.marxists.org/archive/marx/works/sw/course/mscp.pdf.

[51] See on this C. C. Moskos and J. Whiteclay Chambers, *The New Conscientious Objection: From Religious to Secular Objection*, New York, NY, Oxford University Press, 1993, pp. 3-21.

[52] See Brock, *Pacifism*, p. 467.

[53] J. Bowman, *Honor*, locs. 2131-39.

[54] See, for the feminist efforts, F. H. Early, *A World without War: How US Feminists and Pacifists Resisted World War I*, Syracuse, NY, Syracuse University Press, 1997.

[55] C. H. Smith, *Smith's Story of the Mennonites*, Kansas City, KS, Faith and Life Press. 1957, p. 545.

[56] B. Nichols, "The Microbes of Mars," in G. K. Hibbert, ed., *The New Pacifism*, New York, NY, Garland, 1972 [1936], p. 66.

[57] See D. Garbe, *Between Resistance and Martyrdom: Jehovah's Witnesses in the Third Reich*, Madison, WI, University of Wisconsin Press, 2008, pp. 341–367.

[58] J. Greenberg, *I Never Promised You a Rose Garden*, New York, NY, Signet, 1964, p. 99.

[59] The Resolution is available at http://assembly.coe.int/Main.asp?link=/Documents/AdoptedText/ta67/ERES337.htm.

[60] See, for a short overview of the legal aspects of the problem, D. Malament, "Selective Conscientious Objection and Gillette Decision," *Philosophy & Public Affairs*, 1, 4, summer 1972, pp. 363-86.

[61] See, for the way these things work, Conscientious Objection Fact Sheet, at http://girightshotline.org/en/military-knowledge-base/topic/conscientious-objection-discharge#topic-the-process.

[62] "Wenn Soldaten den Kriegsdients verweigern," *Die Welt*, 5.5.2014.

[63] "Wenn Soldaten ihr Grundrecht beaantragen," Google.news, 19.8.2014.

[64] On war and the state see C. Tyler, "Hegel, War and the Tragedy of Imperialism," *History of European Ideas*, 30, 4, 2004, pp. 403-31; on war and the individual, above all S. R. Steinmetz, *Krieg als soziologisches Problem*, Amsterdam, Versluys, 1899.

[65] *Militaerische Werke*, Berlin, Mittler, 1891-93, 4, 1, p. 1.

[66] See on them E. Silberner, *La guerre dans la pensée économicque du XVI au XVIII siècle*, Paris, Recueil Sirey, 1939.

[67] I. Kant, *Eternal Peace*, [1795], at https://archive.org/details/eternalpeaceand00meadgoog.

[68] "The Moral Equivalent of War," 1906, at http://www.constitution.org/wj/meow.htm.

[69] See, for a short list of works on these men and their schemes, van Creveld, *The Rise and Decline of the State,* p. 350, fn. 31.

[70] See, for the list, Permanent Court of Arbitration, Cases, at http://www.pcacases.com/web/allcases/.

[71] See, most recently P. P. Walters, *A History of the League of Nations,* New York, NY, Praeger, 1986.

[72] "General Pact for the Renunciation of War," Paris, 27.8.1928, at http://avalon.law.yale.edu/20th_century/kbhear.asp#treatytext.

[73] The two UN documents may be found at https://treaties.un.org/doc/publication/ctc/uncharter.pdf and http://www.un-documents.net/a25r2734.htm respectively.

[74] "Noam Chomsky Calls US 'World's Leading Terrorist State,'" RT Question More, 7.11.2014, at http://rt.com/usa/202223-noam-chomsky-global-terror/.

[75] "World Ominously Close to Nuclear War," RT Question More, 15.1.2015, at http://rt.com/news/202995-chomsky-rt-nuclear-war/.

[76] See, above all, K. Waltz, "The Spread of Nuclear Weapons: More May Be Better," London, ISIS, 1981.

[77] B. Duignan, ed., *The 100 Most Influential Philosophers of All Time*, New York, NY, Britannica, 2010, pp. 313-16.

[78] "Interview—John Galtung," E-International Relations, 27.5.2014, at http://www.e-ir.info/2014/05/27/interview-johan-galtung/.

[79] See on that objective "Islamic State (IS) Manifesto Reveals 100-Year Plan for a World Caliphate," Security-Risks.com, 14.10.2014, at http://www.security-risks.com/security-issues-south-asia/terrorism/islamic-state-is-manifesto-reveals-100-year-plan-for-a-world-caliphate-3652.html.

[80] N. Machiavelli, *The Prince*, 1527, chapter 15, at http://www.gutenberg.org/files/1232/1232-h/1232-h.htm.

Conclusion: Hannibal *intra Portas*

[1] Memoirs of General Kolchak Denikin, quoted in S. Drokov, "The Founder of the Women's Battalion of Death" [Russian], *Voprosse Historii*, July 1993, pp. 164-69.

[2] G. Berman and T. Rutherford, "Defence Personnel Statistics," 26.9.2014, at http://researchbriefings.parliament.uk/ResearchBriefing/Summary/SN02183.

[3] Grossman, *On Killing*, locs. 138-59.

[4] Matthew 10.34.

[5] Quoted in Th. Merton, ed., *Gandhi on Non-Violence*, Ahmedabad, New Directions, 2007, p. 51.

[6] J. Keegan, *The Face of Battle*, New York, NY, Viking Press, 1976, pp. 318-19.

[7] See on them Sherer, "Warriors for a Living," pp. 13-27.

[8] See on this M. van Creveld, *Wargames*, pp. 285-97.

9 See, out of the huge literature, R. M. Dancygier, *Immigration and Conflict in Europe*, New York, NY, Cambridge University Press, 2010.

10 "Jeder zweiten Haeftling hat keinen oesterricheichen Pass," Unzensuriert, 12.2.201, at http://www.unzensuriert.at/content/0017145-Jeder-zweite-Haeftling-hat-keinen-oesterreichischen-Pass.

11 B. Waterfield, "Mohammed Is Most Popular Boys' Name in Four Biggest Dutch Cities," *The Telegraph*, 13.8.2009.

12 S. P. Huntington, "The Clash of Civilizations," *Foreign Affairs*, 72, 3, summer 1993, p. 25.

13 Associated Press, "Hundreds Attend 'Private' Funeral for Copenhagen Shooter," DTV News, 20.2.2015, at http://www.ctvnews.ca/world/hundreds-attend-private-funeral-for-copenhagen-shooter-1.2245620.

14 W. S. Churchill, *The River War*, London, Longman [1899], 2, pp. 248-50.

15 S. Kern, "Germany: Hooligans Declare War on Islamic Radicals," Gatestone Institute International Policy Council, 10.11.2014, at http://www.gatestoneinstitute.org/4859/germany-hooligans-salafists.

16 FRA, Hate Crimes in the European Union, at http://fra.europa.eu/sites/default/files/fra-factsheet_hatecrime_en_final_0.pdf.

17 J. Galtung, "Violence, Peace and Peace Research," *Journal of Peace Research*, 6. 3.1969, p. 3.

18 Keegan, *The Face of Battle*, p. 336.

19 See, for a discussion of ancient authors who expressed this view, A. W. Lintott, "Imperial Expansion and Moral Decline in the Roman Republic," *Historia*, 2, 4, 1972, pp. 626-38.

20 See, on the "why" of tribal warfare, A. Gat, *War in Human Civilization*, Cambridge, Oxford, Oxford University Press, 2006, pp. 36-113.

21 See, for Rome, *de rebus bellicis*; and, for China, J. Needham, *Science and Civilization in China*, Cambridge, Cambridge University Press, 1981, 30, pp. 101-486.

22 S. Turnbull, *Siege Weapons of the Far East*, Oxford, Osprey, 2002, p. 12.

23 Polybius, *The Histories*, 36.17.5-7 and 40.6.57.

24 Livy, *Roman History*, preface, 4.

25 Juvenal, *Satires*, 6, 292.

26 Aristotle, *Politics,* book ii, chapter ix.

27 Cicero, *De officiis,* 2.26.

28 Polybius, *The Histories*, 32.13.16.

29 See, for Numidius' speech and Augustus' measures, M. McDonnell, "The Speech of Numidius at Gellus N.A 1.6," *The American Journal of Philology*, 108, spring 1987, pp. 81-94

30 *Discourses on Livy*, Chicago, IL, University of Chicago Press, 1996, p. 148.

31 Velleius Paterculus, *Roman History*, 2.115.5; *Inscriptiones Latinae Selectae*, H. Dessau, ed., Berlin, Weidmann, 1892-1916, vol. 1, No. 216. See also W. V. Harris,

"Readings in the Narrative Literature of Roman Courage," in S. A. Dillon and K. E. Welch, eds., *Representations of War in Ancient Rome*, Cambridge, Cambridge University Press, 2006, p. 317.

[32] S. Fidler, "NATO Countries to Vow to Lift Military Spending (Commitment Would Be Nonbinding)," *Wall Street Journal*, 4.9.2014.

[33] Quote from http://thinkexist.com/quotes/George_Orwell/.

[34] "Schuetz fuer schwaengere: Schuetzpanzer kommt spaeter," *Junge Freiheit*, 6.2.2015.

Index

A Few Good Men, 64

Achilles, 68, 116, 118, 125, 149

ACLU, 161

ADHD, 30, 38

adolescence, 15

Agamemnon, King, 143

Air Force Academy, 89

Al Qaeda, 190

Alexander, the Great, 39, 72, 118, 146

Alexander,Clifford, Jr., 84

Alice in Wonderland, 118

Allon, General Yigal, 41

Amazons, 87, 104, 116

American Civil War, 131, 171

American Declaration of Independence, 157

Amish, 17, 18

Amos, General James, 67, 148

Anabaptists, 169

Andersen, Pamela, 106

Aphrodite, 44

Arabs, 1

Aristophanes, 116

Aristotle, 118, 146, 153, 196

Assyrians, 195

Augustus, Gaius Octavianus, 39, 153, 196, 197

Auschwitz, 122

Austerlitz, Battle of, 121

Babylonians, 195

balance of terror, 8

banned books, 28

Barak, General Ehud, 13

Barbarella, 106

Barbed Wire, 106

Bathsheba Syndrome, 54

Battleship, 106

Bayard, Pierre Terrail, 120

Beard, George Miller, 133

Beauvoir, Simone de, 20, 55

Becher, Ernest, 69

Bedriacum, Battle of, 141, 142

Bettelheim, Bruno, 17

Bismarck, Otto von, 178

Blue Angels, 53

Bluntschli, Johann, 177

Bodin, Jean, 153

Boko Haram, 143

Bonet, Honoré, 194

Boorda, Admiral Jeremy, 53

Bowden, Mark, 10

Bray, Captain Linda, 90

Broadwell, Lieutenant Colonel Paula, 54

Broder, Henryk, 197

Bueil, Jean de, 149

Bundeswehr, 86, 96, 138, 176

bungee-jumping, 114

Bush, George W., 5, 53

Bush, Jeb, 113

Butler, General Benjamin, 130

Cabeza de Vaca, Alvar-Nunez de, 129

Caesar, Gaius Julius, 39, 44, 55

Callot, Jacques, 141

Campion, Léo, 173

Card, Orson Scott, 22

Carter, Jimmy, 84

Cavalry Song, 45, 150

Cervantes, Miguel de, 123

Ceuta, Portuguese capture of, 1, 3

Chaeronea, Battle of, 39

Châlons sur Marne, Battle of, 1

Chandelier, 106

Chanson de Roland, 120

chansons de geste, 146

Charcot, Martin, 134

Charles V, Emperor, 73

Charles XII, of Sweden, 40

Che Guevara, 7

Chiang Kai-Shek, 153

childhood, 15

children, restrictions on, 25

Chomsky, Noam, 180

Churchill, Winstom, 192

Cicero, Marcus Tulius, 196

Clausewitz, Carl von, 73, 74, 94, 120, 156, 200

Cohen, Leonard, 182

Cohesion, 94

COHORT system, 146

Cointe, Jourdan de, 130

Cold War, 4, 6, 62, 166

combat fatigue, 135, 140

Confederacy, 131

conscientious objectors, 96, 172, 173, 175, 187

Constantine, Emperor, 169

Convention against Torture, 158

Convention on Human Rights, 159

Cook, Captain James, 130

Cooper, Isabel Rosario, 55

Cortes, Hernan, 2

corvées, 164, 165

Council of Europe, 159, 174

counterinsurgency, 63

courage, 34

Court of Human Rights, 160

Crane, Stephen, 147

Cromwell, Oliver, 169

Cultural Revolution, 180

Cushman v. Crawford, 85

Da Costa Syndrome, 131, 134

DACOWITS, 82, 103

Daesh (ISIS), 7, 11, 58, 143, 181

Daniels, Josephus, 102

Dark Knight Rises, 106

David, King, 54

Day, Hem, 173

Dayan, General Moshe, 5, 55

DeBique, Tilern, 104

Decker, Brooklyn, 106

Declaration of the Rights of Man, 157

Dempsey, General Martin, 85

Diagnostic and Statistical Manual of Mental Disorders, 140

Dickens, Charles, 65

divorce, 109

Duroc, General Christopher, 55

duty, 157, 163, 166, 187

Duty, 164

Dworkin, Ronald, 162, 163

Eisenhower, General Dwight, 55

English Civil War, 169

Epizelus, 126

Eugene, of Savoy, Prince, i

European Convention on Human Rights, 159, 174

European Council, 191

European Pattern of Marriage, 21

European Union, 160

European Union Agency for Human Rights, 193

Falkland War, 144

Farnese, Alessandro, 40

feminism, 19, 83, 167, 176

Fifty Shades of Grey, 59

First Gulf War, 4, 65, 98, 101

Florange, Captain, 141

Fonda, Jame, 106

Foucault, Michel, 118

Francis I, of France, 120

Frederick the Great, i, 57, 67, 121, 153, 154, 178

Frederick William IV, of Prussia, 73

Freud, Sigmund, 19, 106, 113, 134

Friedan, Betty, 20

Froissart, 120

Frontiero v. Richardson, 85

Fukuyama, Francis, 60

Gadhafi, Muammar, 159

Galtung, Johan, 180, 182, 193

Gandhi, Mahatma, 182, 187

Gates, Robert, 166

gender, 116, 185

General Accounting Office, 107

Genghis Khan, 195

genocide, 8, 183

Gingrich, Newt, 17

Global War on Terror, 39

Goebbels, Joseph, 137

Gooks, 10

Gordon, Jean, 55

Gorgias, 126

Gorgias of Herakleia, 124

Goya, Francis, 142

grades, 28

Graf, Urs, 141

Grant, Robert, 68

Graves, Robert, 124

Great Leap Forward, 180

Greenberg, Joanne, 174

Grotius, Hugo, 154

guerrilla, 7, 8

Hadrian, Emperor, 128

Hajjis, 10

Hamilton, Emma, 55

Harari, Professor Yuval, 121, 129, 142

Hathaway, Ann, 106

Haydon, Benjamin, 44

Hector, 149

Hedges, Chris, 56

Hegel, Georg Friederich Wilhelm, 154, 164

helicopter parents, 21

Hemingway, Ernest, 124

Henry V, of England, 95

Heracles, 116

Heraclitus, 194

Herodotus, 126, 194

heroism, 68, 69, 115

Hirohito, Emperor, 153

Hitler, Adolf, 70, 72, 137, 153, 156, 182, 183

Hobbes, Thomas, 153, 154

Hochhuth, Rolf, 143

Hoess, Rudolf, 122

Hofer, Johannes, 130, 131

Homer, ii, 55, 87

Honors, Captain Owen, 52

Houellebecq, Michel, 197

Huns, 1, 195

Huntington, Professor Samuel, 192

Hussein, of Jordan, 79

Hussein, Saddam, 4, 67, 159, 190

Hutterites, 169

hysteria, 134, 135

Ibn Khaldun, 194

IDF, i

Imperial Guard, 44

insurgency, 8

Islam, 194

Isocrates, 196

Israel Air Force, iii

ius ad bellum, 155

ius in bello, 155

James, E. L., 59

James, William, 177

Jeanne d'Arc, 39

Jehova's Witnesses, 173

Jena, Battle of, 120

Jesus Christ, 118, 169, 182, 187

John of Austria, 40

Jünger, Ernst, 123, 124

Juvenalis, Iunius Decimus, 196

Kaldor, Mary, 39

Kant, Immanuel, 163, 164, 177

Kara Mustafa, 1

Keegan, John, 188, 189, 194

Kellogg-Briand Pact, 178

Kennedy, Paul, 194

Korb, Lawrence, 82, 84

Krafft-Ebbing, Richard von, 53

Laden, Osama Bin, 190

Lawrence, T. S., 7

lawyers, military, 62

Le Brun, Charles, 71

League of Nations, 178

Lechfeld, Battle of, 1

Lepanto, Battle of, 1, 40

levée en masse, 165

Leviathan, 153

Leyen, Ursula von der, 86

Liegnitz, Battle of, 1

Lincoln, Abraham, 183

Livius, Titus, 196

Locke, John, 176

Louis Napoleon, Emperor, 158

Louis XIV, of France, 121

low-intensity conflict, 64

low-intensity war, 8

Ludendorff, General Erich, 156

Luther, Martin, 169

Lycurgus, 194, 196

Lysistrata, 116

MacArthur, General Douglas, 55

Machiavelli, Nicolo, 197

Magellan, Ferdinand, 2

Magyars, 1, 195

Mannerheim, Carl Gustaf, 153

Mao Tze Dong, 7

Mao Zedong, 9, 180

Marathon, Battle of, 126

Marche, Olivier de la, 129

Marine Corps Staff College, 65

Marius, Gaius, 89

Marshall, General George, 82, 135

Marx, Karl, 171

masculinity, 113, 114, 115

Masséna, Field Marsshal Andre, 55

Mattis, General James, 67, 78, 148, 149

McWherter, Gregory, 53

Mennonites, 169, 171, 172

mercenaries, 76, 77, 78

militarism, 70, 71, 72, 175, 198

military academies, ii

military-sexual trauma, 111

Mill, John Stuart, 177

Moltke, Field-Marshal Helmuth von, 176

Mongol, 195

Mongols, 1, 195

Monroe Doctrine, 3

Mordechai, General Yitzhak, 13

Mussolini, Benito, 153, 157

Napoleon Bonaparte, 40, 55, 154

NATO, 4, 6, 12, 42, 75, 86

Naval Academy, Annapolis, 48

Nelson, Admiral Horatio, 55, 95, 157

Netanyahu, Benjamin, 6, 13

neurasthenia, 133, 134

New American Militarism, 6

NGOs, 35

Ngram, 15, 157, 161, 162, 167

Nietzsche, Friedrich, 10, 59, 113, 187

Nixon, Richard, 166

No Child Left Behind, 31

non-trinitarian war, 8

Nontrinitarians, 169

Nordau, Max, 135

nose art, 51

nostalgia, 130

Novara, Battle of, 141, 142

Numidicus Metellus Cecilius, 196

Nye, Joseph, 12

Obama, Barak, 7, 42, 60, 96, 116

Odysseus, 150

Omdurman, Battle of, 193

Operation Just Cause, 90

Operation Protective Edge, 13

Orwell, George, 107, 198

Owen, Wilfred, 65

Owens v. Brown, 85

Palmach, 41

Panetta, Leon, 85

Pankhurst, Emmeline and Christabel, 167

Parrish, Nancy, 58

Pascal, Blaise, 155

Patroclus, 125

Patton, General George, 55, 136

Paul, Rand, 17

Pavia, Battle of, 120

peacekeeping, 167

Peloponnesian War, 143

Penn, William, 177

Permanent Court of Arbitration, 177

Persians, 195

Petraeus, General David, 54, 57, 60, 78

Philipp II, of Spain, 40

Philoctētēs, 125

Pilsudski, Jozef, 153

Pizarro, Francisco, 2

Plato, 44, 114, 132, 153, 194, 196

Playboy, 52

Poitiers, Battle of, 1

Polybius, 195, 196

Polycleitus, 51

Pompeius, Gnaeus, 39

Pound, Ezra, 124

Powell, General Colin, 166

pregnancy, 97, 98, 99, 100

Presidential Commission on the Assignment of Women in the Services, 85

Protect Our Defenders, 58

Protestantism, 169

protracted war, 8

PTSD, 10, 11, 125, 127, 128, 129, 130, 131, 133, 137, 138, 139, 140, 141, 142, 144, 145, 146, 147, 148, 149, 150, 172, 186, 187, 189, 199

Pufendorf, Samuel, 154

puppy love, 21

Putin, Vladimir, 74, 179

Quakers, 170, 171, 172, 173

Quantico, Va, 65

Rabin, General Yitzhak, 41

railway brain, 133, 134, 140

rape, 99

Résistance, French, 48

Rice, Susan, 42

Rif War, 3

right of conquest, 179

rights revolution, 175, 187

Ritalin, 38

Roosevelt, Franklin Delano, 60

Roosevelt, Theodore, 147, 148

Rostker v. Goldberg, 95

ROTC, 84

Rough Riders, 148

Rousseau, Jean-Jacques, 177

Royal Air Force, 91

Rumsfeld, Donald, 5

Sajer, Guy, 123

Sallustius, Gaius Crispus, 89

Sandhurst Military Academy, 91

Sarrazin, Thilo, 197

Sassoon, Siegfried, 65, 122, 123, 124

Saxe, Field Marshal Maurice de, 55

Sayers, Dorothy, 137

Schiller, Friedrich, 45, 46, 65, 150

Schlieffen, Field-Marshal Alfred, i

school, 26, 27, 28

Schwarzkopf, General Norman, 69

Scipio, Publius Cornelus Africanus, 39

Second Lebanon War, 13

sexual assault response coordinators, 53

sexual harassment, 80, 91, 110

Shakespeare, William, 95

Sharia, 192

Shay, Jonathan, 125, 149

shell shock, 134

Six Books of the Commonwealth, 153

Saladin, 39

Smith, Adam, 165

Socrates, 36

Soldiers' Heart, 136

Solon, 194

Sophocles, 125

Sparta, 42, 72, 196

Spengler, Oswald, 194

Sports Illustrated, 52

staff colleges, ii

Stalin, Joseph, 158

Stanley, Henry, 2

Stauffenberg, Claus von, 70

Stockholm International Peace Research Institute (SIPRI), 179

subjugation, 179

Suetonius, Gaius Tranquillus, 44

suffragettes, 167

Summersby, Kay, 55

Sun Tzu, 119

Suttner, Bertha von, 172

Tacitus, Publius Cornelius, 141

Taliban, 7, 67, 190

Tarzan, 106

terrorism, 8, 198

Thatcher, Margaret, 164

The Fighter Pilot's Handbook, 58

The Night Crew, 64

The Red Badge of Courage, 147

The Wealth of Nations, 165

Thirty Years War, 141

Thoreau, Henry, 171

Thucydides, 72

Tick, Edward, 145

Timur, 195

Tolstoy, Leo, 121, 172

Toynbee, Arnold, 194

Trafalgar, Battle of, 95, 157

trauma, 34

Treaty of Versailles, 178

Tresckow, Henning von, 70

Trump, Donald, 113

Tsiolkas, Christos, 23

Turks, 1

Uniform Code of Military Justice, 53

United Nations, 158, 159, 178, 179

United Nations Human Rights Commission, 159

Universal Declaration of Human Rights, 158

universal education, 32

upper-body strength, 88, 89

US Marine Corps, 90, 94

US Supreme Court, 160, 175

USAF, 53, 85

Vagts, Alfred, 72

Vattel, Emmerich de, 154, 178

V-E Day, 10

Venus of Milo, 51

Vergillius, Publius Maro, 122, 155

victimhood, 34

victimization, 34

victimology, 34

Victoria, Queen of England, 153

Vienna, first siege of, 1

Viet Cong, 50

Vietnam War, 43, 139, 144, 166, 175

Vikings, 1

violence, 33, 34

violent fantasies, 38

V-J Day, 10

Vo Nguyen Giap, 7

Volksarmee, 138

Voltaire, François Marie Arouet, 154

Wallström, Margot, 74

war among the people, 8

War and Peace, 121

war colleges, ii

war guilt, 178

War of American Independence, 132

War of the American Revolution, 170

War of the Austrian Succession, 55

War Resisters' International, 173

Waterloo, Battle of, 44

Wehrmacht, 42, 48, 55, 123, 136, 138, 143, 144, 145

Wells, H. G., 198

West Point Military Academy, 108, 157

West, Rebecca, 136

William I, German Emperor, 73

Wilson, Woodrow, 102

women, 11, 73, 75, 77, 79, 80, 81, 82, 83, 84, 85, 86, 87, 88, 89, 90, 91, 92, 95, 185, 186

Wonder Woman, 106

Woodward, Margaret, General, 86

Woolf, Virginia, 137

World War I, 80, 81, 102, 136, 141, 172, 173, 178, 185

World War II, 3, 42, 80, 98, 142, 144, 158, 165, 167, 168, 173, 187

Wu Tzu, 11

Xena the Warrior Princes, 106

Yadin, General Yigael, 41

Yokosuka, US base, 47

Ziegler, Maddy, 106

Zumwalt, Admiral Elmo, 83

Made in the USA
San Bernardino, CA
16 July 2016